Business Research
Projects

Business Research Projects

Second edition

A.D. Jankowicz

Teesside Business School
Cleveland
UK

CHAPMAN & HALL
London · Glasgow · Weinheim · New York · Tokyo · Melbourne · Madras

Published by Chapman & Hall, 2–6 Boundary Row, London SE1 8HN, UK

Chapman & Hall, 2–6 Boundary Row, London SE1 8HN, UK

Blackie Academic & Professional, Wester Cleddens Road, Bishopbriggs, Glasgow G64 2NZ, UK

Chapman & Hall GmbH, Pappelallee 3, 69469 Weinheim, Germany

Chapman & Hall USA, 115 Fifth Avenue, New York, NY 10003, USA

Chapman & Hall Japan, ITP-Japan, Kyowa Building, 3F, 2-2-1 Hirakawacho, Chiyoda-ku, Tokyo 102, Japan

Chapman & Hall Australia, 102 Dodds Street, South Melbourne, Victoria 3205, Australia

Chapman & Hall India, R. Seshadri, 32 Second Main Road, CIT East, Madras 600 035, India

First edition 1991

Reprinted 1992, 1993, 1994

Second edition 1995

© 1995 A.D. Jankowicz

Typeset in 10/12pt Times by Gray Publishing, Tunbridge Wells, Kent

Printed in Great Britain by Page Bros, Norwich, Norfolk

ISBN   0 412 63650 6

A catalogue record for this book is available from the British Library

♾ Printed on permanent acid-free text paper, manufactured in accordance with ANSI/NISO Z 39.48-1992 and ANSI/NISO Z 39.48-1984 (Permanence of Paper).

Contents

Preface to the second edition

As you might suspect from a glance at the preface to the first edition, my intentions in putting it together were entirely pragmatic. I wanted to provide you with practical help in preparing your projects in business and management; this objective was achieved tolerably well, to judge by the reactions expressed by my own students, staff from other universities and reviewers in various management journals. I should confess that I also intended to lighten the burdens carried by academics acting as project tutors. They could refer you to this book for the basics of project work and thereby create additional time for more satisfying forms of tutorial activity, in which you and your tutor could concentrate on what interested you both – the meat of the thing: the content, what your particular project was actually about – rather than the basic concepts of research, the processes and the administrative guidelines involved.

Few of the process and administrative issues have changed during the last four years, though some of the guidelines issued by the professional bodies have altered and various support systems have improved in noticeable ways. The Institute of Personnel Management is now the Institute of Personnel and Development; both it and the Chartered Institute of Marketing have amended their regulations. Recent developments in information technology have increased your control in accessing research databases off-line, and other books offering helpful guidelines to project work have appeared, Raimond (1993) in particular. All are described, as appropriate, here.

Much more important, however, has been the development of the conceptual underpinnings to management research and, by implication, to project work. The following themes have been the major reason for my preparation of a new edition; I wanted to alert you to a number of significant developments which were originally somewhat underplayed.

Non-positivist, postmodern thinking about management, and thereby about management research, has developed and made a more prominent appearance in the relevant literature. Both the *Academy of Management Review* and *Management Education and Development* have devoted complete special issues to these topics in their impact on theory-building and research: see section 6.5. While the latter journal continues, its editorial team have decamped to set up a new periodical, *Management Learning*, which emphasizes current thinking about management research. This – the 'New Paradigm', postmodern analysis, call it what you will – is an epistemology whose relevance I argued in my first edition and continue to emphasize in Chapter 6 of the present.

The appreciation of qualitative approaches to the understanding of organizational life has increased during the last four years, approaches seen as complementary to quantitative analysis by many, a substitute by some. The appearance of the second edition of Miles and Huberman (1994) indicates the growing importance attached to qualitative analysis by many management researchers, and I have mentioned some of the techniques they advocate at relevant points in Part Three of this book, without attempting, or indeed being able, to replicate their magnificent work. Discourse analysis, biography and hermeneutic analysis are among the recent approaches to which pointers are provided in Part Three. Similarly, the value of arguing a case, rather than testing a thesis, has been emphasized for some forms of Diploma and MBA work: see section 6.4. But I've also added procedural guides to a number of simple quantitative techniques, believing in the value of combining both qualitative and quantitative forms of analysis and reporting where relevant.

The relativism implied in approaches like these has been particularly important in the export of western ideas (more accurately, the transfer of meaning) by management practitioners, academics and trainers, to the post-command economies of central and eastern Europe. Projects based overseas have been relatively rare in the past, but are increasing as large companies globalize and smaller ones seek out new markets. I have provided guidelines where relevant, particularly in section 7.2.

Some of these changes follow the recommendations of a readership survey organized by Chapman & Hall. Another suggestion was that I provide greater coverage of the production, style and writing of the project document itself. I've done this in the form of a new chapter, 14, although some of the material on document writing and production remains where it was in sections 4.4 and 5.5, because that's where I think it's most useful.

As before, you should approach the book sequentially, the earlier sections when you begin, the later ones when your work is in progress, and the last being tackled just before the main phase of your writing begins.

It remains to express thanks to my kind helpers. To all who assisted in the first edition, and to my MBA students who gave judgement and comment; to Mr Mike Hall and Ms Joanne Taylor, Ms Penny Dick, Ms Jean Shaw and her library colleagues, all of the University of Teesside; to Mr Ingmar Folkmans, my morale-boosting editor at Chapman & Hall; to Mr Mike Ellis for his background support; and finally, to the staff of Volmech Garage of Stockton – discover why for yourself; read on.

A.D. Jankowicz
Teesside Business School

Preface to the first edition

The idea for this book came about one Friday afternoon towards the end of a summer term. I was giving the third project tutorial of the afternoon. The first had been to a BA (Business Studies) student, the second to a part-time MBA student, and the third to a student registered on the Diploma in Personnel Management programme, and a great variety of issues had been dealt with during the course of the time involved.

Nevertheless, I noticed that some of the material was common to all three students. I found myself thinking that I was repeating myself, and wanting to get through the basics as quickly as possible so that we could move on to the specifics of each particular project, which we both, each student and I, found more interesting to deal with. Unfortunately, the basics were precisely those topics which I considered essential to the success of any project. What's more, they dealt with the sort of material which wouldn't, on the whole, have occurred spontaneously to many students, and so it was a necessary part of my job to go through them. One or two could be dealt with by issuing a handout, and the student could be referred to the library for some of the rest, but there wasn't a systematic written compilation of all the points that I needed to make.

I could see this recurring as the series of tutorials continued. A little of the material might be found in textbooks and manuals with the simple title of 'Research Methods', but much of it wasn't available in a written form, being more a matter of 'project methods' than social-science-based research. The more I thought along these lines, the more confident I became that the two represented distinct realms of discourse – with some overlaps, to be sure, but with the differences more significant than the similarities. And this book developed as I began to set down the distinctions, focusing on the basics of 'project work' as distinct from 'research methods'.

As you might imagine, with such pragmatic beginnings, this book owes a lot to its clients, the students themselves. Whoever they might be, whether they're people I met twenty years ago, or yesterday, or the people I've yet to encounter, my thanks to you all.

Next, my thanks are due to the business and management practitioners especially those who have kindly given their permission for me to cite materials developed during my association with them, whether as tutor to students placed with them, or in the course of my own consulting and research activities. Particular thanks are due in this respect to Assistant Commissioner P. J. Moran of An Garda Siochana, and to Mr Bob Mitchell, Chief Medical Laboratory Scientific Officer, Middlesbrough General Hospital.

I'd also like to thank my academic colleagues in the School of Management at Ealing College, in the College of Business at the University of Limerick, and in Teesside Business School: for their interest and assistance in reviewing parts of this book, for providing ideas on project topics and examples, and for helping me with specific techniques initially beyond my ken. They are: Mr Mike Cumming, Mrs Ruth Davidson and Mrs Deirdre Kelly-Patterson in the College; Mr Jim Dalton and Professor Barra O'Cinneide at the University; and Dr Pat Allatt, Mrs Lynn Benson, Dr Frances Brassington, Mr Tim Hemingray, Mr Gerry Kirkwood, Mr Mike Lawrenson, Mr Andec Lillie, Dr Hedley Malloch, Dr Brian Matthews, Mr Alan Welsh and Mr Colin Wimpory of the Business School.

And finally, my thanks are due to my editors, Mr Stephen Wellings, Ms Una-Jane Winfield, and latterly, Mr Mark Wellings, for their firm guidance and help; a quiet word of thanks is also due to my wife Chetna, for putting up with an unsilenced Imagewriter printer, well into the night.

A. D. Jankowicz
Teesside Business School

Getting Started

PART 1

Introduction 1

1.1 WHAT THIS BOOK IS ABOUT

Practically all business and management qualification courses require you to research and write an extended piece of prose as part of the requirements for successful graduation. The final piece of work goes by a variety of names, 'Project', 'Dissertation' and 'Thesis' being the most common. It may vary in length, depending on the requirements of the particular curriculum which you are following; it certainly varies in standard, depending on the level of qualification which your curriculum provides. It's usually done on an in-company basis, for your employer if you're a part-time student, or during a time when you're placed with a host organization if your studies are full-time.

The purpose of this book is to provide you with a set of guidelines, methods and techniques appropriate to in-company work, all of which aim to make the process as straightforward as possible. At times, the guidelines will differ, depending on the nature and level of the programme of studies you're following. Where this is so, I've identified the material which is particularly relevant to your circumstances, with an appropriate abbreviation in the margin, as follows:

- **'undergraduate'** stands for comments directed at people following undergraduate programmes;

  under-graduate

- **'diploma'** stands for comments directed at people following Diploma in Management Studies and Diploma in Business Administration programmes;

  diploma

- **'MBA'**, obviously enough, stands for comments at people following Masters in Business Administration programmes;

  MBA

- **'professional'** stands for comments directed at people following programmes designed to fulfil the requirements of the professional bodies;

  profes-sional

- **'in-company'** is used when I want to make a comment to everyone

  in-company

except undergraduates. I won't mark each paragraph in this way; read on until you encounter one of the other codes, or the code

■ 'all', which indicates that the specific material has ended. While you'll want to read the material appropriate to your own situation in detail, it's advisable to glance at the other cases too: you'll get a better idea of the scope of your own work, by knowing something of the context and contrasts provided by the other levels of work.

all

1.2 A BRIEF OVERVIEW

You're engaged in an exciting venture. Perhaps this is the first piece of extended research you've ever done; possibly it's the first time you've gathered your information inside a host organization; you might have substantial experience of the organization as one of its managers on a post-experience programme, but you're unsure of what's involved in an academic project. How to begin?

Part One is an extended pre-flight checklist. It provides you with guidelines on the reasons for doing project work in the first place, and highlights the implications involved. It gives you assistance in choosing a topic, and information on the standards to which you'll be expected to work; it handles the practicalities of timetabling and scheduling, the usefulness of writing a proposal document, and the minimal equipment that you need for success. These are practical issues – their intellectual content isn't especially deep – yet my experience of 20 years spent in supervising business and management projects suggests that their neglect leads to mediocrity and, all too often, to outright failure. In fact, let that be the first thing you get from this book: an in-company project isn't an intellectual assault-course and you don't have to be brilliant to succeed.

What you do need is a certain clarity of purpose: an understanding of the fundamentals of your assumptions and approach, as they apply to projects in the business and management field. That's what I try to provide in Part Two. You'll find that it pays you to be clear about the nature of research in the first place, so that you can do work which is academically respectable and, at the same time, practically useful to your organization. I'm not sure that the conventional, positivist view of the scientific research process, a view implicitly or explicitly espoused by many of the research methods textbooks to which you'll be referred, is particularly helpful here. I devote Chapter 6 to this issue, and to an outline of more usable alternative views.

The organizational world in which you'll be operating is significantly different to the world which the scientist inhabits. Getting into this world is an issue in the first place, while adopting an appropriate role and attuning to its culture involve activities which pose their own problems.

It's inhabited by people who can hinder you or help, and how you approach them is critical to success: all of which is introduced in Chapter 2, but developed in detail in Chapter 7. Part Two also provides you with guidelines on scholarship, the importance of which is introduced in Chapter 2, and developed in detail in Chapter 8.

You'll notice a lot of this: of ideas and topics introduced early on, and developed later in detail. I've tried to anticipate the sequence in which you're likely to hit various problems in doing your project, and organized the material accordingly. While you might care to skim the book initially, dipping into it in more detail here and there as topics catch your eye, once you get going you'll find that a front-to-back perusal in depth is the best way to approach it.

Part Three deals with the methods and techniques at your disposal. It opens with a consideration of project design, the deliberate arrangement of your data-collection procedures. After considering the distinction between methods and techniques, and providing some guidelines on which method to adopt (Chapter 10), an account of a number of semi-structured techniques in Chapter 11 is followed by material on the more structured techniques (Chapter 12). Finally, Chapter 13 offers you guidelines on techniques which don't fit comfortably into a structure-based classification.

You would never need all of these, and so, after an initial overview, I suggest you handle the material selectively as your empirical work (your own data-gathering) develops. My account is limited in the depth of detail with which particular research techniques can be described – there's little here on analytic statistics and null-hypothesis testing, for example – but where advanced material seems relevant, you can expect to find a reference to appropriate material in depth.

That's particularly true of the last chapter, which consists of material on the writing of your final project document. Writing is a craft to which I can't do justice in the space available; however, there are some standard conventions and stylistic procedures that apply to project work, and these are provided in an outline form.

Certain topics, such as content analysis, or the issue of how best to arrange for the confidentiality and security of your data, apply to several of the different techniques presented in Part Three. Rather than placing them arbitrarily into a separate chapter, I've presented them in the section devoted to the technique with which they're most closely associated or to which they're particularly important. So, even if you're sure about the methods and techniques which you intend to use, you'll still need to skim-read the whole of Part Three, before concentrating on the material which seems particularly relevant to your own circumstances.

Throughout all this, you'll discover that your relationship with your tutor is very important, and I'll be returning to it on the occasions when it's essential that you interact with him or her. However, there will be many occasions when your tutor isn't available at just the right time, and there may be situations in which you feel your query is a bit trivial, and you wish you could just look it up in an appropriate text. Enquire within. (The index is an obvious place in which to look as well as the contents; with the problems of choosing a topic in mind, there's a particularly useful index entry which refers you to every example in the text which might prove a source of topic ideas.)

This isn't to put the tutor on some kind of pedestal, but to make a rather more subtle point. Tuition seems to work best when you've thought about the matter that's troubling you, and have developed one or two solutions (or at least a clearly-articulated problem!) to present to the tutor so that a sensible way forward can be hammered out between you. One purpose of this book is to get you to that stage.

1.3 WHAT THIS BOOK DOESN'T DO

You'll notice that there's nothing here on researching a Ph.D. Research for a Ph.D. is rather different to the work you'll be doing. The approaches, methods and research techniques are very subject-specific, and grounded much more in the personal preference and direction adopted by the researcher, and in the advice and preferences of the personal tutor. A Ph.D. is the culmination of a developing programme of research, rather than of a single investigation. Material on doctorate research is therefore outside the scope of this book; however, before the Ph.D. student turns away and everyone else reads on, you might want to look up the following references in my bibliography. Phillips and Pugh (1987) is the equivalent book to this one, a *vade-mecum* for doctoral students, albeit not confined to business and management students. More to the point, Salmon (1992), while describing the personal side of doing, and living with, the research experience at Ph.D. level, is worth a glance from **anyone** doing research, regardless of the level involved, for the insights it provides into the personal experience of doing research.

1.4 FINAL THOUGHTS

You'll have noticed that this book adopts a fairly informal style. Anyone starting on a six to fifty thousand word project deserves all the help he or she can get! At the same time, your own work will need to follow certain conventions of referencing for bibliographic purposes, and the best way to establish a convention is by example. So all references which I provide will be by name and date, as above. If your regulations require some different referencing method (e.g. the numbered reference), you'll find the ground-rules described in Chapter 8.

The purpose and objectives of a project | 2

The clearer you are about your purpose and objectives, the better your project will be. This chapter reviews the reasons for doing a project and identifies the more obvious implications from your point of view. It shows how the nature of your audience, and its expectations, differ depending on the amount of management experience on which you can draw, and concludes by asking you to carry out an exercise to fit your own preferences to the requirements and objectives of the particular programme on which you are registered.

2.1 THE PURPOSE OF A PROJECT

At the most general level, the purpose of a business/management project can be defined as follows.

■ To create an opportunity for the application of concepts and techniques acquired during the taught programme, in a management practitioner environment, in order to complete the formal learning experience, and to be of use to the sponsor.

Two basic assumptions underly this purpose. The first is that application, rather than sheer exposition by lecturers and absorption by the student, is what makes for effective learning. This assumption matches with the pragmatic and somewhat atheoretic values espoused by business sponsors (who aren't academics and have an organization to run!). Moreover, it is based on pretty solid evidence on the nature of human learning, as you'll recognize from your Organizational Behaviour taught course material. People learn by doing.

The second assumption is that at least part of this learning should take place in the organizational environment. Some people would argue that this is in order to maximize the transfer of learning from the academic to the practitioner environment.

Others would assert that in the case of mature, post-experience students, it isn't possible to learn anything worthwhile unless the learning activity takes place within the context provided by personal involvement in real management issues as they happen. They stress that it's the content of the issue or problem which matters, as much as the principles, underlying theories, or management techniques pertaining to it, and that while case study methods may be useful in teaching, the real thing is better. They feel this so strongly (and on fairly persuasive, though currently incomplete, evidence: see Mangham (1986) that they would advocate that the entire content of any post-experience management programme should be determined by the issues and problems which face practising managers, issues which managers should address by acquiring competencies in handling them. This is the rationale for in-company, tailor-made programmes: a convenient summary, which you should read if you are following an in-company programme, or an MBA of any kind, is provided by Ashton (1989). It's certainly a good rationale for project work.

> in-company

According to this view, then, the project gives you two kinds of experience: the experience of a time (the placement period) spent in a non-academic, occupational situation, while being faced with a partially academic task to complete; and the experience of a task (doing the project itself) which partially simulates some important aspects of a manager's job. In those circumstances in which it is possible to do a project which includes implementation of recommendations, and a degree of evaluation of the consequences (as in the case of many MBA projects, for example), the simulation of some, but not all, aspects will be fairly close.

> all

Notice that my overall definition of your purpose says nothing about making a contribution to knowledge in the academic sense one associates with Master's programmes 'by research', and with Ph.D. programmes. There is no doubt that if your project is any good at all, someone's knowledge will be enhanced: your own, of course; your tutor's, possibly (perhaps through your provision of a good literature review, new bibliographic citations the tutor hadn't come across, or new case study material, confidentiality arrangements permitting); and your sponsoring organization, most certainly. But I omit the academic sense of adding to the generally shared stock of knowledge, or contributing to theory, because I don't believe that successful in-company, practitioner-based projects which form part of a taught management or business programme should have this intent in the way that a 'degree by research' does.

An important exception, which hinges on the words 'as conventionally defined', is presented in Chapter 6. For the moment, I want to make a crude distinction in emphasis, and to consider the dangers involved in adopting an approach based excessively on the style and intentions of academic research. If you subscribe solely to this academic purpose, you'll find yourself handling ideas and concepts in a theory-driven, rather than practitioner, way. (In a project on job satisfaction, for example, you might be tempted to identify and report the best fit of a set of nonlinear regression equations between organizational variables and some measure of job satisfaction, a topic of great academic interest but unlikely to be sufficiently error-free, or generalizable outside your organization, with the sample size at your disposal. Far better to use the same information to identify what the actual factors are, and the level of job satisfaction in general.)

A second danger is that you find yourself adopting methods and techniques based on the research methodology of the social sciences more than you need to. I expect you've noticed how many textbooks on your project reading list concentrate on research methods, and how few on project methods! Finally, you'll be tempted to present your project document laid out in a format more appropriate to a research thesis than a project report.

You'll have noticed that the statement of purpose is very general. You will need to discover the particular way in which your own teaching institution interprets it, and especially, which aspects are emphasized by the particular programme you're following. Moreover, you will need to discover this as soon as possible, certainly before you give much thought to the topic of your project. I would suggest that you do this before giving more than a cursory glance to Chapter 3, which outlines the issues involved in the choice of a project topic.

in-company

If you're doing the project as an employee, as part of a formal agreement between the company and the academic institution, then as well as talking to your sponsor you might consider contacting the manager who first developed the programme with the teaching institution. It is helpful to pick his or her brains about the project purpose, and to take his or her views on what might make for a good project from the organization's point of view, at this stage of their relationship with the educational institution. What has been learnt from previous projects, and what is the direction in which he or she might wish to see the relationship between organization and educational institution develop?

2.2 THE OBJECTIVES OF A PROJECT

all

A good way of clarifying the purpose of your project is to examine the associated objectives in detail: they should be available from your tutor. They tend to vary depending on the type of programme which you're studying; a selection taken from the internal publications of several institutions is given in Table 2.1. They can be classified according to the four major emphases of the general statement of purpose:

■ acquisition and practice of concepts and techniques;
■ the management environment;
■ the personal learning experience;
■ the contribution to the organization.

Acquisition and practice of concepts and techniques

It's difficult to say much about the particular **concepts** which a project should convey: they are, by definition, specific to the subject-matter discipline and the organizational issues, with which you'll be dealing.

There are, however, some general concepts which apply to all forms of research work: issues of validity, reliability, utility, generality, efficiency and effectiveness which you will also be expected to encounter and handle. These are rarely spelled out in institutional handouts (though some reference is made to some of them in some project manuals!). They will be dealt with in Chapter 6, and you should read the relevant section before finalizing your choice of topic.

Again, the **techniques** depend on the subject-matter of your project: anything from discounted cash flow in accountancy, sales projections in marketing, to spreadsheet analysis for corporate planning in a more business-policy related project. And again, this manual does not deal with them, since they're too specific for our purposes.

There are some techniques, however, which are common enough to be relevant to a variety of different projects: those associated with historical review and analysis, case study method, survey method and field experiments. These are dealt with in Chapters 10 to 13 of this book, together with general material relating to the design of your empirical work.

In looking at Table 2.1, you'll notice that undergraduate programmes tend to emphasize the application of conceptual material and techniques, for the first time as it were (and quite appropriately so); they also emphasize the value of initial familiarization with the managerial and corporate environment.

under-graduate

The management environment

While statements of project objectives refer to a familiarization with the environment, you'll rarely find them listed in any great detail in an institutional handout. This is not surprising, as the culture and climate of different organizations vary enormously, between organizations within one country and (for the benefit of those of you who are doing

all

Table 2.1 The objectives of a project: five listings

(a) *In general*: after Balke *et al.* (1978) cited in Baetz and Beamish (1989)

Concepts and techniques:
- To provide a testing ground for concepts presented in the taught programme
- To serve as a basis for developing new concepts not covered in the literature

Personal learning experience:
- To give an opportunity to practise and develop personal skills in an organizational setting
- To provide an initial experience in handling group coordination and conflict
- To create the opportunity for executives to challenge student ideas: a situation from which both parties may learn

Management environment:
- To provide current, first-hand contact with executives, as opposed to the predigested case studies of unknown managers in the taught components of the programme
- To afford the opportunity of organizing a mass of data and observations as a first introduction to organizational complexity for undergraduates

---

(b) *Undergraduate level*: after Hemingray (1988)

Concepts and techniques:
- To provide a basis for applying some of the disciplines and approaches taught in the early parts of the programme

Personal learning experience:
- To assist in the choice of undergraduate specialisms
- To provide an early experience of the scope of employment in the chosen field of interest

Management environment:
- To provide an opportunity to come to grips with the real world with demands and problems which the student might previously not have anticipated

---

(c) *Undergraduate and Master's (not post-experience)*

Concepts and techniques:
- To provide an introduction to data sources and research techniques typical of organizations and their markets, while handling the inadequacies and shortcomings of such data

Personal learning experience:
- To create a sense of responsibility, since analysis and proposals have to be discussed and negotiated with organizational sponsors
- To give experience in the collective effort and process of debate whereby proposals are developed and agreed
- To provide practice in written management report-writing, a skill many students (especially from an engineering, science or mathematical background) may not have acquired

Management environment:
- To identify issues and problems which, in an organizational setting, typically are presented in an unstructured way
- To create a situation in which firm proposals must be made on inadequate information
- To provide an opportunity for meeting senior executives informally, and of forming an objective impression of the values and attitudes of people who will eventually be supervisors, colleagues, or competitors

(d) *Professional*: after Teesside Business School (1988)

Concepts and techniques:
- To demonstrate the ability to apply knowledge and skills, and to define and analyse problems

Personal learning experience:
- To provide an opportunity for personal learning and growth
- To create opportunities relevant to subsequent career choice and organizational entry

Management environment:
- To provide the opportunity, over a relatively long timespan, to identify and explore aspects of the practice of personnel management in specific organizational contexts
- To relate the above to the knowledge and perspectives acquired during the course programme

(e) *MBA (post-experience, in-company)*: after Teesside Business School (1987)

Concepts and techniques:
- To integrate conceptual material from several disciplines with management experience in the place of work

Personal learning experience:
- To develop and test ability to produce a coherent, extended account on a topic of considerable conceptual and/or technical content
- To provide an elective topic of interest to the student and his/her organization, additional to the largely non-elective taught course subjects

international projects) between countries: see section 7.2. Nevertheless, some general statements can be made, and these are summarized in Table 2.2.

The extent to which your project will provide a simulation of this organizational environment, and hence satisfy this objective, depends largely on the level of your course: undergraduate and most Diploma projects expose you to fewer of the pressures associated with the characteristics of Table 2.2 than most MBA projects, and this is one of the factors considered in detail in Chapter 3, when the choice of project topic

Table 2.2 Characteristics of the management environment

Working on your project is meant to give you an experience of the following:

The content of activities, projects, and decisions dealt with by managers
- Events are different to those you encounter in the educational setting
- People's responses to these events are different
- They can't be simulated completely in the educational setting

The ways in which responses are made and decisions taken
- Problems aren't set: they're recognized by an active process
- They're not solved, but resolved: done with, finished with
- Their relative importance must be judged so they can be ignored, postponed, or dealt with as a matter of urgency
- Some of the most important ones have to be anticipated

The uncertainty which managers must handle
- Decisions must be taken on less-than-complete information
- Outcomes may be a long time in appearing
- The standards by which decisions are evaluated may not exist, and may themselves involve judgement on the part of the manager

The fragmentation of experience and activities
- Issues aren't dealt with to completion in a neat sequence: several issues may compete for the manager's attention
- Some of them will have short timespans; with others, the time between recognition and 'being finished with' will be considerably longer
- Some issues will re-present themselves at a later date; others will be different, but look the same; others will look different, but be the same

The human and interpersonal element
- Managers get work done through other people
- Many of their problems will therefore be human ones
- The manager may be extremely competent at the tasks s/he must deal with, but not as effective in handling the people

is discussed. Secondly, it depends on the basis on which you're doing the course. If you're a part-time student, doing the course on a post-experience basis, you're likely to tackle project topics which involve you more in the issues mentioned in Table 2.2.

under-graduate

It is likely that your project placement is the first time that you've experienced this environment. If your placement is a long one, the chances are that you'll have additional, non-project responsibilities to your employer, and will encounter some of these factors directly. If you're on a short placement, your opportunity will be limited to the medium of the project itself. In either case, what are the implications for your project?

First, your time should not be as fragmented as that of the permanent employees. In this sense, the project should only be a partial simulation of a manager's job, and you should expect to be protected from excessive demands on time that's meant to be devoted to the project. You can satisfy this particular project objective partly by simply being in the environment, and observing how other people operate; if your other responsibilities impinge on project time or, in the case of a brief, project-only placement, you're asked to take on other duties, **talk to someone fast**. This should be your immediate supervisor at work: **always** deal with him or her first, even if you suspect the issue will only be resolved by calling in your next resource, the tutor from your institution.

If all goes well, however, you'll obtain direct experience of some of the other items listed in Table 2.2. Choosing a topic and progressing the project represent tasks and problems which you set for yourself; and the topic, if properly chosen to be relevant to the organization, will be sufficiently open-ended as a problem to simulate some of the uncertainties handled by full-time employees. You'll have to exercise considerable social and interpersonal skill in obtaining help and cooperation from other people, though it should be said that you'll be very unlikely to have supervisory responsibilities arising directly from the project, and so this aspect of organizational life won't be simulated completely.

Finally, you should ensure that one item from the list in Table 2.2 definitely does not affect you! Namely, you should be crystal-clear about the standards by which your project, and the decisions you have made in doing the project, will be evaluated. Chapter 4 deals with this in particular.

While the best way of satisfying this project objective is simply to be there, in the organization, a useful way of preparing yourself in anticipation is to do a little reading. I've highlighted a number of imaginative and readable texts in the bibliography. They're all easy reading; the sort of book you can enjoy as bedside reading before your project placement begins.

In your case, it is assumed that you already know plenty about the management environment! At first blush it would appear that the project is simply one more task for you to carry out, one more pressure, among the other responsibilities involved in your fragmented day-to-day job. However, the task is **different** to your other jobs. It has to satisfy standards of academic, rather than pragmatic, content and rigour. It represents an opportunity to tackle a work-related issue which you wouldn't normally handle in your day-to-day work. And in the case of MBA courses, this has to be an issue in which you stand back from the normal flow of events and consider matters of strategic or corporate importance or, indeed,

in-company

recognize and explore the strategic aspects of the normal flow of events: a much more valuable exercise, some would say.

More subtle, perhaps, is the consideration that the nature of the task, and the kind of information which you'll need to complete your project, can be agreed in advance with your tutor and with your sponsor to some degree. This has the function of legitimizing what you're doing in a way which isn't always possible with a normal management problem. (In this sense, a project is a technical, rather than management, task, with some fairly firm ground rules and evaluation criteria.)

So, while it's 'just one more job to do', it's worth treating it as distinct and somewhat special. Whatever techniques of time management you habitually use or don't use for your other activities, it will be very important to manage project time deliberately and explicitly. There are a number of techniques for doing so (see section 5.2); in the meanwhile, it might be worth thinking of the project as sufficiently distinct to merit its own separate weekly day or half-day: a time when you do nothing else. More of this below!

The personal learning experience

all

If you're following a programme which assumes little substantial prior working experience, you'll find that a major emphasis is placed in your project objectives on the acquisition and development of a variety of technical, developmental, interpersonal and persuasive skills required in dealing with the other people on whose goodwill and cooperation the success of your project will depend. Some of these are shown in Table 2.3. By and large, it is assumed that you already possess most of these skills if you're following a post-experience programme and are already a practising manager.

This issue of experience is important, because it will help to determine the scope and difficulty (see Chapter 3) of the topic which you decide to tackle in your project. If, as a mature post-experience student, you've acquired some of these skills already, then this will be taken for granted when your project is assessed. If, as an undergraduate, you've had little experience in dealing with chief executives, persuading reluctant informants, or working with a team of colleagues, then, while you will be expected to achieve some of these objectives by learning the relevant skills, you won't be judged too harshly if your project shows weaknesses arising from the fact that people have been bloody-minded, from your own insensitivity, or, more likely, from a combination of the two.

For example, one of my undergraduates ran into severe difficulties when he was seconded to a different department and omitted to tell his line manager when the head of his new department sent him to a factory

Table 2.3 Characteristics of the personal learning experience

Some technical skills which you will need to acquire and use:
• techniques of time management
• writing letters requesting support
• composing memos and interim reports
• using libraries and information services
• gaining access to respondents
• interviewing respondents
• speaking to an audience

Some social and interpersonal skills to be acquired and used:
• dealing and feeling comfortable with senior managers and chief executives
• persuading people to cooperate
• providing assurances and evidence of confidentiality arrangements
• working with a team of people, usually in a colleague relationship

Some personal pressures which you may need to overcome:
• uncertainty about the approach you are taking
• doubts about the credibility of some of your academic concepts and purposes in the organizational environment in which you work
• dislike of the relatively long periods which you spend in working alone
• tension arising from the need to reschedule timetables
• uncertainty about the data: will they or won't they confirm the arguments you are expressing?
• a highlighting of your general uncertainties about your capability for successfully completing the qualification programme

120 miles away to gather some data for his project. The student knew all that classical management theory has to say about unified command, the problems of having two bosses and so on, but wasn't quick enough to make the connection with his own circumstances. The line manager, who came from a production background, didn't give a damn for the theory but knew an unreliable employee when he saw one, and as for the head of the new department, he was away on holiday when the student came back to base. Upsets all round, the line manager's subsequent cooperation refused, and missing data in the final project report, for which the tutor made allowances in the light of the circumstances.

There is one personal aspect which tends to be underestimated, both in written accounts and in informal dialogue with tutors. Working on a project is a long and somewhat lonely endeavour. Some projects last over a one-term timespan, others last a whole year; and most curricula are arranged in such a way that you're not following any taught courses during this time. Are you familiar with Jaques' concept of timespan? Briefly, the assertion is that the experience of effort, and hence potential stress, is related to the period during which a manager must exercise discretion: the longer the interval between being given a task, and the point in time at which an assessment and feedback are possible, the greater the perceived weight of responsibility (Fox, 1966). In some cases, your project will have a longer time-span than many of your taught courses!

A number of tensions may arise: they're included at the bottom of Table 2.3. Most of these are probably worse for undergraduates, familiar and hence more tolerable for those Masters and Diploma students who have completed academic projects before, and probably least acute for post-experience students. The last item, though, is particularly relevant to post-experience people who gained entry to the qualification programme on an 'experience' rather than 'prior academic qualifications' clause: in my own experience, Institute of Bankers students and senior police officers tend to find their first written examination, and the final year project, particularly troublesome in this respect, and I'm guessing this is true for other people with a similar background.

To know that a problem is likely to occur, and to anticipate it as a typical concomitant of project work, is surely some comfort as and when it might arise. If it's typical, then it's banal, boring, to be lived with in a fairly relaxed way and to be handled with a sense of humour, a trouble to be shared with friends over a pint, and not worth troubling over excessively. It just happens, that's all!

If you find that, nevertheless, the tensions I have listed persist, don't do your worrying by yourself. At the very least, share them with someone else in your class: you'll find you're not alone. Try and share them with your tutor. I'm not sure how the learning experience involved in handling these issues can be summarized in a neat list of skills to be acquired, which may be why it doesn't appear in a highlighted form among the official lists of objectives in Table 2.1. However, I have a feeling that the completion of a project in which these problems have arisen, and been lived through constructively, is a particularly valuable experience in personal development, and is surely related to the experience of management for which your programme is preparing you, or in which your programme is providing further development. And I'm not alone in this view: you might care to dip into Salmon (1992) for a very readable account of the research project as an experience in personal development.

under-graduate

If you examine Table 2.1 carefully, you'll notice that the objectives for programmes which don't assume prior management experience tend to present the project period as a time in which career directions are explored, whether in the immediate sense of exploring the possibilities of specializing in a particular kind of business function later on in the taught programme, or in the longer-term sense of gaining experience in a particular kind of industry, organization, or business function with future job applications in mind. You might care to choose a topic which is going to be useful in this respect.

Though it isn't immediately apparent from the objectives in Table 2.1, you probably already know that a substantial number of post-experience MBA students make fairly major career changes as a result of their MBA programmes. To be honest, I suspect that this is as much because the letters 'MBA' still carry a special magic to the employers of senior managers, as it is because of any specific skills you might acquire, or experiences which you might encounter, while engaged in your project. Nevertheless, you might bear the issue in mind when you choose your topic. It may suit you, or your employer, to use your project as a way of positioning yourself for your next move within your organization. I doubt if it would suit your employer if you were to use the project to facilitate an outwards move! But such moves do happen, and I leave this issue as a matter for your own concern, planning, and, perhaps, conscience.

MBA

A final factor, which underlies the post-experience Masters statement of objectives in particular, is that you are expected to integrate material across disciplines, rather than confining yourself to a single discipline or business function. This is as it should be: as someone with general management experience, you know that issues and problems do not present themselves neatly wrapped in the cloak of a particular specialism, and your choice of topic should reflect this. Undergraduates, and some Diploma candidates, in contrast, can afford to choose topics which are more specifically related to a discipline or function and which are, in that sense, more artificial.

The objectives in your own case are quite clear: the topic you choose should reflect your business function, although corporate and strategic aspects must be dealt with, and it would seem a poor strategy to choose a topic which eschews a significant treatment of the latter. See section 2.3 below.

profes-sional

The contribution to the organization

Somewhat surprisingly, there is relatively little in the general or institutional literature about this fourth factor. I've added it to the general definition of purpose myself because I know it to be implicit in the practice of many academic institutions, and because I believe it to be important. It does appear in the guise of a rationale for collaborative research and for teaching company schemes, and for some single-company MBAs, but it's rarely spelt out among the written objectives for in-company project work in general.

all

Some general publicity brochures produced by educational institutions occasionally state the advantages to the organization of acting as hosts for undergraduate industrial placements. And so, if a project forms part of such a placement, it would seem sensible to view it as a culmination of a placement, apply the placement objectives to the project and generalize them to all projects whether they form part of a placement programme or not. Table 2.4 lists a number of advantages and benefits for the sponsoring organization. These should be treated as objectives for all projects: in short, the results should be valuable to the organization in some way. A good indication that your project has this sort of value to the organization is given when you're asked to make a presentation of your final report to the organization, in addition to any presentation you have to make to your academic institution.

under-graduate

In the case of undergraduate projects, it has to be said that the results may not be directly of the same generality as if you were a full-time employee. This is no reflection on you, the undergraduate: sometimes a good topic from the academic point of view may be somewhat limited from the organization's perspective, being seen more of an exercise, or of only local interest. A lot depends on the support and keenness of your sponsor or direct company supervisor. However, in choosing your topic (Chapter 3), you might give a thought to the needs of your direct supervisor, and try to choose one which will be of direct personal or departmental use to him or her personally, even if the wider usefulness within the organization is problematic.

all

It's very helpful, but not always possible, if the project involves a topic in which the academic tutor's input provides expertise which is otherwise

Table 2.4 The benefits of a project to the sponsoring organization

- The project tackles an issue of relevance to the organization: it should not be a purely academic exercise.

- It represents an opportunity to examine an issue of corporate or strategic importance which might be otherwise ignored in the pressure of more immediate, operational demands.

- It draws on the back-up of the educational institution, and if carefully chosen, represents an inexpensive form of consultancy expertise.

- A carefully chosen project topic will be useful to the immediate company supervisor of the student who is doing the project.

- In the case of non-in-company based students, and depending on any non-academic components of the work involved, it may release a permanent employee for other responsibilities.

lacking in the organization. The combination of your own efforts (and if you're an employee, you know the company well!) and the tutor (who has relevant subject-related expertise) could well add up to a very powerful form of outside consultancy, which, note, is free of consultancy fees.

A successful project under this objective is one which has the sponsoring organization crying out for more: expressing a wish to sponsor another undergraduate placement, or wanting to put another of its managers through an MBA, Diploma, or professional programme.

2.3 THE SPECIAL OBJECTIVES OF PROFESSIONAL PROGRAMMES

Project work done in order to satisfy professional bodies differs sufficiently from the previous types of project to merit a brief section to itself. Such projects take their subject-matter from activities within the business function served by the professional body, and do not primarily address issues and topics in general management (though the corporate implications of functional issues may well be considered). Primarily, they serve the purpose of entry into the profession, and particularly, of giving you membership of the professional body itself. The other purpose and objectives outlined in Sections 2.1 and 2.2 apply in addition, however.

The most important issue for you to be clear about is the status of the programme you are following, as much as the status of the project within the programme. Some professional bodies, like the Chartered Institute of Marketing, remain entirely responsible for the content and assessment of the project, which in their case is a report on work done in the past. Others, like the Institute of Personnel and Development, run a dual system in which different regulations for the project apply, depending on whether the responsibility for the programme of which the project forms a part has been devolved on to the educational institution. No doubt you will know which regulations apply to your programme, but you may not be clear initially how these translate into objectives for your project. Your tutor should have issued you with a handout outlining the intent, objectives, and practical regulations of the project, or possibly a longer, purpose-written project handbook.

However, even if there is such a handbook, you might find it useful to do some further personal research by getting in touch with the professional body in question and obtaining a copy of their regulations, to see how your own institution has interpreted them. Have there been any shifts of emphasis? To what degree has the professional body devolved responsibility on to the institution, and to what extent does this reflect local or regional knowledge or staff expertise on which you might draw in deciding on a topic for your project or in finding a tutor (to the extent that you have any choice in the latter matter!)?

For a few examples of professional programme objectives, see Table 2.5. The Institute of Personnel and Development structures the bulk of its Stage 2 curriculum in a way which requires the completion of a major management report (quite apart from the written examinations and six work-related assignments by which the taught courses are assessed), the purpose of which is described in similar language to my general statement in section 2.1.

The emphasis here is very much on analysis, planning, and problem-solving. In this sense, these objectives are similar to the objectives of many MBA programmes. There is also an emphasis on the presentation of recommendations for action, by people who are already in full-time employment and hence able to make meaningful implementation proposals. In contrast, in those programmes following the IPD general guidelines which have been devolved on to educational institutions as Exemption Programmes (called by names such as 'Diploma in Personnel Management' or 'Masters in Human Resource Management'), the objectives of the project may differ in emphasis, having been set by the institution, albeit approved by IPD. The students may be part-time or full-time; in the latter case the project would be carried out during a period of industrial placement. One such set of objectives appears as listing (d) in Table 2.1.

in-company

Projects are sometimes used to give entry to otherwise unqualified post-experience candidates. Thus, the Chartered Institute of Marketing uses a formal paper as a form of direct entry in the case of mature senior marketing practitioners who do not possess a degree or membership of one of a number of Chartered Institutes. The characteristics of this paper translate into objectives as shown in Table 2.5.

The formal paper differs from those described hitherto, in one major way: project activity and topic would be historical and, at the time of application to the Institute, largely complete; it is the write-up which would be current. Recommendations would have been implemented, the consequences assessed, and some interim or final outcomes evaluated. Implementation and evaluation of the results is rarely part of an undergraduate project, isn't common at Diploma level, but may occur in some MBA programmes.

Table 2.5 Sample objectives from three professional bodies

Institute of Personnel and Development.
To demonstrate that the student:
- comprehends principles underpinning the matter being investigated
- has considered alternative approaches to investigating and analysing the issue
- has examined, by obtaining primary and secondary data, alternative solutions to the problem
- has demonstrated a critical evaluative approach
- has drawn relevant conclusions
- has considered the feasibility of the introduction of the recommendations that have been made within the context of the organization
- can present data in a clear and logical form using charts, diagrams, etc. as appropriate
- is able to prepare an implementation plan
  (Tel. 0181 946 9100)

Chartered Institute of Marketing
The formal paper should:
- normally be not less than approximately 5000 words
- cover a marketing programme which the applicant has personally planned and implemented during the preceding three years
- demonstrate the application of marketing skills or market diagnosis, analysis and planning
- deal with an actual business situation or problem where the applicant's management and marketing expertise can clearly be shown to have accomplished measurable results
- demonstrate intellectual rigour, quality of analysis, relevance of findings, and evidence of managerial competence following six criteria (as specified)
- demonstrate an ability to understand and apply the marketing principles underlying the specific actions described in the report; a report which merely describes such actions is not acceptable
- must be written by the applicant him/her self but may contain extracts from e.g. advertising agencies, market research reports, so long as acknowledgement, and a critical commentary, are provided; previous reports written by the applicant e.g. a marketing plan are acceptable if properly integrated into the paper
- avoid a mere analysis of the applicant's current or previous responsibilities; nor is an anecdotal approach to the applicant's achievements acceptable
  (Tel. 016285 24922)

Chartered Institute of Public Finance and Accountancy
Aims:
- To develop research techniques and demonstrate their application to the planning and carrying out of a sustained financial review
- To develop skills of collecting, analysing and evaluating complex financial and non-financial information

Table 2.5 continued
• To test the ability of candidates
  to plan and carry out a sustained financial review in a systematic way without detailed supervision
  to collect and critically evaluate relevant information
  to select, apply and evaluate the usefulness of problem-solving methods and techniques
  to identify potential options, and to select and substantiate the most suitable
  to communicate orally and in writing
  (Tel. 0171 895 8823)

IPD (1993); CIM (undated); CIPFA (1993)

2.4 IN CONCLUSION: MAKING THE OBJECTIVES YOUR OWN

all

All of the foregoing should surely suggest the importance of tailoring your project to the requirements of your particular audience. What you have to do is to prepare a project report which applies programme concepts and techniques in a practitioner environment in a way which completes your learning experience and is of use to someone in the sponsoring organization. The objectives which specify this purpose in greater detail may vary a little according to the level of programme (first degree, Diploma, MBA) which you are following, but vary much more with the extent to which you do or don't have prior management experience. Thus there is a substantial difference of emphasis and expectation between undergraduate and post-experience/in-company students. There is also a distinction in expectations according to type of programme being followed: between professional entry and academic qualification programmes.

In all this discussion of objectives, there is one person whose interests may have been forgotten: and that is **yourself**. As well as working to satisfy your tutor and your sponsor in a way which reflects the particular programme which you are following, it is important that you satisfy your **own** wishes and needs. The best way of doing this at this stage is to try to personalize the objectives which you will have to address, in the light of the factors I have outlined above.

So: what is your experience base, and what type of programme are you following? Perhaps, while you were reading this chapter, you have been making notes on the purpose and objectives as they apply to you. If you weren't, now is the time to go back over the material and identify the particular emphases and expectations as they apply to your own circumstances. You will need to think through the following issues:

■ What are the concepts and techniques in which you're expected to demonstrate competence?

■ To what extent are you likely to be required to integrate material across disciplines, or conversely, emphasize the particular interests and perspectives of a particular academic discipline or professional/business function?

■ What kinds of skills it is likely that you will be asked to demonstrate, which ones interest you, and which ones will you want, as well as need, to acquire?

■ In the case of people following a competency-based programme, which competencies from your individual learning contract are likely to be demonstrable through the medium of the project?

■ In the case of post-experience and in-company students, what kinds of past experience might you highlight and draw on during the project period? Have you done any projects on similar topics in any previous courses which you have studied? (But see section 3.1 on this issue.)

■ Depending on your experience base and location, what kind of contribution to your Sponsor is it feasible for you to make, what kind of contribution might you personally like to make, and at what organizational level? (Supervisor? Sponsor? Departmental? Whole-organization?)

You can only begin to answer these questions if you have a copy of the institutional, and, possibly, professional, regulations as they apply to your particular programme. Now is the time to get hold of them, if you haven't already done so.

I'm not sure how far you will be able to answer these questions at present. Certainly, you won't answer them completely until you have a clearer idea of the topic which you wish to choose for the project, and so I imagine you'll want to return to the questions after you have read Chapter 3, and finalized your choice of topic. It may be that your final answers will be clearer after you have familiarized yourself with the standards and criteria which will be applied to your project work, and so you might return to them again after you have read Chapter 4.

The reason for posing them at this stage, and returning to them periodically, should surely be obvious, however. At present, the objectives are someone else's. There they sit, in institutional black and white print. The knack of good project work lies partly in making the objectives your own, that is, in familiarising yourself with the objectives of your own particular programme, and by thinking through your own preferences and circumstances, of expressing the purpose and objectives in ways which are relevant and interesting to **you**.

Choosing a topic

3

I'll hazard a guess that, at the outset, two issues will dominate your thinking about the project: 'What shall I choose as a topic?', and 'What sort of standards are involved?' Common sense will suggest that both must be resolved for the project to be successful, and that the sooner this is done, the better. The purpose of this chapter is to help you deal with it expeditiously and as effectively as possible. The second issue is more problematic, and it's my suspicion that weak projects are often unsuccessful because the issue of standards was scarcely considered, and insufficient help given: a theme which merits a separate chapter, Chapter 4, to itself.

3.1 BASIC CRITERIA

Let's assume that you haven't yet fixed on a topic, and are considering a range of possibilities. Some will be vague, others more precise; the ones about which you're confident don't necessarily interest you; the ones which you like seem a little too ambitious; you'd like to link one idea with another, but aren't sure if it will be acceptable to your tutor; you quite like the sound of another, but can't express it sufficiently clearly in writing. All a bit messy, and time is passing. What to do? Treat the following as a set of guidelines which you apply to each topic idea, regardless of the clarity of the idea at the moment. You might find it useful to jot down ideas, and make notes relating to possible ideas, as you read.

Does it interest you?

You're going to be living with this topic for quite a long time. If you're considering it because you feel you ought to, because your lecturers said it was important, or because it's currently fashionable in the literature, the chances are that you'll be sick to death of it before you're through, and are likely to do the minimum required to bring the project to completion. Ideally, the topic should be one about which you're curious, and one in which you feel you can interest your reader too.

One reason for choosing a less-than-fascinating topic is that you've left things too late, and must choose any old thing that feels 'do-able' in the time available. Don't leave things too late! Try and collect ideas well ahead of the deadline. ('Deadlines already? For choosing a topic?' Oh yes indeed. See section 5.2.) Jot them down as they occur to you; make mini-lists of interesting concepts as you first encounter them in your course; when you read over past papers during your revision for examinations, copy out the questions that sound intriguing, whether you know anything about the issue or not. Some you might deal with during your taught course as time becomes available, others you might never return to; but the rest form a list which you might consider when the time comes to start work on the project. So: which of these listed topics interests you most?

How much do you know about it already?

Clearly, you'll have less work to do if you choose a topic which you've encountered and worked on before. Analysis, evaluation, and judgement will come more easily, and you'll be more aware of the issues that arise, if you've covered the basic ground already. You'll know what aspects of the topic are likely to repay in-depth investigation. Any topics which you've already researched, for an essay or assignment, are worth considering for their potential as projects, so long as you feel that they have the depth to carry an extended treatment.

Perhaps the best guide here is provided by the marks you have received for the prior work you have done. Choose something you're good at! And certainly, avoid your weak areas. If your mark for an assignment was poor to average, you are unlikely to be able to expand it into a project successfully unless you're crystal-clear about where you went wrong, and have a good idea about how best to improve. If you struggled to gain an average mark in a 2000-word report, you're unlikely to do well by expanding it into a 20 000-word project.

Choose a topic within a business function, or discipline, in which you're comfortable. The 'interest' criterion will save you from choosing a heavily statistical or accountancy-based topic if these are your weak subjects, as performance and interest tend to be strongly related in these subjects. However, even if you have the interest, you need to bear in mind that certain topics can only be adequately approached in a numerate way, and if you lack the skills, they're best avoided.

MBA

For you, familiarity may have its dangers. If you read Business Studies or Management at undergraduate level, or for a Diploma, then topics you've dealt with before may be a little stale: especially if you've already done an undergraduate project on the same topic, and the first degree was very recent. To some extent you'll have made up your mind and foreclosed on the conclusions. In other words, it could be difficult for you to say anything fresh, at the level and depth required in your project (which is likely to be longer than your previous treatment of this topic). On the other hand, the earlier comments about the advantages of familiarity apply.

Advice to strike a happy medium is never terribly explicit, don't you find? Here are some concrete suggestions.

- If your previous work has included very similar ideas and concepts, handled the same way as before, it would seem useful to alter the topic to one which brings some new ideas to bear.
- If the data you're planning to gather are similar to the data you've gathered before, the same comment applies.
- If your project is being done to complete an MBA, then you shouldn't be contemplating a purely functional-area topic, even though this might be familiar from undergraduate work.

in-company

If you're a part-time student following a professional programme, or an in-company-based MBA, your work experience gives you a great advantage, since your topic is likely to deal with your own organization. The danger is that you choose a project which you would have been covering already as part of your day-to-day responsibilities. While your project should be relevant, it should also have a measure of academic content!

This issue is dealt with in greater depth in Chapter 8; for the time being, your best action is to remember that the intent of your course is to add to your personal development as a professional, or as a general manager: choose a topic which draws on your experience by all means, but also one which helps you to grow in a desirable direction. 'What sort of topic will assist me in my next career move?' is a very helpful and legitimate question in this context, and one with which you are familiar in any case since it is part of the reason for undertaking a period of academic study in the first place.

How difficult is it likely to be?

all

Your previous studies will have given you an idea of which topics you find easy, and which ones more difficult. However, you need to bear in mind that some topics are intrinsically more difficult than others, and before you tackle them in depth, you may not realize what you've let yourself in for. This is an issue which your tutor will want to address at your first project tutorial, though he or she may use the word 'Scope' rather than 'difficulty'. It helps to know what issues he or she will have in mind. 'Difficulty' in this sense breaks down into five aspects:

- the level of qualification to which you're working;
- the intrinsic complexity of the subject-matter;
- the availability of expertise on which you can draw;
- the ease with which you can access data;
- the time required to complete a project based on the topic in question.

Level of qualification. Some topics lend themselves to an under-graduate project, while others are more appropriate to treatment at Masters level. Some merit a more scholarly treatment, others are ideal for an in-company based project. Many, I must admit, cross these boundaries! Table 3.1 gives some examples of each, where the distinctions, though arguable, are fairly clear-cut. You will also get a better grasp of this issue in the next chapter, which deals with the issue of standards.

Intrinsic complexity. Some topics deal in ideas, or require the application of techniques, which are difficult to handle in themselves. There they sit, out on the frontiers of knowledge, making demands on the most experienced researchers. How can you recognize them? Here are a few obvious clues.

- People talk of them as being 'leading-edge', and your common sense suggests that they're not talking about currently fashionable, 'flavour of the month' issues.
- You notice that there is relatively little material available in your otherwise well-stocked library.
- They're dealt with in language and concepts which belong to your main subject of study, but which you haven't encountered in lectures. Perhaps they rely on statistical, mathematical, or financial techniques which are more advanced than your course expects of you.
- Finally, you notice that your basic textbooks make little reference to them, practitioner journals are sketchy, and only the most advanced refereed journals provide a thorough coverage, using language that you find difficult to understand.

Conversely, of course, you shouldn't embark on a project which is too easy! You see why the first tutorial session is important?

Table 3.1 Samples of topics by area, field and aspect

Area	Field	Aspect and topic
Undergraduate		
Behavioural/ personnel	Organizational culture	A repertory grid-based study of how companies construe their trade in the post-command economies
Finance	Cost accounting	Cost analysis and cost behaviour in relation to production in Company X
Policy/strategy	Economics	An economic analysis of the process of privatizing catering services in the NHS
Production	Process control	Profitability and efficiency in a process firm
Marketing	Market analysis	Barriers and possibilities for sales into China
Diploma		
Behavioural	Organization structure	The organization and structure of a church voluntary group
Finance	Credit control	Evaluating customer credit arrangements
Finance	Management accounting	Development of a ward-based financial information system for Hospital X
Personnel/IR	Employee participation	Improving quality by employee involvement
Business policy	Marketing	Development of alternative markets for handknitting yarns from a UK yarn mill which used to supply a hometrade market
Policy/strategy	Marketing	The marketing of the College to SE Asian students
MBA		
Behavioural	Organizational structure and culture	Is the Basic Command Unit the way forward for policing in year 2000?
Personnel/ behavioural	Organization development	Introducing an employee participation scheme into Company X: the consequences for staffing policy
Finance	Cost/management accounting	An analysis of transfer pricing methods

Marketing	Market analysis	Possibilities for entry into the on-shore and offshore petrochemical/ oil and gas decommissioning market
Marketing	Marketing strategies	Strategic partnerships between providers and major clients as a move towards globalization
Strategic management	Company mission and market	How Company X can best position itself in the waste minimization consultancy market
Strategic management	Local government	How should Local Authority Leisure depts. prepare for LG reorganization with respect to their discretionary services?

Availability of expertise. Very few teaching institutions have expertise in all of the areas within which you might choose your project. Staff have their specialisms in which they can show excellence; their humdrum competencies; and their conceptual black holes, subject-matter which they'd rather you didn't mention with any great enthusiasm. Ideally, you should have been placed with the tutor in whose field of excellence your topic will lie. A very good, and fairly common, arrangement is for your tutor to call on a relevant colleague when you require greater help than your tutor can provide. It helps, therefore, if you're familiar with your tutor's preferences before confirming your topic, and you should certainly discuss this issue during your first tutorial.

A second form of institutional expertise is the library and computing resource on which you might wish to draw. It's worth scanning the library holdings to see if your proposed topic is adequately covered: section 8.1 will tell you how. If all else fails, ask a librarian! Similarly, if your topic will depend on computing facilities, it's best to explore their availability at the outset. Is the hardware there, and accessible at convenient times? Check out how the booking system works. Are non-project students likely to hog all the terminals for word-processing their assignments just when your project timetable indicates that your data require analysis? Another reason for early timetabling: see section 5.2. Is the appropriate software available? How well do you get on with the technician or programmer whose help, believe me, you'll be requiring in due course?

In-company based projects have their own expertise base. You'll find two kinds of help particularly important. Firstly, your sponsor, whose role is complementary to your academic tutor: section 7.3 gives you more details. As with the tutor, it helps if the sponsor is knowledgeable about

in-company

your topic; if he or she is more of an administrative appointment, it's useful to cast around for other people who might be expert in the in-company issues which your topic addresses. Secondly, you may find it helpful to have someone who is more of a personal friend to act as mentor and coach (if your sponsor can't do so), particularly someone who has already completed the level of course which you're studying. If there is such a person, you might bear in mind this expertise when choosing your topic, so long as your topic is different to theirs; but then in-company pressures will almost certainly ensure that this is the case, since the practically useful and relevant topics required for in-company projects are rarely repeatable in quite the same way as academically based topics.

If you are thinking about an internationally based topic, it may be that you will have to rely on local expertise in the country in question. How feasible is this? Are communications with the foreign-based manager involved sufficient for your purpose?

Ease of data access. All business and management projects require you to present empirical material (that is to say, research evidence of some kind), whether you've originated this yourself or worked from secondary sources. Is your topic one for which data can be readily found? The data may be too difficult to generate, or too expensive. They may take you too long to acquire. Confidentiality, industrial relations climate, and the internal politics of the organization from which you are drawing the data all have a bearing on your choice of topic.

MBA

Many survey-based topics at this level require you to be particularly careful in drawing up a sampling frame from which you decide on the particular sample of respondents to approach (see section 9.2). Your choice of topic will require an early decision based on whether the sampling frame already exists, or must be created by you. A recent topic which I tutored depended on the existence of a database of ethnically owned businesses in the county, from which the sample could be drawn. Unfortunately, while some individual boroughs had this information, others didn't, and the ensuing problems made for a weak project. It takes time, and money, to create a directory of businesses, and while funding can be found, it's unusual that a project timetable can be easily shaped round the background work required.

in-company

Some in-company projects are easier than others because someone, perhaps your sponsor, is interested in the results. This interest may be predicated on his or her activities, responsibilities, budget, or personal and hidden agendas. So your topic will be partially determined by political interests (which you might as well think of as legitimate without taking sides: why make problems for yourself?); a measure of discretion and sensitivity to other people's needs will be required. Certainly, if the topic is otherwise worth doing, and you have strong internal support, your project is likely to be successful: after all, one of the signs of practical importance and relevance (criteria your project must address) is that people in your organization are intrigued, engaged, and feel strongly about it. This is particularly true of the more strategic, policy-related, and corporate issues which make for good topics at MBA level.

Data access can pose particular problems in international projects. One of my students doing research on new product development found that her Bulgarian managers were extremely careful about what they were willing to tell her, and this became apparent in a particularly frustrating way: having agreed to help in advance, they subsequently avoided her inquiries and ignored all of her phone calls. She'd have preferred them to have said 'no' at the outset, but that isn't the east European way! In the end, she got what she needed through gentle pressures applied through family contacts, but the delay put back the completion of her project by over three months.

Time required for completion. This is associated partly with the difficulty of the topic, and partly with the natural timetabling imposed on you by events largely outside your control. Focusing on the latter, if your topic is likely to depend on other people's work, hitherto unpublished research, or the completion by others of personal, in-company, agency, or government reports, you need to be very careful in estimating timing and feasibility. If you are likely to have to travel to interview respondents, to look up archival data, or to spend time at head office or outlying company premises, these need planning for at an early stage. A second opinion by tutor and/or sponsor will be very valuable, and your own decision, or their advice, may lead you to abandon an otherwise promising topic at the early planning stage.

all

In summary

The basic criteria in choosing a topic are, therefore, your interest in it, the state of your prior knowledge, and the difficulty of the subject-matter in question. Difficulty is in itself a complicated issue of scope, involving the suitability of the topic to the level of qualification for which you're studying, the intrinsic complexity of the material, the availability of expertise afforded you, the ease of data access during the project, and the time required for completion of the particular topic which you might have in mind.

At this stage, you should ask yourself if the rather vague ideas you had at the outset of this section are any clearer. Have you eliminated any initial topic ideas as unsuitable, and firmed up on any others?

I suppose there are two possibilities at this stage: a notion that you might tackle one of a small number of topics, each of which is still underspecified but deserving of more detailed thought; alternatively, a sense of panic because nothing plausible has come to mind. Section 3.2 deals with the former case, while section 3.3 is intended as a soothing security blanket, offering a number of heuristic devices for generating project ideas.

3.2 WORKING UP AND NARROWING DOWN

One of the criticisms that tutors and examiners make of unsuccessful projects is that the basic idea was too vague at the outset, and wasn't sufficiently worked up during the early stages of project work. This is betrayed by a woolly project report, that is, by a lack of direction in the introduction, or by a mismatch of objectives and achievements. Much of the material will be irrelevant, being directed to issues which, while related, have no direct bearing on the topic as declared at the outset. The purpose of this section is to help you work up your topic ideas, and thereby minimize problems of this kind from the outset.

Make a start as follows. Take each of your possible ideas separately. Imagine that all knowledge can be classified under three headings: Area, Field, Aspect. Make a list in which each idea is assigned to one of these headings.

An **Area** is a broad field of scholarly or business endeavour. It can be a basic discipline dealt with in your course, such as 'Economics' or 'Behaviour in Organizations'. It might be one of the business functions, like 'Production' or 'Accounting and Finance'. It could be the title of one of the more interdisciplinary course components of your overall taught course, like 'Business Strategy' or 'International Marketing and Trade'.

A **Field** is a component of an Area. It represents a sub-discipline, like 'Macroeconomics' or 'Employee Motivation'; alternatively it might be a theme within a business function, like 'Process Control' or 'Trading Terms'; or, finally, it may be an issue dealt with by an interdisciplinary course, like 'Small Business' or 'The Exporting Function in Organizations'.

An **Aspect** is just that: a more detailed facet of a Field. To complete the running example of the last two paragraphs, it might be 'The Impact of UK Monetary Policy' or 'Employee Incentive Schemes'; it could be 'Profitability and Efficiency in a Process Firm' or 'Evaluating Consumer Credit Arrangements'; it may be 'Local Businesses as Contractor-Suppliers to the Larger Firm' or 'Critical Analysis of Export Marketing Strategy'.

This represents a very rough-and-ready classification, and it may be that those of a more purist, taxonomic cast of mind (business encyclopaedia writers? professional indexers? who knows?), would quarrel with its consistency. However, the scheme is immensely valuable in narrowing down your project ideas, since it allows you to consider the level the ideas have reached. There are other, more subject-specific ways of narrowing down (see Sternberg, 1988: 14, if you have a background in the behavioural sciences) but this particular classification scheme has the advantage of generality across all the business and management topics.

At the outset, it's worth regarding an idea as a good one if you can assign it fairly readily to any of the three categories. I'll say that again in a different way. Early on in your choice of topic, it doesn't matter that all your ideas are at the Field or Area level. It's okay! Don't worry! As time and your thoughts progress, then certainly, your ideas should be represented at the Aspect level, but it is comforting to know that much project and research development progresses from the general to the specific, and that there is a natural timespan in which this occurs.

Having said that, it is also true that a good topic is one which has been through the Area-Field-Aspect process, and that your ideas must be progressed through these stages before the bulk of your project work can begin. One problem with weak projects is that, to all intents and purposes, the material is dealt with at the level of Field rather than anything more specific, and a second one, that the Aspect stage was reached too late in the day. A third, and probably less common difficulty, is posed when you are certain of your topic at the outset and remain stuck at the Aspect level, without any broader framework to guide your ideas and your reading. This can be a particular problem for in-company students, and is dealt with later on in this chapter.

Certainly, by the time you have your second project tutorial, the Aspect stage, together with one further very important task, should be achieved. The Aspect stage is still not the final step, however: it needs narrowing down yet again, to focus your idea into a final topic which could well constitute the title of your project report, if you chose to do so. This final step does two things.

- It informs your tutor (and, if the result is a title, the reader) of which issues you have, by implication, **excluded** from your topic, and is the result of some initial reading (see Chapter 8 on literature reviewing).
- It demonstrates the way in which your project will be more than a description of the subject-matter.

To take just one of our running examples, Area: 'Behaviour in Organizations' – Field: 'Employee Motivation' – Aspect: 'Employee Incentive Schemes'. A focused topic in this case might be 'A critical evaluation and comparison of employee share participation schemes in two manufacturing companies'. By implication, it excludes other forms of incentive scheme (though the literature review would briefly describe the excluded alternatives) and it focuses on manufacturing, rather than retailing or other forms of privately owned service organizations where such schemes exist. Secondly, it avoids pure description by promising an evaluation and a comparison of specific and, possibly, contrasting practices in two particular companies.

A topic which excludes and restricts is in no danger of being too broad, or, at least, its scope and difficulty can be easily judged by your tutor. A topic which does more than describe is required by all the levels of study (undergraduate, professional, and Masters): see Chapter 4 for more on this theme, and section 8.4 together with Table 8.7 for a treatment in detail. For the moment, you might like to consider a few additional words and phrases which indicate that your work is doing more than describing. As well as evaluation and comparison, there are 'analysis', 'synthesis', 'assessment', 'the importance of', 'the impact of', 'the influence of', the latter three indicating some exploration of cause and effect, and hence some degree of explanation.

Table 3.1 gives you some further examples of this process of narrowing down. If you are considering topics at a particular level of study, it is a good exercise to look at topics in the table which are described as appropriate to some other level, and ask yourself what would have to change (a complexity factor? a different emphasis in narrowing down?) to make it appropriate to your own level. To the extent that the topics as they stand in Table 3.1 could conceivably be appropriate at several levels, what assumptions do you have to make about the topics to be clear that they are at your level, rather than some other? Check your reasoning with your tutor!

**profes-
sional**
For those of you who are following a professional programme, working up your topic follows the same rationale as above, except for the expectation that your Area pertains to the interests of your professional body. This is likely to involve you in issues and problems pertaining to the relevant business function, but not exclusively, since your professional curriculum may well require you to address policy issues, from the perspective of, or applying to, subjects of professional interest.

For example, if you are following a post-experience programme aimed at Institute of Personnel and Development membership, then management report topics dealing with the implications for corporate strategy of particular manpower policies are as likely to be encouraged by the IPD as more function-specific topics within the Fields of employee resourcing, relations, or development. So you may wish to combine the functionally relevant with the corporate and strategic, and this will involve you in keeping an eye on the links between your own, and the other, business functions.

The problems of working up a topic are somewhat different if you're working on an MBA programme. The need to spend time in thinking through your topic is just as acute but, because of the general management emphasis, the process is not so much one of narrowing down, but of striking an appropriate balance between generality and in-company specificity.

It's likely that your choice of topic will be dominated by the need for fairly specific relevance to your organization, a division within it, or possibly your own department. At the same time, as I indicated in section 2.2, the stress is on topics which are of general management interest, which usually means that you'll be involved in the exploration of an issue of corporate importance. The idea of a continuum of knowledge levels remains useful, and you may find the Area-Field-Aspect approach useful if you have no immediately pressing in-company issue to offer as a topic. **Ideally, though, your approach should be to work from the more specific, outwards, to the more general.** You start with a specific organization-related issue and attempt to discover two things: is it of strategic or corporate importance, and secondly, how does it relate to, and draw on, the various academic subjects covered in the taught part of your programme?

Issues of strategic importance will vary depending on the nature of your organization. (The various contingency factors mentioned in your Organization Theory taught course are relevant to your thinking here: type of business sector, industry, technology, ownership, size, age, and the rest.) They will also vary with what is contemporaneously important and, to an extent, fashionable. At the time of writing (1994), for example, topics which relate to the form of corporate ownership of public-sector organizations, to cultural issues within organizations, to various forms of strategic partnership, and to new markets in central Europe and China, may possibly predominate the strategic orientation of your topic. It is possible that over the next five years, issues of selective disinvestment, business ethics, and strategic management in small businesses will become more important, but this is perhaps too speculative to be useful. It does demonstrate one useful approach which you might adopt in searching for the wider relevance of your in-company topic, however: try to leaven the dough of contemporary relevance with the yeast of the immediate, but developing, future. If strategic issues deal with a five- to eight-year horizon, don't limit yourself to what is of current concern.

Secondly, your topic needs to draw on the material which you have encountered during the taught elements of your MBA programme. In going from the specific to the general, then, you should use the Aspect-Field-Area continuum in that order, attempting to identify and draw on the various concepts and techniques dealt with in relevant components of your taught programme. Be explicit about the provenance of the themes on which you draw. For example, the Aspect for an MBA project done by a senior nursing tutor might involve 'Structural and cultural changes affecting nursing training'. The Field could be 'Management of Change' and the Area 'Organizational Behaviour'. Alternatively, the Field could be 'Strategic Management' and the Area 'Corporate Strategy'. Which emphasis does the manager wish to give to this specific issue in the nursing school and therefore, which ideas and concepts covered in the taught programme might be relevant? As this is an MBA programme, it would be surprising if at least some reference were not made to both taught courses, whatever the emphasis.

all

This is not an abstract exercise: a knowledge of which course components are relevant to your topic will be essential in organizing the background reading, and specialist tuition, which you will need to organize during your project.

3.3 IN CASE OF EMERGENCY

This section contains procedures and ideas to help you cope in situations where the rational approach has, for whatever reason, been found wanting. It offers you a number of heuristics whereby you might generate a number of project ideas. Note them down as you read the section, then run them through the guidelines outlined in sections 3.1 and 3.2.

There are, firstly, a number of wheezes suggested by Mason (1988). (His article is aimed at projects in the information technology rather than management field, but is very useful nevertheless.) For the next week, keep a notebook with you at all times and jot down any idea that is triggered off by events in your daily round; at the end of that time, put them through the narrowing-down procedure. If they're still at the Area or Field level, go to the library and try to identify a substantial amount of material pertaining to each. Abandon any which aren't supported by library holdings, and try narrowing down on the remainder in the light of a brief reading of relevant-sounding book chapters or journal articles.

Alternatively, build a 'relevance tree'. As Mason describes it, this is a rough-and-ready directed graph which starts with a general title, and branches out into three aspects of the general title that may occur to you. Anyone familiar with Buzan (1989) and his graphic, non-hierarchic technique for notemaking, will recognize exactly what I mean. You think about each branch, and jot down a further three branches to that, at a more specific level. Go through as many iterations as it takes to come up with an idea which interests you. Then, I'd suggest, take it through the steps of Section 3.1.

Mason's final suggestion is morphological analysis. This is a variant of the 'automatic jargon generators' which appear at rare intervals within in-house management and technology publications. You know the sort of thing: a column of adjectives, a column of nouns, and another column of nouns are written down side by side, and the reader takes various combinations of adjective-noun-noun from different rows in the three columns, having a giggle at the absurdity of the buzz-word produced. It may not make you laugh, but it does serve a useful function of stimulating possible mental connections if, when you try the exercise, the columns consist of key factors pertaining to an Area or Field with which you're working. Table 3.2 shows an example; you can find further examples of relevance trees and morphological analysis in Howard and Sharp (1983: 29).

Secondly, you might consider going to the library and locating bound volumes of past projects. Do the titles and abstracts suggest anything to you? Be careful to think through contemporaneously, personally or occupationally relevant variations of any titles which catch your attention, and use these just to stimulate thought. (To reproduce the themes and topics of existing, completed work too literally will drive you to the same body of literature and data-gathering, and is an insidious form of plagiarism which you must avoid.)

Thirdly, you could come clean with your tutor about the depths of your difficulty, and ask him/her for a topic. This is a counsel of desperation, and he or she may not cooperate directly. But he or she will give you further guidance, and it's far better to adopt this last-ditch approach than to delay too long in your choice of topic.

If you're having problems with a topic which is to draw heavily on, and contribute to, the workings of your organization, why not involve your company sponsor, mentor, or closer working colleagues in your choice? It would be worth the price of a few drinks if you got two or three colleagues together during lunch to brainstorm the issues which concern the department specifically or the organization in general. It's surprising how a mind unfamiliar with your academic studies can throw fresh light on your problem. Write down everything that sounds plausible, then run the suggestions through the stages outlined in sections 3.1 and 3.2.

in-company

It is very easy to recognize the differences between an initial idea for a topic, and the same topic when it has been worked up and narrowed down, after the latter event; it is quite difficult to imagine the latter event at the outset! If you want an illustration of what I mean, and some useful additional guidelines to my own, have a look at Raimond (1993); the first two chapters have some excellent examples of good, and not so good, topics, in their initial and developed form.

Table 3.2 An example of morphological analysis

Steps:
(a) Place the possible topic idea (failing that, the Field) at the head of a page.
(b) Identify three key attributes of the Topic and place them at the head of three columns across the page.
(c) In each column, list several examples of these attributes.
(d) Consider different combinations of the examples, taking one from each column
(e) What thoughts about the topic suggest themselves with each combination?

Example

(a) Field: Managers as leaders

(b) *Definitional problems*   *Behaviour*   *Contingencies*

(c)

Type of manager	Assumption of role	Size of organization
Leader as agent	Task-oriented style	Position power
Leadership as a transaction	Person-oriented style	Existing relations
Substitutes for leadership	Personal satisfaction	Nature of task
Effective leadership	Interpersonal skills	National cultures

(The attributes reflect your own reading in and around the subject of leadership. Putting the examples into the columns reflects an association of ideas: one item suggests a second, which leads to a third, and so on.)

(d) Combination 'Type of manager–Personal satisfaction–Size of organization' may suggest . . .

(e) . . . that senior managers in small organizations may be more satisfied than senior managers in large organizations. Something similar, you might possibly recall, was done by Porter in 1963. Provided the Porter questionnaire was replicated and just two companies of varied size were chosen, this could make a good undergraduate project.

(d) Combination 'Effective leadership–Task-oriented style–National cultures' may suggest . . .

(e) . . . that the definition of what sort of behaviour counts as task- rather than person-oriented style may vary with culture. An up-to-date issue (see Smith and Peterson, 1988; Mączynski, 1991) and a good topic at MBA level for someone employed by a multinational.

(d) Combination 'Leadership as transaction–Interpersonal skills–Nature of task' suggests . . .

(e) . . . that appraisal systems may be unsuccessful because insufficient training is given the managers concerned, rather than because inadequate appraisal questionnaires are used. A good project for part-time IPD students.

3.4 MAKING A DRY RUN

Some teaching institutions require you to write a project proposal document before you begin work on the project itself. The purpose of this requirement is to encourage you to think through four things: **what, how, with whom**, and **when**.

- **What**: your Topic, and the kinds of issues I've covered in this chapter.
- **How**: matters of technique and methodology, as described in Part Three of this book.
- **With whom**: addressing the need for you to make the necessary personal contacts (tutor and sponsor in particular).
- **Within a deadline** so that you can start on the project without undue delay.

A document of this kind is also a convenient mechanism for assessing performance on any taught course in project/research methods which might precede your hands-on project activity. It may not be a requirement in your own institution, but you might nevertheless want to prepare a brief, two- to five-page document which has the same purpose, and show it to your tutor for his or her comments and feedback. That will mean skim-reading the relevant sections of this book; a very brief glance at section 3 even at this stage is well worth your while!

What do you intend to do?

Firstly, after stating the topic, it is useful to provide a brief account which states why this topic is interesting and important: to you, to the academic discipline within your course or course specialism, to your placement company, or to your permanent employer, as the case may be. Next, provide a paragraph or a diagram locating the topic within its Area, Field, and Aspect structure, giving the reader an idea of where you're coming from. A brief list of the main authors, and academic concepts on which you will be drawing, can also be placed under this heading.

How do you intend to do it?

State the main research method and techniques which you intend to use, your research design, and an indication of the sample or samples of people who will be providing you with your data.

The chief mistake when you're describing the method and techniques is to include everything: 'interviews with senior managers and customers, questionnaires to customers and staff, participant observation of employees, focus groups to establish the main issues, and comparative case studies of selected competitors' may be an indication that you haven't really thought things through. (When I act as tutor, it's usually that plural in the word 'questionnaires' that starts the warning bells ringing.) Be selective.

The design involves a careful research plan by which you intend to establish your main assertions; it's a technical term, and you can find out more in Chapter 9, where issues of sampling are also covered.

With whom

This is an opportunity for you to record the main helpers on whom you'll be dependent, and record their basic address, telephone number, and other contact details. This is also the place in which to state what formal level of support you will need, and will have negotiated, with your data providers or sponsors.

When

By when are you likely to finish the main stages of the project? It is very useful to provide a brief timetable for the project in five to ten lines.

It seems far too early to be thinking at this level of detail, as you're grappling with the issue of what topic to choose! And so much of what goes into the proposal depends on material in subsequent chapters of this book. A fair point; but it would be useful if you regarded this level of detail as the minimum which you will need to establish before you have done with 'choosing your topic', and aimed to achieve it before your project begins.

Standards of assessment $\boxed{4}$

While you attend your taught courses before starting your project, you are likely to hear people talking about the standards which are applied. Your lecturers might be heard talking about 'good projects they have known', and you might come across the students who have completed their projects exchanging gossip and war stories about individuals who did particularly well, or spectacularly badly, when their work was assessed. You'll hear talk from both parties of 'contributions to knowledge', and you'll find yourself wondering just what standard will be required of you.

The purpose of this chapter is to give you some information about the standards applied to project work. It begins by offering some general guidelines, goes on to discuss a number of attributes which characterize all good investigatory work (originality, generality, pragmatism, balance and the nature of evidence used), outlines some samples of formal assessment criteria used at various levels of project work, outlines some of the practical requirements of format and presentation prior to a fuller treatment in Chapter 14, and concludes by looking at assessment from your examiner's point of view.

4.1 GENERAL GUIDELINES

Your project is going to be examined when it's finished. Someone, or some group of people (your tutor, other academics, your sponsor perhaps and maybe another in-company colleague) are going to be assessing the standard you've reached. It's important to have some idea of the level of excellence which they will expect from you, as it will enable you to anticipate their judgements, monitor your progress towards the standard, and do something about it if you get the feeling that your work is unsatisfactory. In effect, you become one of the examiners, which is a good thing to be, if only because you have greater control when you're self-assessing than when you're being assessed.

Let's start with the banal assertion that standards are related to level of study: in some sense, less is expected of the undergraduate projects, more of the postgraduate Diploma, and more again of the Masters-level project. But less and more of what? Let's focus on academic standard in general, leaving aside, for the moment, the issues arising from the involvement with in-company relevance which characterizes a business or management project.

Putting it very crudely, there are three types of information which you will be supplying for assessment:

- ■ Concepts, rational argument, the use of existing ideas, and the links you establish between these existing ideas and your own
- ■ The methods and techniques which you use to obtain your evidence
- ■ The evidence itself: data derived from your empirical investigations, together with inferences leading to conclusions and recommendations.

Now, 'information' is defined as anything which removes uncertainty: anything which is new to its recipient. So one way of thinking about standards is to ask what is new about your work.

A Ph.D. student (bear with me), who is conventionally required to make 'a significant contribution to knowledge', will do well if he or she develops new concepts (developing an existing or new theory, for example); develops new methods or techniques; or comes up with new findings – and preferably two of these, the first and second, or the first and third. In addition, the student's technical expertise (the rigour with which the methods are used, whether existing methods or newly developed) must be perfect.

Why talk about the Ph.D. student? Simply because this level of work offers you a useful rule of thumb. You're expected to do less, and specifically:

- ■ at Master's level: one of the above (new concepts, new methods, or new findings), and the technical expertise must be perfect;
- ■ at the postgraduate Diploma level: one of the above, perhaps at a lower standard of difficulty, with some tolerance for the odd mistake or incompleteness in method;
- ■ at undergraduate level: almost always the last one (new findings), with some tolerance for mistakes and greater tolerance still for incompleteness, in your use of methods and techniques.

under-graduate

Do remember, this is just a rough-and-ready expression of standards. If you're an undergraduate aiming for a First, while you're not expected to make any substantial contribution to theory, it would be nice if you did;

and you'd certainly aim for perfection in your use of ideas (e.g. no holes in your reasoning), and in the methods you use (e.g. a really adequate sampling of respondents; some sophistication in your data analysis).

Come to think of it, shouldn't everyone aim high and strive for perfection? Yes, indeed. This rule of thumb, however, is a general statement which describes the average expectation at any one level of study; a crude statement of the standard which ought to put you in the 55% to 60% bracket at each level. Aim to do more if you can; and take your tutor's advice on the feasibility of this intention, given the topic you choose.

Is there a corresponding non-academic, in-company based rule of thumb for specifying the standard which you must reach? Indeed there is, and it focuses on the issue of **relevance**. You will be judged on the extent to which your work illuminates an issue which concerns your sponsor, and on the extent to which you come up with findings which are important to the organization involved. When you apply the rule of thumb outlined above, do two things. Add 'relevant' to the wording. And, secondly, notice the emphasis on results: in general, your sponsor would much rather you offered new data and conclusions, than new concepts or new methods and techniques. (There may be an exception in the case of some professional projects: a new application of a technique, or indeed an amendment to a technique, would be most acceptable.)

4.2 THE ATTRIBUTES OF A SUCCESSFUL PROJECT

The general guidelines focus on the differences between levels of work: they identify the expectations of undergraduate, as opposed to Diploma, as opposed to Master's, project work. In addition, you need to give some attention to five characteristics which apply to project work at any level of qualification.

Originality

There are two senses in which this word is used, each interrelated. I introduced the idea of novelty when I outlined the rule of thumb in the previous section: the fresher your use of concepts, methods and findings, the more informative the project will be. Tutors grow old and grey in direct proportion to the number of retreads they read; indeed, it's quite common, and on balance justifiable, for a tutor to steer you away from a project you're planning because something very similar was offered by a student last year, even though the topic is exciting to you. In-company sponsors will alter their views of what they find relevant if your project goes over old ground. Aim, if you can, to write something which excites them; which gives them an insight; which has them saying 'aha!'.

You do so for a very good reason. As well as being named individuals with whom you have a relationship, your tutor and sponsor stand for the wider community of readers implied in the very notion of standards of assessment. To satisfy these readers, and give them an experience of something new, you will have to discover what's old: you'll need to learn about what has gone before, what's been covered in the academic literature, and what's taken for granted in the organizational setting. And so you'll automatically be satisfying one of the objectives of your project, as I outlined in section 2.2.

You'll know that your work is original when you discover that other people want to hear about it. Your sponsor wishes to circulate the executive summary of your project to other people in the organization. You are asked to give an oral presentation after any oral examination has been completed. It gets written up in the company magazine. Perhaps your tutor encourages you to present a selection from the project report as a paper at an in-college seminar, or external conference. You've achieved something you never expected: your ideas have arrived in the wider arena, beyond the confines of the assessment process!

The second sense in which your work must be original is that it has to be your own. It mustn't be plagiarized. **Plagiarism**, 'copying' from someone else's work, is a matter of degree, and can arise unintentionally if you're unaware of the rules for reporting, acknowledging and referencing direct quotations. The rules are outlined in section 8.1 and Table 8.3. Very occasionally, tutors encounter deliberate plagiarism, where an entire project report, or a significant section, is taken from someone else's work. If they can prove it, the consequences are ruinous and terminal for the student concerned. And it's surprising the lengths to which a disenchanted tutor can go to verify what is, after all, an extremely serious suspicion.

I remember a colleague who imposed a three-month delay on graduation while microfiches of a five-year-old marketing project were tracked down in a remote Mid-West American university, to establish that an undergraduate on this side of the Atlantic had plagiarized. Don't.

Generality

In research-driven projects, it is comparatively simple to ensure that project work has generality, that is, a relevance beyond the situation and setting in which the data were gathered. Research projects identify the issues to be investigated by referring to a theory, concepts, or group of ideas, and make their contribution by extending or adding to that theory in some way. Since theories are general by nature, and the purpose of research is to make general statements, then the projects achieve generality when they draw out the implications of the data for the theory.

Business and management projects aren't quite the same. They don't relate to a theory in quite the same way (as outlined in Chapter 6), but the issue of generality still matters. If your conclusions apply only to this year's accounts; if your recommendations about employee participation address just one office or one part of a department; if your marketing plan ignores a closely related group of products to the product on which your findings are focused, then your project is unlikely to be successful. Your project will be acceptable to the extent that its recommendations can be extended to different times, locations, markets, departments and so forth. More subtly, perhaps, they'll only be useful if they state or imply the circumstances which constrain this extension.

For example, in a personnel management project on communicable diseases which examines the practices and hazards of night-shift workers, a recommendation which advises a local authority cleansing department to provide plastic gloves to sewer workers on the night shift is weaker than one which advises the department to provide them to all sewer workers – unless there is evidence that the day shift is not exposed to the hazards which require the use of gloves in the first place, and this evidence has been highlighted.

Many projects at these levels base themselves on a case study of an organization, usually your own. The issue of generality is particularly important in this instance, and you'll need to check that your conclusions apply in some wider sense to your organization, than simply to the department or section in which you gathered your case study data.

MBA

diploma

in-
company

Pragmatism

A good project should be applicable; that is, someone somewhere should be able in principle to put the recommendations into effect. This is partly a matter of practicality and of what is possible on both technical and common-sense grounds. A project on 'managing change' which recommended that the employees of all departments should take part in Quality Circles would be impractical if it arose from work carried out in a large multinational organization and took no account of the location and nature of the departments concerned.

all

It would be unsuccessful on technical grounds if it didn't consider the number of employees in each department, the functions served by those departments, and any departmental restructurings which the company was planning to implement. I call this a 'technical' issue, since the evidence about quality circles which would qualify the recommendation is known, and easily available in the literature: see, for example, Frazer and Dale (1986).

Finally, there is the matter of common sense: a project may be poor because the recommendations fly in the face of more general information which a few moments' thought, or a discussion with sponsor or tutor, would have identified as a constraint on the actions being recommended.

under-graduate

This is sometimes true of undergraduate projects in particular, and is revealed by a hectoring or censorious style in which the author attacks the organization for not doing what the literature, or the lecturers, or sometimes the industry, advocate as good practice. For instance:

- 'As is well known, job satisfaction is not just a matter of pay; the company must introduce a job enrichment scheme into this department.' Wham!
- 'It is vital that the company stops neglecting the EC Directorate's recommendations on quality standards if it is to maintain its share of the export market.' So there!
- 'The local authority must privatize its refuse collection since private services have been shown to be more cost-effective.' All right?

Of course, these statements are taken out of context, and I could imagine the kind of information and evidence which would justify the sense of urgency (though 'vital' is a greatly overused word – do you really mean that the issue is a matter of life or death?). Where the statements are problematic is in situations:

- where qualifying evidence has not been considered;
- where it is assumed, without looking for evidence, that the organization has not considered the issue before;
- where the organization is believed to be perfectly free to act on the recommendation.

all

You can ensure that your project is sufficiently pragmatic if you are clear about the distinction between efficiency and effectiveness. **Efficiency** has to do with technical possibility and feasibility, and answers the question 'Could it be done?' If your recommendations are supported by evidence, and follow logically from the evidence, then they're efficient. **Effectiveness**, on the other hand, has to do with the constraints on the applicability of technically acceptable recommendations. It answers the question 'Can it be done?', given the wider implications. The main implications are usually financial (what will it cost?), temporal (is the timing right?), resource-based (have we the skills or the equipment to do it; can we do it in another and better way?), political (what interest groups will be affected?) and policy-related (does it fit with the way we wish to do things?). Research projects can sometimes ignore the issue of pragmatism; in-company projects can never ignore it.

Balance

This is my own word for an issue which you will recognize if you've ever done an academic, research-based project before, or if you have a background in a scientific discipline which conducts its research by the formal testing of hypotheses. You'd recognize it under the name of 'symmetry of hypotheses', and a good account in these terms is provided by Howard and Sharp (1983).

The issue addresses your expectations of the outcomes of your project, and how they are confirmed by the data you gather. To talk of 'expectations' is not to say that you ever know the results of project work in advance (or that you're going to bend the evidence to fit your preconceptions!). What I'm saying is that if you've done your background reading properly, you'll know what kinds of outcomes are possible when you've asked all your questions and the data are in. A balanced project is one in which the outcomes will be equally valuable whether your expectations are confirmed or negated; an unbalanced project is one in which evidence which agrees with your expectations will leave you helpless, or, equally, one in which evidence which disagrees with your expectations will have no value.

Suppose you're doing a project on corporate strategy in the water supply business. You're exploring the idea that companies which have diversified into new products and services (manufacture and retailing of domestic garden hoses and fittings, for example) are more resistant to takeover than those which have not. A positive finding would be very interesting, and would permit some fairly powerful recommendations. A negative finding would be equally interesting, and would suggest that diversification is a poor strategic option. The topic of this project is balanced.

On the other hand, imagine that your reading suggests that venture capital firms prefer to invest in business start-ups where a market niche is likely to be created, rather than in start-ups in which a commodity product is being sold. Evidence which confirmed your expectation would be banal, given what's known about this topic already (Gorman and Sahlman, 1986). It's what you'd expect! Evidence which negated your expectation would be extremely exciting – but highly unlikely. The topic in this instance is very unbalanced.

Balance is a matter of what is known already; of the potential value of positive and negative findings; and of the likelihood of either kind of finding. A topic in which your expectations and hunches are unbalanced is a risky one in which to engage. A good way of checking the balance of a project topic is to ask yourself whether your findings and recommendations are likely to make a difference to the decisions made by a manager in the company involved in your study.

The nature of evidence used

A final issue which your examiners will address is the nature of the evidence you provide. This depends largely on the extent to which you are dependent on primary data as opposed to secondary data. **Primary data** consist of material that you've gathered yourself: systematic observations, information from archives, the results of questionnaires and interviews, case studies which you have compiled. **Secondary data** include everything else, being the results of other people's primary data-collection as reported in a wide variety of formats: company annual reports, technical manuals, government and trade body publications, books and journals.

You might find the distinction between primary and secondary difficult to draw at times. After all, if you're compiling a case study (primary) you may wish to include financial reports drawn up by the company's accountant (secondary). If you take the line that there's nothing new under the sun, why should you bother with the distinction?

There's one very good reason. Data are primary if they have been gathered according to your own rationale, and interpreted by yourself, to make a point which is important to your own argument: in other words, if they're relatively original. Data are secondary if they come to you with someone else's rationale and assumptions about what's important; that is, if they carry the possible risk of constraining your own freedom to interpret findings because of the author's emphasis or selectivity. (If you want more on this, see Williams and Stevenson (1963: 7) for a cogent account, and Goldstein and Goldstein (1978: 258) on the broader issue of the originality of evidence.)

You can see why the distinction is important. You'll be assessed on the clarity of thinking you've shown in gathering and interpreting your own data, and you'll have to satisfy the examiners on the expertise you show in recognizing and demonstrating the relevance of secondary data to your own argument. The groundrules for primary data are outlined in Part Three, in quite some detail. The standards which will be applied in the case of secondary data may not be quite so obvious, however.

Basically, don't believe what you read! The information in secondary data may have been derived by eminent people (by definition, you might argue, since their work has been published and yours hasn't), but unless the source is widely known to be idiosyncratic but essential, it is you who will be held responsible for the accuracy and interpretations which you reproduce from the source. Your project reaches a high standard when:

- you state the assumptions under which the information was compiled, as well as presenting it, and show that these assumptions are relevant to your own situation;
- you identify the obvious biases in the information (as, for example, the

sampling limitations of a particular set of survey evidence, or the known political constraints or public-relations intentions under which company handouts and reports were compiled);
- you qualify or evaluate other authors' inferences or conclusions, in the light of other information known to you.

MBA students must be a hard-bitten lot: I haven't come across many MBA projects which took secondary sources as Gospel. On the other hand, it does seem to be a particular problem at the other levels of work. Believe what the author says by all means, but check it out as I've suggested above. And, in addition, ask the following questions.

- Have you heard the same thing said, or the same kind of data quoted, in other sources?
- If everyone else agrees on a statement but forgets to quote the evidence, is a stereotype operating?

Finally, the balance of primary and secondary data can make the difference between a good and a poor project. It would be very unusual to find a good project with no reference to other people's writings, whether the references are presented as a formal separate literature review, or are interspersed among your own material. Similarly, a project with no empirical content which you'd originated yourself, would be unlikely to be successful.

4.3 ASSESSMENT CRITERIA

Most teaching institutions have their own project standards, published in the form of a handout which is distributed to students when they begin their project work. Some will incorporate guidelines published by professional bodies where these apply. All of them vary substantially, from a single page which identifies the main headings under which projects are evaluated, to detailed manuals of up to 50 pages which give reasons for the standards, and a mass of useful information on project work besides. I'd suggest that you get hold of any such handouts before you read on, and in the case of the one-page productions, make notes onto the handouts to amplify them in the light of the earlier parts of this chapter. If anything I've said conflicts with your local standards, then ignore what I say and stick to the local version, since it is that which will apply!

Some of the handouts which state the standards to be achieved are criterion-referenced, that is, they specify the level of your performance against each criterion, as well as describing the criterion itself. These are offered to the staff who will act as your tutors and examiners, who use

under-graduate

them as they think fit in marking your work. Some tutors find them very helpful, and stick to them fairly closely when assessing your project; if you know that this is true in your own institution or of your own tutor, you should make a particular effort to get hold of them. Examples of such handouts are shown in Tables 4.1 and 4.4.

all

You'll notice that they occasionally refer to **scholarship**. All institutions at all levels expect this of you, and, though they don't necessarily think about it in the same words, so do all employers involved in project work. It's a word of the finest pedigree: but what does it mean? The primary meaning is quite clear:

■ careful and accurate use of evidence;
■ care in the discovery and attribution of sources;
■ thoroughness in the coverage of subject-matter;
■ respect for truth and the validity of data and assertions.

There is also a connotation to the word 'scholarship', a connotation which conveys a value. Namely, that in a fallible and fragmented world, in which fashion, the 'easy way out', charisma, prejudice and bigotry contaminate our understanding of what's happening around us, there is some merit in struggling to achieve the attributes listed above. To ignore scholarship is to make you prey to the charlatan and the demagogue: to the proponent of the latest management 'flavour-of-the-month'. So if you're aiming at a moderate to excellent assessment for your project assessment, I feel that you need to subscribe to the value I've expressed.

in-company

The same comment applies to in-company based projects.

The remaining tables provide examples of assessment criteria at other levels.

Table 4.2 is an example of a professional programme project assessment, which reflects the requirements of a professional body (the Institute of Personnel and Development), and highlights some of the specific comments made in section 4.2 above, for example the need to maintain a balance between informed criticism of the organizational setting and an understanding of the organizational constraints which prevent the ideal from being implemented. There is also the suggestion that, if time permits, the project done for a professional programme may involve you in the implementation of recommendations, and their evaluation, rather than just a simple coming to conclusions and recommendations in your project report.

diploma

Table 4.3 outlines some of the requirements involved in one particular Diploma in Management Studies programme and illustrates the variety of assessment systems which apply to this qualification. As well as indicating the possibility of implementing and evaluating recommendations, it represents the relatively rare situation in which you are explicitly assessed

Table 4.1 Assessment criteria: modular Business degree

Definition of appropriate problem: 10%
1st Hons: 70% and above
Thoroughly related to an appropriate academic area of business/management in a wider context; scope accurately delimited and justified; outline of treatment entirely appropriate.
2.1: 60–69%
Well related to an appropriate academic area of business/management in a wider context; carefully delimited and/or justified, but not unarguably so; outline of treatment almost entirely appropriate.
2.2: 50–59%
Related to an appropriate academic area of business/management, seen in but hardly related to a wider overall context; delimitation/justification present but lacking in rigour; outline of treatment fairly appropriate, and clearly outlined.
3rd: 40–49%
Related to an appropriate academic area of business/management, but not explicitly so and not seen clearly in wider context; area defined but without convincing justification or rigour; outline of treatment clear but of doubtful appropriateness.
Fail: 39% and below
At most: relationship to an appropriate academic area of business/management tenuous, unrelated to the wider context; area ill-defined; outline of treatment muddled/inappropriate/absent.

Source and method of data collection: 30%
1st. Hons: 70% and above
Selected from all appropriate sources only those which can be handled in time available; methods reflect scholarly attention to detail at highest level available at this point in the course; sources and methods show much originality and considerable initiative.
2.1: 60–69%
Almost all appropriate sources consulted, well researched and without serious misunderstanding; methods show fair amount of possible scholarly attention (as above); originality and initiative clearly important in researching topic.
2.2: 50–59%
Some important sources omitted, but mostly showing quite sound grasp of those consulted; methods uneven, not altogether appropriate; some signs of attempted originality/initiative, but in a minor role; awareness of need for scholarly approach detectable.
3rd: 40–49%
Sources unimaginative and/or omitted and showing little understanding beyond relevance; methods unimaginative, uneven, with marked inappropriateness and no evidence of scholarly awareness; initiative/originality missing/misplaced; very dull and pedestrian.

Table 4.1 continued

Fail: 39% and below
Important sources ignored/misunderstood/misused; methods inappropriate
and/or wrongly applied; originality and initiative missing/misplaced.

Methods of analysis: 30%
1st. Hons: 70% and above
Shows awareness of and uses all appropriate academic and/or experiential
background; techniques wholly appropriate, showing awareness of scope and
limitations; scholarly; techniques applied systematically, fairly and accurately,
and shows awareness of limitations, if any.
2.1: 60–69%
Aware of almost all relevant academic and/or experiential background; uses
them appropriately; evidence of some scholarship; analytical techniques relevant
and appropriate but without necessarily showing awareness of scope and
limitations; systematic and accurate application.
2.2: 50–59%
Definite but incomplete awareness and application of academic and/or
experiential background; techniques of analysis fairly well chosen and applied,
but with little/no critical consideration; application of techniques fairly systematic
and accurate; some room for error.
3rd: 40–49%
Some awareness of academic and/or experiential background, fairly well applied;
techniques of analysis appropriate enough, allowing for some misapplication; no
critical acumen applied; some attempt at systematicity but with little accuracy.
Fail: 39% and below
Academic and experiential background absent/entirely misapplied; analysis
lacking/techniques wholly inappropriate; methods inaccurate and unsystematic.

Validity of conclusions and recommendations: 20%
1st Hons: 70% and above
Logically derived and fully supported by foregoing evidence; well organized (e.g.
by importance/hierarchically); evidence of intuition/initiative/originality;
awareness of future avenues for investigation and research/proposals for such;
awareness of limitations of project and methods employed; constructive criticism
of such.
2.1: 60–69%
Logically derived but less strong in evidence of intuition/initiative/originality;
some evidence of organization; simple awareness of need for further
investigation; awareness of limitations of project and methods employed.
2.2: 50–59%
Logically derived but lacking intuition/initiative/originality; shows a fair grasp of
implications of project but without deep insight; may show some slight awareness
of future needs and/or limitations of content/method.
3rd: 40–49%
Not fully logical; some obvious conclusions/recommendations omitted; insight

into value of work not demonstrated; no awareness of further areas for research; conclusions and recommendations valid but random in organization.
Fail: 39% and below
Based upon uncertain evidence, frequently illogical; conclusions and/or recommendations omitted; little evidence of organisation of conclusions; no/mistaken views about the value of work undertaken.

Quality of presentation: 10%
1st Hons: 70% and above
Fully documented including title page, contents page, appendices, bibliography, references; presentation commensurate with academic excellence; text free from errors of spelling, punctuation; grammatically mature and fluent; vocabulary appropriate; style consistent with subject and content of report; typescript perfect (through proof-reading).
2.1: 60–69%
Documentation full (as above); presentation free from major faults with very few errors of spelling, punctuation and structures; style and vocabulary reasonably mature and appropriate to subject and content.
2.2: 50–59%
Documentation almost complete, could really be improved (e.g. some minor appendices missing/inadequate); some noticeable carelessness in spelling, punctuation, structures; style lacking final polish/not entirely consistent with content; nevertheless readable and showing overall awareness of presentation.
3rd: 40–49%
Documentation reasonably complete; shows awareness of appropriate pattern of presentation but has not pulled it together cohesively; errors of spelling, punctuation and structures just too evident for comfort; style rather awkward yet still readable; inconsistency with content quite noticeable.
Fail: 39% and below
Documentation seriously at fault, e.g. sections missing, wrongly ordered; presentation careless and extremely difficult to find one's way around; text full of errors, e.g. in spelling, punctuation, sentence structures, solecisms, faulty grammar, making it very difficult to read; vocabulary and style immature and inappropriate; typescript messy and full of uncorrected errors.

Hemingray (1994)

Usage
The weightings beside each major heading suggest the relative importance of that criterion to the overall assessment. Tutors using this table would choose one honours category under each heading, using the verbal description, percentage band, and honours category as a guideline in marking under that heading, going on to combine marks under all five headings to give an overall mark. The weightings might vary depending on the business specialism being followed by the student, and the criteria are meant to be used with sensitivity. The table is made available to students, with substantial explanatory comments.

Table 4.2 Assessment criteria: Diploma in Personnel Management

---

Statement of the problem
Summary of organizational background
Concise statement of the situation and problems to be resolved
Terms of reference clearly defined
Evidence of intended analysis as well as pure description
Definition and description of method of investigation

Use of appropriate concepts
Evidence of study and application of relevant literature
Evidence of knowledge of current 'best practice'
Evidence of consultation with experienced personnel practitioners

Use of evidence
Presentation of all the relevant facts
Definition of relevant organizational constraints
Use of appropriate methods and techniques, e.g. surveys, interviews

Adequacy of evaluation
A critical (but tactful) analysis of the existing situation
Sufficient consideration of all reasonable alternative solutions

Conclusions
A logical flow of conclusions from the facts and from the analysis of them
Indication of what cannot be done, with reasons
Indication of areas requiring further investigation
Adherence to terms of reference

Recommendations
Clarity and specificity of recommendations
Feasibility of recommendations in terms of cost, practicability, acceptability
Potential for implementation, where feasible
Evidence of implementation, where implementation was feasible
Provision for review and validation of recommendations as they are implemented

---

Taken from Teesside Business School (1988)

on the quality of an oral presentation to an invited audience (some of whom will belong to the sponsoring organization, but some of whom will not) and reminds you of the efficiency–effectiveness distinction.

MBA

Table 4.4 provides an example of a set of criteria at MBA level. In some respects, these are similar to the DMS (indeed, in the linked management development programme of the institution in question, the DMS constitutes year 2 and MBA constitutes years 3 and 4); in others, as in the concern for the nature and adequacy of your recommendations as a contribution to management thinking and practice, they reflect the nature of the programme: a Master's rather than a Diploma. The concern with

Table 4.3 Assessment criteria: Diploma in Management Studies

Background and situation in existence: 10%
Details of organization sponsoring research
Situation and its history, context of problem and why considered to be a
problem, with evidence
Reason for undertaking the project
Anticipated outcomes and results at the outset

Brief and terms of reference: 10%
Account of work and responsibilities involved in setting up the project
Terms of reference initially agreed; major changes subsequently made
Objectives, with particular reference to sources of information and data

Methods of investigation: 15%
Research strategy, methods, and approach adopted
Details of research methods, sample, and techniques
Statement of methods of recording data and their analysis

Findings: 20%
Presentation of data in analysed form
Technical adequacy of empirical foundation for subsequent conclusions and
recommendations

Conclusions and recommendations: 15%
Adequacy of conclusions in the light of the data and analysis
Adequacy of recommendations (defined as managerial implications of findings
and conclusions)
Completeness of conclusions in the light of the alternatives possible
Feasibility of recommendations in terms of cost, personnel, capital and
equipment
Relationship between recommendations and terms of reference
Evaluation of implementation if implementation carried out

Quality of written presentation: 15%
Adequacy of referencing, bibliography, illustrations and glossary
Adequacy of executive summary

Quality of oral presentation: 15%
Adequacy of presentation to invited audience
Adequacy of presentation in private meeting with examiners
Quality of response to questions from both above audiences

Taken from Teesside Business School (undated)

strategy and the strategic implications of the topic and issues addressed, are also in keeping with MBA objectives: see section 2.2. Overall, there is a great concern for the development and presentation of a critical argument, supported by primary and secondary data. While implementation of recommendations is not a requirement in an MBA programme (since the opportunity may not be there in many cases), it is welcomed and will then be taken into account in the criteria as shown.

4.4 FORMAT AND DEADLINES

all

You'll have noticed that most of the statements of assessment criteria make an explicit reference to presentation, some of them going so far as to state a relative weighting of marks to be assigned to the quality of your written project document. Again, my general rule is as before: if your teaching institution provides you with a written brief which tells you what is required, then make sure you follow it carefully and disregard the rest of this section. If it doesn't, or if some of the issues are underspecified, you might like to use the following as guidelines, checking them with your tutor before you put them into effect. The major points about format follow below, to give you an early indication of what's involved and what you're aiming at. When the time comes to begin writing, you'll need to look at Chapter 14 in detail.

Length

I wouldn't be surprised if this is the first question that occurs to you! It's certainly the first thing you should clarify with your tutor, since the requirements vary very widely, from a minimum of around 5000 words in the case of some professional bodies, (e.g. Chartered Institute of Marketing give a benchmark of 5000 words, and CIPFA look for 6000 to 8000 words plus appendices), to a maximum of some 40 000 words, depending on the level and nature of qualification. At a rough 300 words to the page, that's a range of between 17 and 140 pages; at the lower level, statements of length usually exclude appendices, title and content pages and the like; for example, the IPD Management Report regulations (which require no more than 7000 words, excluding appendices) explicitly require you to place details of methodology and organizational context in an appendix. You'll soon discover that the problem isn't finding enough to say to match the minimum requirement, but rather, one of trying to fit your material within any maximum that might be specified.

Table 4.4 Assessment criteria: Master in Business Administration

---

Introduction and background

'A' Grade level: 70% and above

Overall aim and reason clearly stated; strategic importance to organization high and clearly presented; objectives clearly stated and relevant; issues (and thesis, if any) entirely appropriate, with the approach to be taken clearly described, appropriate and rigorous; organizational background interesting and relevantly stated.

Good: 60–69%

Overall aims and objectives clearly stated; strategic relevance indicated; most of the issues (and thesis) indicated; approach generally appropriate with some argument possible over its rigour; organizational background relevantly stated.

Clear Pass: 50–59%

Overall aim can be inferred but some lack of clarity in objectives; strategic or wider relevance can be discerned with some assumptions necessary; approach not entirely clear and/or justified; organizational background a description without consistent demonstration of relevance.

Marginal Pass: 40–49%

Overall aim and/or objectives in doubt; uncertainty over strategic or broader relevance; approach unclear, with some arbitrariness discernible; key aspects of the organizational background appear to be omitted. Overall, reader placed in a position of having to assume or guess at appreciable elements of the above components.

Fail: 39% and below

Aim unclear, some or all objectives missing; little or no strategic relevance as stated; approach unstated, confused and/or arbitrary; organizational background, where present, irrelevant/reads like a company brochure. Overall, the reader left in a position of guessing or ignorance over above components.

Conceptual analysis

'A' Grade level: 70% and above

Material selected from all appropriate sources; scholarly, professional and practitioner detail consistently high, with good evidence of originality; material followed logically, systematically and persuasively with direct relevance to objectives. Where review is presented separately from evidence, reasons for asking the questions are obvious; where integrated with evidence, this is done flawlessly.

Good: 60–69%

Almost all sources used and generally understood; scholarly, professional and practitioner detail high with occasional omissions with respect to the argument; some originality; generally systematic presentation without complete persuasiveness; generally relevant to objectives. Where review is presented separately from evidence, reasons for asking the questions clearly summarized; where integrated with evidence, this is done persuasively.

Table 4.4 continued

Clear Pass: 50–59%
Some sources omitted but with reasonable grasp of those consulted and with
sensible relevance to the argument; no particular originality; some unevenness in
presentation; occasional doubt as to relevance to the objectives. Where review is
presented separately from the evidence, reasons for the questions asked aren't
always obvious; where integrated with the evidence, some omissions of either
concepts or evidence.
Marginal Pass: 40–49%
Obvious omissions of sources relevant to objectives, some seriously so; some
misunderstanding; argument not following a clear thread, unconvincing where
discernible, with no attempt to summarize the gist; objectives rarely referred to.
Where review is presented separately from evidence, the reasons for the questions
asked are often unclear; where integrated with evidence, substantial confusion arises.
Fail: 39% and below
Key sources omitted, much misunderstanding; argument must be guessed at,
with little or no case made; reader confused as to the thrust of the argument,
having to refer constantly to the objectives and/or conclusions, where available.
Where review is presented separately from evidence, the reasons for many of the
questions are unknown; where integrated with evidence, major and serious
omissions of either concepts or evidence.

Evidence and argument
'A' Grade level: 70% and above
Methodology crystal-clear and entirely justifiable, with awareness of limitations;
research design explicitly discussed, interesting, and exactly appropriate to
objectives and/or thesis; sampling appropriate and as complete as possible;
methods and techniques appropriate and well executed; results drive the
argument onwards, completely and fairly, with contrary findings used to
illuminate or extend the argument.
Good: 60–69%
Methodology generally sound, limitations mentioned, research design dealt with
as an issue and appropriate to objectives; sampling appropriate and complete
enough for the purpose; methods appropriate, with occasional incompleteness
or lapse in technique; results substantiate the argument/test a thesis, with some
triangulation attempted, and are generally fair with occasional unawareness of
scope and/or limitations.
Clear Pass: 50–59%
Issues of methodology mentioned with incomplete awareness of limitations;
research design little considered; sampling occasionally incomplete or
unconsidered; methods and techniques show occasional errors in use and
interpretation; results related to the argument, but without deep awareness of
limitations in supporting/progressing the argument; triangulation not attempted:
a one-source set of evidence.
Marginal Pass: 40–49%
Methodology confused with description of methods and techniques; unaware of

or confused about research design; sampling incomplete; methods and techniques appropriate enough but insufficiently interpreted with some errors apparent; results patchy, and presented without progressing the argument; assertions frequently presented as evidence; little if any critical awareness; no triangulation.
Fail: 39% and below
Little or no awareness of methodology; methods and techniques inappropriate or incomplete; unaware of research design; sampling unconsidered as an issue; results scrappy, doing little if anything to progress the argument; unwarranted assertions rather than evidence; illogical, with appreciable non-sequiturs; no critical awareness.

Conclusions
'A' Grade level: 70% and above
Logically derived and fully supported by previous evidence, well-organized; evidence of originality with respect to the argument; alternatives fully discussed and dealt with; utility, scope and relevance critically considered; strategic consequences understood and presented; all with reference back to aims and objectives.
Good: 60–69%
Logically derived and generally supported; evidence of organization; less strong evidence of originality; some alternatives discussed; reference to utility, scope and relevance; strategic consequences considered; reference back to aims and objectives.
Clear Pass: 50–59%
Logically derived and supported but with no great originality or organization other than a list; little discussion of alternatives; gaps in issues concerning utility, scope and relevance; reference to strategic issues but perhaps not explicitly or fully competently; some reference to aims and objectives.
Marginal Pass: 40–49%
Not completely logical; gaps in reasoning; some obvious conclusions omitted from the list; value of own work not demonstrated and alternatives little considered; little awareness of further work required; strategic relevance little understood; achievement of objectives mentioned but unwarranted.
Fail: 39% and below
Based on assertions and uncertain evidence. Frequently illogical or arbitrary; conclusions disorganized; mistaken views, if any, of the value of the work; alternatives not considered; strategic relevance unmentioned or merely asserted; little discernible relevance to objectives.

Recommendations
'A' Grade level: 70% and above
Driven obviously by the conclusions as best related to strategy; eminently practical, feasible given resources, with possibility of paying for themselves clearly outlined; some creativity and originality present. Where implementation and evaluation possible, a clear account of what was achieved, successes and failures with reasons given and related to the foregoing; the 'value added' outlined, with a logical rationale and discussion.
Good: 60–69%
Based clearly on the conclusions; practical, feasible given resources, which are explicitly considered. Where implementation and evaluation possible, an account

Table 4.4 continued

of what was achieved, some discussion of successes and failures with reasons, and an attempt to relate to the foregoing.
Clear Pass: 50–59%
Related to the conclusions; generally feasible, with some consideration of costs and practicalities. Where implementation and evaluation possible, some account of what was achieved, with gaps in discussion of reasons for successes and failures, with insufficient discussion of the latter.
Marginal Pass: 40–49%
Little relationship to conclusions; feasibility and practicality incompletely dealt with; leads the reader to wonder if they mightn't have been possible 'by common sense' without the need for the study. Substantial work would be required for implementation and evaluation.
Fail: 39% and below
Scarcely related to conclusions; serious impracticalities; costs not thought through; a 'common sense' list, with some doubts about the sense. The reader would be seriously worried about any attempt to implement the recommendations as stated.

Presentation
'A' Grade level: 70% and above
Fully documented and styled according to the brief; text free from spelling and grammatical solecisms; vocabulary appropriate to topic with all specialist terms defined; illustrations and tables well prepared; data presentation logically integrated into discussion in body of text/appendices; appendices relevant.
Good: 60–69%
Fully documented and styled according to the brief; free from major faults of spelling and grammar; vocabulary appropriate; illustrations and tables well prepared; data generally integrated into discussion.
Clear Pass: 50–59%
Some incompleteness of documentation, e.g. appendices, bibliographic items; carelessness in spelling; vocabulary and style lacking polish but understandable; illustrations and tables adequate; data occasionally misplaced without detracting from the thrust of the argument.
Marginal Pass: 40–49%
Some incompletenesses of documentation, e.g. appendices; bibliography incomplete/largely missing; carelessness in spelling and grammar; vocabulary and style uncomfortable but on balance acceptably conveying meaning; some data, illustrations and tables missing.
Fail: 39% and below
Documentation seriously at fault: missing, misplaced, difficult to find one's way around; persistent errors in spelling and grammar, solecisms or occasional failure in conveying meaning; typescript messy with uncorrected errors; key data, illustrations and tables missing; missing bibliography.

Teesside Business School (1994)

Layout and make-up

You are aiming to produced a typed, bound document. The print should be double spaced, with a 4 cm margin at the left and a 2.5 cm margin elsewhere, except in the case of direct quotations and highlighted material, which can be single or one-and-a-half spaced and indented from the left margin by a centimetre or so.

The type should be clear and black, with the minimum of Tipp-Exed corrections; it's best to use a word processor and a laser or inkjet printer, but other arrangements are possible. As you'll have to provide at least two copies of the project document, you'll be using a photocopier: so you might like to try the effect obtained by increasing the intensity of the copier in the case of dot-matrix and daisywheel print, submitting only the photocopies rather than the original.

Timing

While the factors of length, layout and make-up can make a difference between an adequate and a somewhat more than adequate project, there is one factor which can make a difference between complete success and abject failure: and that is the matter of deadlines. If your project document has to be submitted by a certain date, then you simply must comply, if you are to succeed.

Structure

The minimum requirements for a project report are as follows.

- A title page;
- a summary, which can be of two kinds: sequential or executive summary;
- contents pages;
- acknowledgements;
- a general introduction, which states the topic, defines the scope, lists related objectives and describes the organization, in that order;
- the main body, comprising material describing other people's relevant work, your own conceptual material, your methods and results, your discussion and conclusions;
- bibliography;
- appendices

in that order. If you are clear on this sequence, and aware of the additions which you are required to make to suit your institution's special requirements, you'll go a long way towards satisfying the presentation requirements.

Your project document is more of a management report than a research dissertation, so the summary is particularly important. It gives your reader the first inkling of the structure you will adopt, as well as specifying the content of your project. In the case of undergraduates, it's sequential: it states the topic, gives the background and rationale for what was done, briefly mentions how it was done, lists the main conclusions and highlights the recommendations. In the case of Diploma and MBA projects, it's more likely to be an executive summary, in which this sequence is more or less reversed: topic; recommendations; evidence for recommendations; the methods only if the recommendations depend on them (in the sense that they lead to different and better recommendations than the use of some other method); the background which led to the project; and the importance of taking action, given this background.

4.5 WHAT THE EXAMINER WILL BE LOOKING FOR

The way in which your project document hangs together is particularly important to how it is assessed. The bulk of the content begins with the Introduction, the purpose of which is threefold. Firstly, it provides your reader with everything he or she needs to understand your organization, your topic and your reasons for choosing it. Secondly, it attempts to create interest in what you have to say. And thirdly, it provides an overview of your thinking on the issues covered by the topic, and is never assessed in isolation, but in context with the Findings, Discussion and Recommendations which you will present at the end of your project document. The problem with many weak projects is that the author never makes this connection, and leaves the reader to flounder within the structure, not quite sure whether everything which the author intended to achieve was in fact achieved.

under-graduate

Turning to the material that comes in between, Figure 4.1 provides an example of a more detailed breakdown of the structure of an undergraduate project document which follows the minimum requirements listed above. You'll notice that it's shaped like a goblet, and offers you an image of a commonly used structure for undergraduate project reports. How you structure your project report will betray how you think to your examiners, while a good structure can help you to think more clearly as you write. It's worth examining in detail.

Many weak undergraduate projects are 'broken-stemmed'. The bowl has come off from the stem: in other words, there is no link between the presentation of other people's work (the literature review, in undergraduate projects) and your own empirical work. The writer says all he or she knows about the background, describes what he or she did, but shows no awareness that the two are related. The bowl in Figure 4.1 is roughly flute-shaped, since

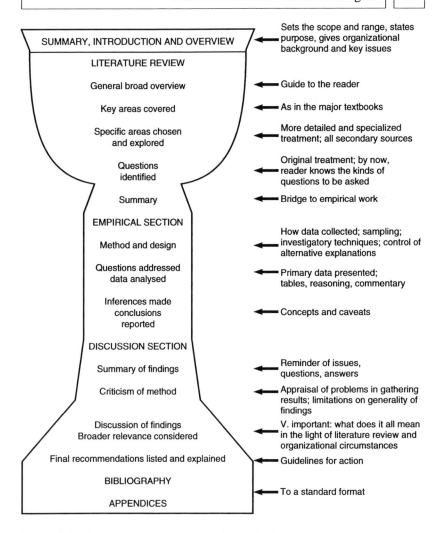

Figure 4.1 The structure of an undergraduate project.

the review of background information should begin with a wide scope, and narrow down to a more detailed consideration of issues which relate directly to the topic of the project. The bowl rests firmly on the stem, in the sense that the research questions which you ask, and report results on in the stem, should follow logically as the obvious questions to ask, given your discussion which leads up to that point.

The examiner's thoughts

'Well, here we go again. Um. Interesting title; I wonder what that means? Let's see the Abstract.' He or she skims the contents and might glance at the bibliography to see whether key authors are present: an impression of what might be involved is being formed, and he or she looks for a context of company background as provided by the introduction. 'Seems okay; now, what exactly is the intention? Okay, now why did the student feel these were useful objectives to choose . . . and is there any indication of how they're to be achieved?'

The examiner continues to read, looking for information relevant to the criteria which he or she has in mind (depending on the nature of the course involved) and hoping that this information will be readily available in the form of a coherent, readable and interesting argument. For much of the time, he or she is concerned with the structure of the argument being presented.

Inadequate structure. 'Well, in this project about employee selection methods, he's told me everything he knows about selection methods in the lit. review. Not a lot, but that matters less than the fact that I can't see the relevance of much of it. And on the next page here's a set of results; that's a bit sudden. How did he obtain them? Oh, I see, he says he prefers interviews to questionnaires but doesn't say why, and in any case it looks as though he ran out of time to do the questionnaire properly. Here's some answers to questions on the way in which the company trains its staff to use psychological tests, and there's some more in the appendix which look very relevant to the main discussion. Why those questions in particular, I wonder? And finally, here's a list of conclusions. Um, don't think much of that: he could have arrived at these kinds of conclusions without all the data-gathering. Now, hang on, what did he say the objectives were?' And the examiner will leaf back to an earlier chapter, hoping that objectives are there, reminding him- or herself what they were (often necessary at the end of a woolly account), and trying to decide if they have been achieved.

An adequately structured account. This is one in which in clarity of thinking is revealed by the structure; here, the examiner is more likely to be thinking something like the following. 'Okay, here are the generalities that apply to the selection process as a whole, and they're followed by the more specific issues that relate to some commonly used selection methods. She's considered the issues relating to the use of psychological tests for employee selection, and highlighted ones relevant to her company circumstances which relate to training in the use of tests; she summarizes the argument by listing a number of interesting and important questions. I wonder if there's anything on validity and meta-analysis? Aha, yes; good so far.'

If you look at Figure 4.1, you can see that the examiner has reached the bottom of the 'bowl' at this point. 'Now, how is she going to answer the questions she raises, and what's her rationale for the methods she uses? Given the constraints on her time, and the technical arguments and rationale she's provided, it's not a bad methodology; can't wait to see the answers she obtained.' We've reached the stem. 'If I'd got answers like these . . . hang on, what exactly were her objectives? Well well, I don't have to turn to Chapter 1, she's restated them here for me, excellent . . . if I'd got answers like these, I'd be coming to conclusions X, Y and Z. What are hers?'

The examiner reads them, and is ready for a clear discussion in which the conclusions are interpreted in the light of relevant wider information about selection, and related issues in the company in question. 'Okay, if that's as it is, what recommendations make sense? Good . . . yes . . . plausible given her previous argument, oho, and some costings too, excellent.' The examiner has reached the base and is in the mood for a suitably generous mark.

Structural variants

A frequent problem with undergraduate projects is the inadequacy, or absence, of a proper base. If the discussion and recommendations are missing, or if the recommendations are based on an inadequate discussion, the project document will be top-heavy and fall over. If the material which should be in the appendices is put into the empirical section, the same will occur. The first is self-evident; as for the second, you might care to note that the empirical section is the place for evidence directly relevant to the expression and evaluation of each of your results and no more; and the appendix is the place for the background material essential in supporting your argument. (More detailed guidelines are provided as part of my description of each empirical technique in Chapters 11 to 13, with a brief summary in Chapter 14.)

under-graduate

The structure for many in-company projects, and practically all MBA projects, is usually somewhat different. Only rarely can you narrow the issues down to a single, clearly-separated query to be resolved by a closely related set of questions. Perhaps you will find the candle-and-holder image offered in Figure 4.2 more helpful. The project starts with a particular issue of significance to you, your department, or your organization. Its company-wide and/or strategic implications lead you into a consideration of a variety of related issues or problems, each of which

in-company

MBA

needs describing in its organizational context. This candle, you recognize, sits within a body of knowledge which your study suggests is relevant and which you outline and draw on: a candleholder which will guide you in narrowing down to some specific research questions for each issue. Given the complexity of the issues you're considering, the base of the candleholder is quite broad, and you'll find yourself combining conceptual argument and empirical data in several sections or segments – before narrowing down to a series of conclusions. Finally, the same kind of broadening occurs as in the undergraduate model, in which conclusions, recommendations and the rest follow.

With this sort of structure, the best way you can help the examiner is to signpost the argument: summaries, bulleted lists of points that have been made and points that will next need to be made; all help the examiner to make his or her way systematically through the material and the various issues involved, each with its own conceptual and empirical analysis.

profes-sional

MBA

If you have an opportunity of taking action, to implement recommendations and to evaluate the results, it might be useful to see this as a further narrowing and broadening of the candleholder: there will be a point at which you need to become specific again, directing the examiner's attention to particular decisions and outcomes, before returning to the general level of the broader implications for your organization.

Finally, the MBA project document should be preceded by an executive summary. This should be on one page, with recommendations placed at the start. I'm not sure of the image to offer: a candleflame, perhaps, which results from, and illuminates, the contraption below.

diploma

It's difficult to offer a separate image for the professional and the Diploma projects. Sometimes these will relate to a single issue structured more like the undergraduate form, and sometimes they will be more akin to the MBA structure. The nature of the corporate implications, and the extent of dependence on a single academic discipline, will help you determine the structure to adopt and influence the ease with which the examiner understands the points which you wish to make.

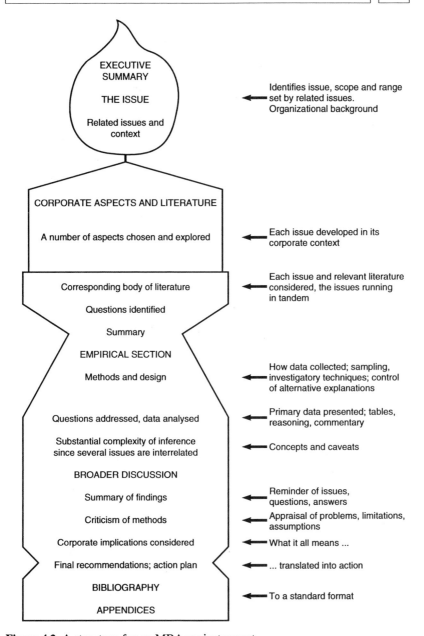

EXECUTIVE
SUMMARY

THE ISSUE

Related issues and
context

← Identifies issue, scope and range
set by related issues.
Organizational background

CORPORATE ASPECTS AND LITERATURE

A number of aspects chosen and explored

← Each issue developed in its
corporate context

Corresponding body of literature

← Each issue and relevant literature
considered, the issues running
in tandem

Questions identified

Summary

EMPIRICAL SECTION

Methods and design

← How data collected; sampling,
investigatory techniques; control
of alternative explanations

Questions addressed, data analysed

← Primary data presented; tables,
reasoning, commentary

Substantial complexity of inference
since several issues are interrelated

← Concepts and caveats

BROADER DISCUSSION

Summary of findings

← Reminder of issues,
questions, answers

Criticism of methods

← Appraisal of problems, limitations,
assumptions

Corporate implications considered

← What it all means ...

Final recommendations; action plan

← ... translated into action

BIBLIOGRAPHY

← To a standard format

APPENDICES

Figure 4.2 A structure for an MBA project report.

Getting organized for takeoff

5

all

The purpose of this chapter is fourfold. First, it acts as a practical summary of the ground covered in the first four chapters, and provides a checklist to a number of preparatory activities dealt with in those chapters. Secondly, it helps concentrate your mind on what is to come, by addressing the issue of planning and timetabling. Thirdly, it discusses a number of physical resources which you will need to organize for yourself before you begin work. Finally, it focuses your attention on the direction you'll be taking, that is, the argument or thesis you're about to address.

5.1 YOUR PREFLIGHT CHECKLIST

Regardless of whether you have to prepare a formal project proposal document, there is a number of activities which you should think through in detail before your flight begins. They're shown in Table 5.1; some of them are worth highlighting.

The regulations

You'll need to spend some time gathering handouts, scanning material in the library, reading regulations, aims and objectives, perhaps telephoning to professional bodies for further information, and, primarily, thinking about the implications, for your project, of the information you gather at this stage.

The topic

You will find yourself spending time in the library, doing an initial information search to help you decide on the topic to choose. You might wish to glance ahead to section 8.3, to find out how to use the library's

Table 5.1 Getting started on your project: a checklist

The regulations	Comment
• Get hold of a statement of aims and objectives from your academic institution	Check that your topic matches the Aims and Objectives in broad terms
• Identify your own personal objectives for the project	What would you like it to achieve for **you**?
• Get hold of any statements of special requirements	e.g. the professional guidelines, in the case of projects done in a professional programme
• Form an initial impression of the standard to aim at	
• Identify the anticipated level of originality, generality, pragmatism, balance, and type of evidence demanded	In general terms: many of these items will become clearer further on into your project work

The topic	
• Finalize your choice of topic	Get to the Aspect stage; form an idea of how the topic is more than a description
• Check the professional-body requirements	e.g. does the Area match with those required by the professional body?
• Check breadth, scope with tutor and sponsor	Is it sufficiently general and strategic?
• Ensure that the topic meets your own requirements	Interest, prior knowledge, difficulty
• A title isn't essential as yet	But give it one now if you like
• Do some preparatory reading to give you a feel for the company environment in the case of undergraduates, or if working in a different organization to your own	Try company handouts, annual reports, projects done in that organization Don't forget the suggestions in section 2.2
• Map out an initial structure for the eventual project report	This will become clearer as you progress; for the moment, what relative emphasis to be placed on data and recommendations as opposed to implementation and evaluation?
• If you're still unsure of your topic, use	the emergency procedures of section 3.3
• If these still don't help	**See your tutor immediately**

Your helpers	
• Identify your tutor and sponsor	Depends partly on your topic
• Identify the name of any other person in the organization who might offer advice	e.g., the person who agreed the in-company project scheme with your institution
• Establish to whom you are expected to report in the organization while doing the project	Try and avoid reporting to two bosses
• Clarify expectations	e.g. work on other projects at the same time?
• Identify other supporters	e.g. a mentor

resources in this task. You'll probably want to obtain written information from sources within your host organization as well.

A network of helpers

An early task will be to locate the people who will be your tutor and sponsor, together with the associated helpers listed in the table. Until you firm up on the Area and Field of your topic, you may find yourself negotiating with whoever in your academic institution is responsible for administering projects and allocating tutors. You might find yourself calling to see more than one potential tutor before you finalize the topic, and these might be people whom you haven't met before, because they don't teach on your main programme. This will be an opportunity to decide whether you are likely to get on with them, and to identify their personal style of tuition and assessment: there's more on this in section 7.3. This might just have a bearing on your choice of topic, assuming you have several in mind!

in-company

Somewhat similar comments apply to the sponsor. I feel it's legitimate to be aware of the politics and personalities inside your organization and, to the extent that a particular topic would have you working closely with someone whose relationship with you is problematic, considering the choice of a different topic.

If you're based in an organization and have substantial management experience, you'll probably be aware of the usefulness of networking, though it may not occur to you to draw on your network for an 'academic' activity. You'll know that the purpose of a network is to provide you with support from people who share similar job interests and values to yourself, who don't mind being contacted at odd times, and who expect you to respond in your turn when they need assistance.

If you think about it, you'll recognize that a project is a good time for extending your network as well as using existing people, because you're dealing with broad, cross-departmental issues. You might wish to consider:

- your own department head if he or she's not already involved;
- heads of departments in which you plan to collect information;
- someone in the training or personnel departments, because the project is part of your own development as a senior employee;
- the members of any Friday night drinking group to which you belong;
- the keeper of the organizational history, if there is such a person in your organization: it's often a person with long service, someone who has been in a variety of roles and survived reorganizations and mergers by keeping their head down and staying in a quiet backwater;

■ the network of secretarial staff. Think about it: they know what's going on across the organization, sometimes rather better than yourself, because they often transfer from one boss to another, retaining personal contacts as they do so. They can predict how their boss will respond to your approaches, and can usually be relied on to indicate the best time to approach him or her. They may be quite powerful gatekeepers; and they'll give an administrator's perspective on the managerial implications of your project ideas and proposals. You'll never join their network, but you might tap into it to a degree.

It's important to complete the preflight stage as soon as possible. You're likely to be at this stage while taught courses are still running, and the temptation to put things off, or to neglect the legwork involved in running elusive staff to earth, is appreciable. Don't procrastinate! There is more on this stage in section 5.2; for the time being, let me emphasize that the shorter the time allotted to your project, the sooner you should try to finalize on your choice of helpers. Very short projects (and some professional projects on full-time programmes spread themselves over no more than three months) mean a very rapid progression through the checklist. Aim at a week in this case, or better still, try and complete it before the project period officially starts.

If your project is to be done while you're in an industrial placement away from your institution, it seems very sensible to complete the tutor- and library-related items of the checklist well before you leave for the placement, unless your regulations specify otherwise.

all

under-graduate

5.2 PLANNING AND TIMETABLING

A little time spent in drawing up a timetable at the outset may save you much bitter regret at the end. This is common sense, yet so few students seem to do so in appropriate detail.

all

The first step is to be clear about the various stages of your project, and to order them sequentially. What counts as a 'stage' depends very much on the topic you choose, but it seems sensible to regard the main headings shown in Table 5.2 as major, and applicable to all topics. The idea is to divide the stages into the total time available to you, allocating time to each; then, as you begin work and develop a better idea of the details involved in each stage, allocating smaller amounts of time to each activity within each stage.

The items I've provided within each stage are there to give you a flavour of the kind of activities involved; what you put in their place will depend on your topic. The time demands of some of the activities will be easy to estimate, of others, more difficult. I've suggested some standard times in

Table 5.2 The major stages of a project which require timetabling

Preflight checklist activities
- Regulations
- Choice of topic: including preparatory reading
- Arranging the helpers: including arrival 'on placement'
- Writing an outline project proposal document

Basic familiarization
- Library work and literature review
- Organizing in-company written information
- Meetings with initial informants; confidentiality arrangements
- Writing and major notemaking begins

Identifying main thrust of arguments and their critical features
- Expectations: hunches and hypotheses, models and theories
- Thinking through the implications for data collection
- Deciding on the details of methods and techniques for data collection
- Deciding on the analytic techniques to be used, quantitative and non-quantitative
- Reading and talking to people continue; writing and notemaking continue

Data collection and analysis
- Initial pilot work
- Revision/fine tuning of expectations and techniques
- Main data collection
- Scanning the data, 'eyeball' testing, thinking
- Further data collection
- More systematic analysis, tentative conclusions
- Checking the plausibility, reliability, and robustness of these conclusions
- Further data collection with cross-checks; perhaps different technique or method
- Possibility of implementation and evaluation of some recommendations
- Reading and talking to people continue; writing and notemaking continue

Writing up
- Systematic and organized writing
- Checking that objectives as stated at the outset have been achieved
- Checking of drafts with tutor, sponsor, and other relevant people
- Reading continues; final update of literature review elements

Production
- Typing or word-processing
- Frequent revisions
- Last-minute panics over bibliographic references
- Further typing or word-processing
- Binding

Delivery
- Distribution of project document
- Presentations

Table 5.3; some are taken directly from, or are based on Berger and Patchner (1988), and Howard and Sharp (1983). Many are my own estimates, based on recent personal activities; the rationale for these is occasionally obscure, but they seem to work and will do as a rough guide. (For example, on cross-checking a respondent's assertions: has it ever struck you that you can find out any nonclassified piece of information by asking and refining your question in a sequence of four phonecalls? The first call will refer you to someone more likely to know, the second, to someone much more likely to know, and so on.) Many should be amended in the light of your own circumstances by use of a little common sense. Far better to rely on experience, and who is more experienced than your tutor? If in doubt, ask him or her.

Some activities are particularly vulnerable to neglect, and it's worth discussing these in more detail. We'll work backwards through the main sequence, since this is a good way of designing a project timetable and since, in an unplanned project, the problems always seem to come home to roost at the end.

Delivery

Deadlines matter! And because no one cares quite as much about your project as yourself, it's safest if you deliver the document, by hand, yourself. Allow time for any travel that may be involved; allow time to prepare yourself for any oral presentation that is required. If yours is a group project, this activity in itself may take up to a fortnight.

Production

Often neglected because it comes at the end! Think of this stage as involving a cumulative, '1-2-3' rule of thumb. Talk to a typist now, and take his/her estimate of the time it will take to type up your manuscript. (A working week in which the typist does nothing else is a fair estimate for projects of around 20 000 words.) That's '1'. Now add another two weeks at least to allow for the interaction between you as you proof-read, amend, and retype. That's '2'. Finally, add another three weeks for final corrections, (particularly to the bibliography and all the references which you thought you had filed safely but seem to have lost), more editing, last-minute retyping, and collating and binding. That's '3'. A total of six weeks to go from manuscript to finished article always seems excessive before you begin, and always seems accurate, or even an underestimate, when you've finished.

If you have, or can arrange, constant access to a word processor, and know how to use it, it's a good idea to do your own typing. You'll have

Table 5.3 Estimates of standard times for some project activities

Reading an empirically based journal article thoroughly	*3 hours*
Reading a book thoroughly	*10 hours*
Absorbing and using a statistically based technique based on five texts	*50 hours*
(with a total elapsed time of	*6 weeks)*
Preparing a 10-question interview schedule	*1 day*
Pretesting the schedule on two interviewees and amending the result	*1 day*
Destroying a relationship through lack of pretesting an inept interview schedule	*1 minute*
Conducting an interview	*1 hour*
Conducting four interviews in the same location (five possible but very tiring)	*1 day*
Transcribing one hour of tape recorded interview	*7 hours*
Cross-checking an interviewee's assertion	*up to 4 phonecalls*
Content analysis of 300 one-sentence written items already typed on to cards	*7 hours*
Reliability cross-checking of the result	*6 hours*
Final version: add another	*2 hours*
Informal pretesting of a questionnaire by five respondents located on one site	*1 day*
Piloting a larger questionnaire more formally	*up to 4 weeks*
Pretesting a single summated rating scale for internal consistency	*2 days*
Reaching postal questionnaire sample by first-class mail	*1 week*
Time for respondent completion	*2 weeks*
Time for postal return	*1 week*
Add lag time since many respondents peak at 2 weeks, but some take longer	*2 weeks*
Time to post, complete, return chase-up letter and questionnaire	*3 weeks*
The 'psychological week' (at the end of which period, an inquiry to a respondent made at the beginning of the time will be forgotten)	*5 days + weekend + 5 days*
Creating a six-field (mixed numeric and textual) database ready for printout	*4 hours*
Filling the database with 50 records each of 400 characters across 6 fields	*5 hours*

The sample size below which it probably pays to hand-analyse a simple 15-question questionnaire with no appreciable cross-tabulations	*100 people*
The sample size above which it usually pays to use a computer, even though you aren't familiar with the software in question	*200 people*
It all depends	*100 to 200 people*
Time taken to absorb SPSS manual sufficient to do one analysis, assuming you understand the basic statistical procedures involved but don't know SPSS	*3 days*

more control over production, and the cost will be substantially less. If you're used to using it, you'll most probably write directly into the word processor, dispensing with the manuscript stage completely. The evidence is that the process of writing electronically is different to the pen-and-ink procedure, and there are some pitfalls peculiar to the medium; have a look at Turk and Kirkman (1989: 119) for the details. Apart from this, you'll need to remember:

- that the '1-2-3' process, particularly the '1', holds even if you've been typing up as you go along: allow six weeks for final production;
- to use a backup disc regularly, and take the trouble to keep it in a different physical location from your main disc;
- unless you have your own printer, to make arrangements for print-outs while you are writing as well as for the final production run: the word-processing of long documents depends on the repeated amendment of print-outs.

Writing up

As you can see from Table 5.2, writing is something you do throughout. Many people find it relatively easy to get the Introduction out of the way early on, to write up their methods while they're collecting their data, and to write up their data during the main analysis stage. Time estimates for these, as well as for the major stage in which you pull together the various sections, should be made well in advance. There's more information on the writing process itself in Chapter 14.

Don't forget that writing also involves talking – with your tutor and sponsor. If you can allow time for either or both of these people to read your project report in a draft form, chapter by chapter or the manuscript as a whole, you'll find that their comments can make a substantial – no, major – difference to the grade you finally receive, provided of course that you note them and act on them. And this is true regardless of the amount of tutorial contact you've had while carrying out your project. A lot will depend on how busy and willing they are; but it's well worth negotiating this with them, and allowing time for necessary rewrites, preceding, and separate to, the '1-2-3' time which you need for producing the finished article.

Data collection and analysis

Time requirements vary enormously, depending on the method you choose. This is the stage at which you're most dependent on other people; you might want to note that using a method and its associated techniques requires that you should know how to do so, and this will mean setting aside time to learn it in practical terms, as well as knowing it in principle from previous lectures on the subject. This will involve asking other people for their help – for example, a computer technician whose help you can request when you're stuck with the package you use for the analysis of your data. Contacting your respondents always involves a lead time: they don't just sit there in suspended animation waiting for your call and your visit!

Questionnaire-based surveys always involve chasing up non-respondents, which increases your initial estimate of how long to allow for postage and questionnaire completion. Information obtained from interviews, especially if they're carried out to write case studies, needs cross-checking with other interviews; content analysis of interview data requires twice as much time as you initially assign, since someone else has to carry out the basic procedure (described in section 11.2), as well as yourself, to ensure reliability.

Identifying the main thrust of arguments

This stage is the most difficult to plan ahead. It often runs contemporaneously with the preceding and the succeeding stages, since, in many in-company projects, ideas are developed, critical analyses undertaken, and hypotheses generated in parallel with the collection of information and data which test them out. (This important contrast with the main model used in scientific research work is developed in detail in Chapter 6.) It also involves selecting, and learning about, the main method and techniques which you will be using, and your first practical point of contact with these might well be the last Part of this book. Include the time to read the rest of this book in your time estimates!

Basic familiarization

The problem here is often one of locating information. You'll need to allow time for arranging visits to various information centres, commercial and academic libraries, and interviews with key informants. Chapter 8 provides you with guidelines for bibliographic searching; for the moment, it's a useful rule of thumb to see this process as one involving three stages:

- Stage 1, in which you refer to immediately accessible sources already known to you;
- Stage 2, in which you draw up, and read and interview a list of sources somewhat more systematically (e.g. the formal library bibliographic search);
- Stage 3, in which you read and interview a list of sources to which your Stage 2 reading and interviews have referred you.

There is an appreciable timelag between Stage 2 and Stage 3. For example, it takes ten days to three weeks for items to arrive via inter-library loan; it may take two to four weeks for yourself and your planned informant to find a mutually convenient time in your diaries.

Of course, many of these activities can take place at roughly the same time. Many are critical, in the sense that your subsequent work depends on their prior completion. The way to handle these issues, and produce a very clear timetable for your whole project, is to use some form of critical path analysis. Although microcomputer-based software exists, you would probably be better to carry out a simple version by hand. The rules involve listing the activities in time, putting simultaneous activities in parallel, associating time estimates with each activity, and taking care to identify the activities which are critical in the sense indicated above. A brief and useful description of a simple form of critical path analysis and associated control charting is provided in Howard and Sharp (1983: 46).

5.3 PHYSICAL RESOURCES

When I was a graduate student, I knew a colleague who had a brilliant idea for his Ph.D. thesis on knowledge acquisition in management. Why not present his thesis document in a multimedia format, including all the physical resources he had used in collecting and generating his ideas, as an example of the ways in which, in practice, knowledge is acquired? One chapter might consist, for example, of the bus-ticket on which a notion was first recorded, the back of an old envelope on which it was developed, various inter-library loan request forms through which the notion was pursued and grown, and some inspired writing to link it all together. It was one of those wheezes which seem like a good idea at the time (3pm, in the days when pubs closed after lunch), but proved far too self-referential to be a good risk as a Ph.D. topic. He went on to do something banal with expert systems instead.

The project diary

This does illustrate the variety of media which you'll find yourself using, however, and suggests that there is a need for some intermediate recording system between the idea, the chance conversation, the memory of possibly related events, and the more formal written account which you will develop into your project document.

You need to begin a project diary right from day one of your project work. A simple hardbacked notebook will do; one of the thin ledgers sold in Boots gives plenty of space. Its purpose is to:

- act as an immediate (same-day) recording system for the 'bus-ticket' ideas;
- act as a record of developing ideas;
- use as a planner for appointments and schedules;
- help in the management of activities and people (being especially valuable in group-based project work);
- act as a record for names, notions and bibliographic references that you just happen to come across when doing something else;
- provide you with a personal briefing in preparation for meetings with tutor and sponsor;
- form the basic store of data for any intermediate reports which you might be required to provide in the course of your project work.

under-graduate

Many undergraduate regulations require you to keep such a diary as a formal requirement, for submission along with your project document. The intermediate report is also a requirement of some undergraduate projects.

all

But the project diary is an indispensable part of project work at any level; it's tremendously useful, and I'm surprised that many guideline documents don't mention it. Apart from the list I've given above, it's up to you how you organize it and use it; my only thought is that it shouldn't be a diary with pre-printed dates, since you'll have varying amounts of material to record in it on different days. If you're comfortable with personal organizers, their specialized pages and looseleaf format can be helpful, provided you're careful about cross-referencing, and provided, I feel, you keep one dedicated solely to your project. Personally, though I use a type of organizer diary for other things, I prefer an A4-sized ledger for each separate project in which I'm involved, as organizer pages aren't large enough for my needs.

Record cards and notetaking media

You'll find that a stock of A5 record cards is useful for making notes on the authors you read and the people you talk to. Use them for the following.

■ **Précis**: a note which summarizes an argument in briefer form while staying faithful to the source's assumptions and mode of expression.
■ **Paraphrase**: a note which reproduces an argument in about the same length while reflecting your own emphases and expression (most usefully cast in a form which links the material to other ideas which you plan to use).
■ **Synopsis**: a note which summarizes briefly, but in your own words; unlike the previous forms of notetaking, it needs substantial reworking and expansion before using the material in your project document.
■ **Quotation**: a note which reproduces the source's utterance word-for-word.

Each of these should include a bibliographic reference in the case of reading, or a speaker-date-place reference in the case of conversation. See Figure 5.1 for an example; there's more on the craft involved in each kind of notetaking, in Parsons (1973: 21) and Williams and Stevenson (1963: 95).

Many people prefer to avoid cards, and use punched paper and a ring-binder instead, but this is clearly less economical if your separate notes are relatively short. You'll need one or more ring-binders in any case, for the main sequence of material in your write-up.

You'll certainly find it helpful to obtain a stock of smaller-sized index cards on which to record your bibliographic references, one reference to a card, following the conventions outlined in section 8.1 and Table 8.3. Alternatively, if you have constant access to a microcomputer, you might prefer to keep your references on that. I find that, while databases are very convenient for sorting and searching, they're often more complicated to set up and manage than a simple word-processing program. 'Sorting' is achieved by insertion of a new reference in the appropriate alphabetic position when you first add it to the list of references: after all, you'll never want to present the bibliography in any other order but alphabetically by author. The database is very useful if you like to organize your thoughts on an issue by searching and selecting all mentions of that issue across the whole set of references, however. Remember to do a print-out now and again, as well as keeping a backup of your disc!

Tape recorders

These are useful in some kinds of systematic interview-based survey work, for recording conversations with key informants and for collecting verbatim comments in case study preparation. You might argue that the pocket dictaphone kind is a useful way of recording ideas as they occur to you, in addition. The decision to use a tape recorder for the former

Schön's original text

In management as in other fields, 'art' has a twofold meaning. It may mean intuitive judgement and skill, the feeling for phenomena and for action that I have called knowing-in-practice. But it may also designate a manager's reflection, in a context of action, on phenomena which he perceives as incongruent with his intuitive understandings.

Managers do reflect-in-action. Sometimes, when reflection is triggered by uncertainty, the manager says, in effect, 'This is puzzling; how can I understand it?' Sometimes, when a sense of opportunity provokes reflection, the manager asks, 'What can I make of this?' And sometimes, when a manager is surprised by the sucess of his intuitive knowing, he asks himself, 'What have I really been doing?'

Filecard used for précis

'Art' has the same two meanings when used in management, as elsewhere: the exercise of subjective judgement, ('knowing-in-practice') or a reflection on events which seem counter-intuitive ('reflection-in-action').

Managers reflect-in-action when they're uncertain, when they mull over possible opportunities, and when they seek to understand a successful intuition.

Schön D.A. *The Reflective Practitioner* London: Temple Smith 1983: 241.

Filecard used for paraphrase

The term 'Art' carries the same connotations in management as in other disciplines. It can stand for the way in which experience and gut feelings give rise to competent performance, as a form of 'knowing' in itself. Additionally, the term can be used to express the manager's attempt to make sense of events which his intuitions didn't anticipate: his private effort to 'know about'. This attempt at deliberate and explicit explanation is made whenever the manager acts as a scientist, to comprehend unexpected events; or when s/he behaves as an entrepreneur, to exploit opportunities; or when s/he acts as a psychologist, trying to understand the ways in which his/her intuition works.

Schön D.A. *The Reflective Practitioner* London: Temple Smith 1983: 241.

Filecard used for synopsis

'Knowing-in-practice': way in which competent performance is itself a form of knowing. 'Reflection-in-action': deliberate problem-solving (solving a puzzle or seizing opportunities); trying to understand process of own intuition.

Schön D.A. *The Reflective Practitioner* London: Temple Smith 1983: 241.

Filecard used for quotation

ART 'may mean intuitive judgement and skill, the feeling for phenomena and for action...' OR '...reflection in a context of action, on phenomena which he perceives as incongruent with his intuitive understandings.'

Schön D.A. *The Reflective Practitioner* London: Temple Smith 1983: 241.

Figure 5.1 The use of filecards for notemaking.

purpose is a major one. On the one hand, it increases the completeness of the data you record; on the other hand, it only results in useful information if you transcribe the data accurately, and you can see from Table 5.3 that this is a very time-consuming process. This is a decision best discussed with your tutor. The decision to use a tape recorder for the latter purpose is more of a personal whim: and why not?

5.4 YOUR ARGUMENT

You may recall that the word 'thesis' was used in Chapter 1 in association with the more advanced and academic kinds of research-based document associated with Ph.D. work: a word which I've decided to eschew in favour of 'project'. There is a second use of the word '**thesis**', which I feel is very important to the success of your project, and which I'd like to commend to you.

Used in this sense, a thesis is a statement of your belief and intention in doing your project; in other words, a statement of your argument: what exactly you're trying to establish, or in other words, the kind of conclusion which you believe your data may support. The more you are aware of what you're setting out to establish, and the clearer you are about what your thesis is, the more successful you're likely to be.

This is what I had in mind when I discussed the issue of balance in section 4.2. And as I mentioned there, the fact that you hold a thesis doesn't necessarily mean that you run a risk of biasing your findings. On the contrary, having a clear notion of your thesis will alert you to what kinds of findings would support it, what kinds would refute it, and help you to think more clearly in interpreting the meaning of your data. Also, as I mentioned in discussing balance, it will help you to avoid excessively risky topics. So, you must have a thesis to be successful.

For instance, you might have a topic involving the use of psychological tests in the selection of computer operators. But that doesn't include any kind of argument, and to write a project with that as your thesis is going to lead to a very woolly and waffly description; to write a project around the thesis that 'the introduction of tests for this grade of staff will make for more effective selection than using interview methods alone', if that indeed is the belief which you set out to establish, would be much more effective.

undergraduate

In your case, you may be evaluating a thesis which is obvious to your project, such as that 'deregulation permits building societies to diversify services effectively only if they pay more attention to policy and strategy than hitherto' for a topic dealing with the impact of UK monetary policy on the development of services provided by the building society in which you work. Alternatively, you might not be obviously testing out a thesis, so

MBA

diploma

much as fitting and evaluating some conceptual model, for example, by using the Ansoff matrix and some technique of portfolio analysis such as the Boston Box in a project on the strategic choices facing a company seeking to trade in eastern Europe. But a thesis is still in there somewhere (as, for example, in recognizing that the Boston Box is two-dimensional and that issues of market penetration and horizontal strategy might well need to be taken into account), and the clearer you are about the data you need to support your thesis (and, conversely, what data would negate it), the more focused your argument will be.

all

Why leave it so late? If the thesis is so important, why not deal with it earlier? Well, my experience is that, while a thesis follows logically from a topic, as soon as the topic is enunciated, psychologically it takes you some time before you really become clear about what your thesis should be. You begin to be clear about it as you start planning and timetabling your work, and especially, as you start to think through the kinds of data you will need to collect, and the method you plan to use. So now is the time to set down your argument and clarify the thesis which you will seek to support.

Take your newly-acquired project diary, and enter the following items on the first page:

- your Area, Field and Aspect;
- one or two sentences which state the issues excluded in moving to your topic;
- an indication how your topic will be more than a descriptive account;
- a formal statement of your topic in one sentence;
- a statement of your thesis.

That's all you need on this first page. Put the date on it, and there you are: you've made a solid beginning and are well under way. You've a head start on the student who neglects the beginnings and background; you're taken off and on course!

Key Issues in Depth

PART 2

What is research anyway?

6

I imagine that you view your project as a form of research. Academic staff use the term, as do your fellow students. You expect to be referred to books with titles like *Research Methods* to help you in your project activity. If you're in-company based, you may hear your colleagues using it as a convenient word to describe the time which you spend in your organization when you aren't engaged in the more usual, daily round. And, used loosely, the term is fairly appropriate – after all, you're setting out to 'find something out in a systematic way, in order to increase knowledge'. It would seem sensible to examine what this activity of research involves, and the prior assumptions to which you will be expected to subscribe.

There is a second reason for examining the term. If you use it precisely, and model your activities on it too closely, I believe you'll be led astray. To put it bluntly, the research process as conventionally defined is incapable of handling many of the issues with which you're presented in a management or business project. The word 'research' (particularly if preceded by the word 'scientific'), as a description for what you're doing, is misleading in principle, and positively dangerous in practice.

The first part of this chapter describes the conventional view of research, and examines the underlying assumptions. The second part highlights some of the difficulties this view presents for management and business project work, while the third part offers an approach expressly designed to cope with these difficulties. Finally, the last part outlines the practical implications, highlighting the issue of confidentiality in particular.

All of this is basic **epistemology**: an enquiry into how it is possible for people to know things, and how best to think of the process in which you're engaged. If that sounds rather abstract and dry, let me offer you an image for what we're doing.

I want you to join me in a quest: a campaign for understanding. Our opponent is Ignorance, and our goal is knowledge itself: the understanding and wisdom your project will bring.

6.1 RESEARCH AS A MILITARY CAMPAIGN

People conduct research, as I've suggested above, in order to increase knowledge; they do so by finding things out, and by being systematic about the process. The approach always involves an interplay of three elements:

- an assertion that certain things might be true;
- information relevant to the truth or otherwise of the assertion;
- some method for bringing the first two elements together.

The assertion may consist of a belief, a hunch based on past experience, a hypothesis which suggests that two things might be related, or a set of statements about interconnections which form part of a theory. (There's a progression here, from belief to theory: a progression from the less formal and undefined, to the more formal and predefined.) The information may consist of conclusions arrived at by inference from knowledge already available. When the two are put together by the method of 'just thinking about it, mulling it over', one talks of rational thought and decision-making. The rules of logic and of common sense apply.

When the information also consists of **empirical data** (the results of new observations made in order to check out the assertion), the method remains somewhat similar in that thinking and reasoning are involved. However, there's also a concern that the observations be accurate and reliable, and that the thinking takes account of the limitations and advantages arising from the way in which the data were collected; the method involves somewhat more careful inference-making, and in this case, one talks of scholarship. You might recall the rules which apply to this method: they're given in section 4.3.

This method of combining assertions and information is usually reserved for situations in which the researcher wants to understand and explain particular events. However, when the researcher wishes to construct or add to a theory, that is, to make general statements which have the power to explain a whole range of events, the bare bones of the procedure are the same (empirically collected information brought to bear on an assertion), but an additional method for combining the two is used: scientific method. (That's why people debate whether the work of historians can ever be viewed as scientific. People who feel that it can't, would argue that history has no generality to offer, being simply an understanding of particular events (Goldstein and Goldstein, 1978: 202).)

Scientific method is also known as the **hypothetico-deductive method**. It's made up of the following minimal components:

- a formally expressed general statement which has the potential to explain things: **the theory**;
- a deduction that, if the theory is true, then you would expect to find a relationship between at least two variables, A and B: **the hypothesis**;
- a careful definition of exactly what you need to measure, in order to observe A and B varying: **the operational definition**;
- the making of the observations: **measurement**;
- the drawing of conclusions about the hypothesis: **testing**;
- the drawing of implications back to the theory: **verification**.

The groundrules for the making of observations are very well developed, possibly because measurement is the stage over which the researcher has most control. Measurements must be **valid** – that is, they should be accurate: some alternative measurement method should arrive at the same answer. They must also be **reliable,** that is, precise: the same answer should be obtained on re-measurement, assuming the situation has not changed, of course. See Goldstein and Goldstein (1978: 232) for a brief further discussion, Berger and Patchner (1988: 55) for a good summary, and Brindberg and McGrath (1985) for a comprehensive approach at Masters level.

The last component, verification, is always seen as provisional, in the sense that, while you can cast doubt on, or even overturn, a theory by disproving the hypothesis, you can never verify a theory as true by proving the hypothesis. All you can do with a proven hypothesis is to say that the theory remains intact for today; mind you, if it remains intact for a long time, despite repeated testing of various related hypotheses, your belief that the theory is true will certainly increase.

Hypothetico-deductive method has a variety of techniques appropriate to various situations. The most powerful of these is the formal experiment, in which the hypothesis is stated as an association between A and B (the variable A is correlated with the variable B), or as a causal relationship between A and B (variable A is seen as independent, causing changes in variable B, which is seen as dependent). In the former case, the influence of other variables which might contribute to the association is controlled by careful design of the experiment, and by a statistical technique called 'partialling out'; in the latter case, experimental design is the main method of control and statistics is used mainly for analysis. There are other techniques, used in the analysis of survey questionnaires, which model themselves on the experiment and also look for the influence of one variable on another (see section 12.1).

There you have it, in brief. If you want more, you'll find a thorough treatment of scientific thinking in Giere (1979). Our army consists of skirmishers (the method of deduction, or 'just thinking') and lightly armed reconnaissance troops (the method of scholarship). But the big battalions in the search for knowledge, the real McCoys as it were, are the hypothetico-deductive method and the experiment.

So runs the conventional view. Indeed, these troops can be formidable; but an army made up of big battalions has severe disadvantages. It's ponderous and slow in its movement over the terrain, and it may not be suited to all territories or to all forms of conflict. It demands an excellent level of staff work to be effective: intelligence about the enemy's movements must be well developed, the implications of decisions must be worked through very carefully, and it demands an adequate level of time, support and resourcing. Finally, it requires a high level of morale, a belief in the power of the big battalions. This belief arises from a number of basic assumptions it makes about itself.

These assumptions arise from a philosophical position which is called **positivism**, and they look like this.

- Empirical science is not just one way of knowing things, it's the only one which avoids the dangers of stereotyping, myth and superstition.
- It should be applied, in the form of theories which provide an underpinning to technology.
- Ultimately, and all talk of probabilities aside, people can identify whether an assertion is true or false: we're always capable of making this distinction, and our objective is to seek the truth 'out there'.
- We recognize truth in only two ways: by seeing that an assertion is consistent with deductions made from it (the basis of truth in logic and mathematics – what I've called 'just thinking'); or by recognizing that it is supported by empirical evidence (the basis of truth in everything else). The only alternatives are either sheer emotion, which is unreliable, or poetry, which is nice but not to be taken too seriously; anything else is nonsense.

Giere (1979: 32); Schön (1983: 57).

6.2 PROBLEMS FOR APPLIED RESEARCH: THE TERRAIN TO BE FOUGHT OVER

This sort of army is unbeatable whenever it's used for pure research in subjects such as chemistry and physics; however, it runs into difficulties when it's used in engagements by other disciplines, and these can be severe when it's used to handle a business or management project. Projects represent a form of applied research, and applied research presents it with very rough terrain.

Figure 6.1 shows you a picture of the battleground. Research is seen as an activity which draws on the instruments available in the academic community – including the hypothetico-deductive method – in order to serve society on the one hand, and build knowledge about what is true on the other.

Think of yourself as being located in the box labelled Research, the business school in which you're studying in the box labelled the Academic Community, and your organization in the box labelled Society at Large. If you were engaged in pure research, particularly in a classical, experimentally based subject like physics (Figure 6.1(a)), then the hypothetico-deductive method would make eminent sense. If you were a management consultant doing consultancy work (Figure 6.1(b)), clearly, it wouldn't: your job wouldn't be to build theory but to help resolve problems. There is considerable debate about the usefulness of the hypothetico-deductive method in applied research (Figure 6.1(c)): the issues presented by the Practitioner Field don't readily lend themselves to it. Finally, when the applied research takes the form of a project in business or management, I would argue that there is no place for the method at all: though there is room for scholarship.

Many people involved with the problems of consulting, professional practice, and applied research in general would agree with me, people known collectively as the supporters of the 'New Paradigm' (Reason and Rowan, 1981a). The difficulties they identify are serious, and can be summarized under five headings, as follows.

The issues are inherently complex

The issues dealt with by professionals (and for the sake of this argument, I include managers) are frequently very complex: there are many variables, some modifying the relationships between others. To say, as scientists frequently do, that the theory incorporating these variables needs further development to handle the full complexity arising in professional practice is of little use to the practitioner, who needs to take immediate decisions. And in the case of issues which primarily involve people, there is some suspicion that sufficiently precise and comprehensive scientific theories will be a very long time in arriving, if they ever arrive at all; you might care to read a good discussion of this theme in Allport (1981).

Problems cross discipline boundaries

Part of the complexity arises because practitioner problems don't sit within the neat boundaries of academic knowledge, or within categories

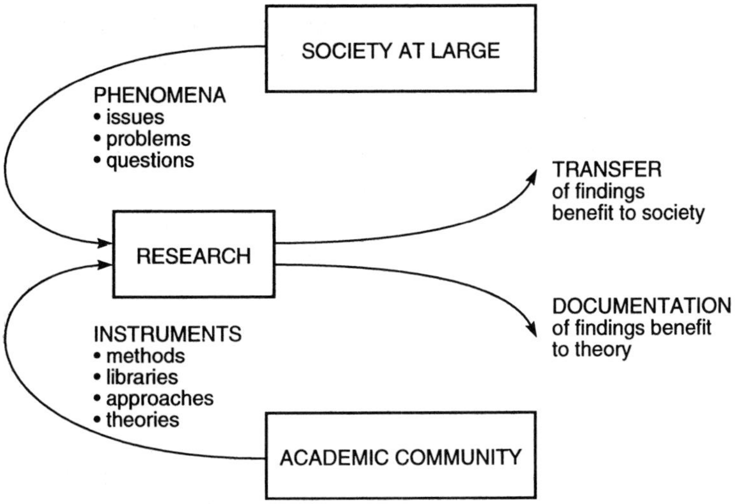

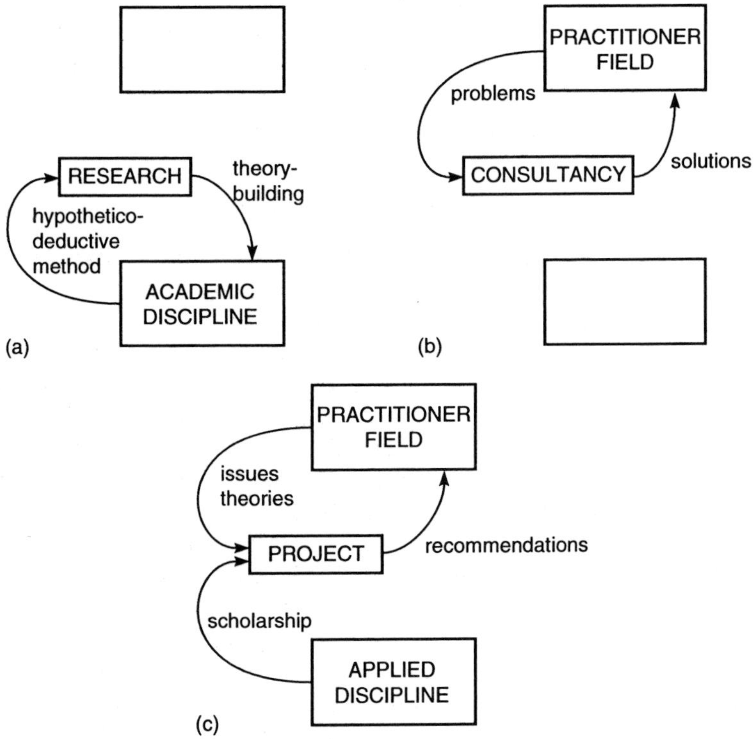

Figure 6.1 A description of the battleground. (a) Pure research; (b) consultancy; (c) project work as applied research. (After Riebel and Amini, 1985.)

which might suggest an appropriate technique to apply; they're frequently messy (Eden *et al.,* 1983). A variety of knowledge bases and methods, each based on different assumptions, must be used, each being at different levels of development. None of them fit coherently together, in a way which would allow the hypothetico-deductive method to operate (Schön, 1983). This is particularly true of the corporate issues tackled by senior decision-makers, and of questions which involve policy-setting and strategy determination. Yet, as we saw in Chapters 3 and 4, these are particularly fruitful fields for investigation in project work, especially at Diploma, professional, and Masters level.

The technical issue is rarely the problem

Professional problem-solving is value-driven (e.g. most issues of corporate strategy and business policy), it may have social consequences (e.g. issues of quality in manufacturing and service management), and it is frequently intertwined in contradictory assumptions about social policy (e.g. the problems of management in the health, the social, and the police services). The problems of professional practice arise from these kinds of implications, and less from the technical or scientific questions which the professional is required to address. But management, in this sense, is pre-eminently a professional, rather than a technical activity.

Problems have no independent life of their own

Professionals don't think in ways which are easily analysed by the hypothetico-deductive method, which assumes a dispassionate 'observer', the existence of problems and truth 'out there', and a situation which sits still enough for the effects of scientific interventions to be noticed.

Intuition, gut feeling, and flair are involved in management decision-making, and this is true at senior corporate level (Eden *et al.*, 1979) and at middle management level (Isenberg, 1984); whether the business one's in is architecture, engineering design, training, town planning (Schön, 1983) or banking and venture capital (Jankowicz, 1987). Much of the manager's time consists, not of testing out the truth of questions, but of framing the questions in the first place. The evidence does not exist in the form of variables to be measured; the manager has to determine what counts as evidence by recognizing it as it goes by in the flow of events, and this recognition is an active process of construction and judgement, rather than a dispassionate assessment of what is objectively 'out there'. (Glance back at Table 2.2 for a description of the managerial environment that brings about this state of affairs.) However, the manager is a product of his or her own culture with its particular history, and operates within a language which slices up phenomena in a culturally idiosyncratic way; if he or she is operating in a foreign market, he or she rapidly discovers that what counts as evidence to the foreign business partners may radically differ: Boisot (1994); Woodall (1992). Imagine how differently problems are construed by the eastern European manager, whose language has no indigenous word for 'marketing' and a rather different meaning for the word 'management' to our own (Jankowicz, 1994)! As part of the very activity of management, interventions and decisions become part of the problem itself, and change the situation being researched.

Using over-simplified methods will distort the problem anyway

Of course, you could argue that I'm confusing the difficulties which exist in the subject-matter being researched, with the activity of research in itself. You may grant me that the field to be researched is unreasonably complicated in the ways I've described above, but that this shouldn't prevent the application of scientific method. After all, even insanity – unreason itself – can be studied scientifically!

The difficulty with this is that in order to carry out scientific research in management, you have to distort the issues so much to get them to fit into the language of hypothesis, variables, and theory; you have to elide the intuitive and the judgemental; you have to ignore so much of what makes the issue worth researching in the first place – that the result of your labours may turn out to be largely irrelevant.

It looks as though the big battalions are beaten: they're floundering in a morass of uncertainty, and the enemy just won't stand still long enough to be brought to battle. The hypothetico-deductive method seems inappropriate for many of the topics with which you might want to deal in your project.

If all this is new to you, you might want to read an alternative account which covers the same ground and comes to similar conclusions. Bennett (1986: 10) is very useful at any level of study, but is particularly helpful to undergraduate readers, some of whom may be doing the very specific and technical projects in which hypothetico-deductive methods have some place. The other levels of project will simply have to confront these difficulties head-on; there is a good account of the problem in Harré (1981).

6.3 PROJECT WORK AS GUERRILLA WARFARE

It seems as though we need a different kind of army, one which is better adapted to the terrain in question. Perhaps we should stand down the big battalions, and adopt guerrilla tactics instead. We have some troops who would do very nicely, after all: the skirmishers, our deductive method of systematic reasoning or 'just thinking'; and the lightly armed reconnaissance troops, the method of scholarship.

All we have to do is deploy them sensibly, and this involves a discipline just as strict as the one which applies to the big battalions themselves. We can't afford sloppiness in method or reasoning. If we drop our adherence to hypothetico-deductive method with its search for the truth 'out there', we must still retain a rigorous approach to ensure that our understanding is complete enough to permit workable prediction (note the difference in emphasis); there's no excuse for playing the old soldier, or for being a barrack-room stanchion. It's still a matter for cold steel, and this is supplied in the form of a number of procedures advocated by the New Paradigm approach, which address the problems of terrain identified in the previous section.

Inherent complexity

You have two courses of action: you either refuse battle (find a simpler, but perhaps less important or realistic topic amenable to scientific method); or accept the complexity. The best way of accepting complexity is not to think solely in terms of variables which some theory tells you are relevant, but in terms of issues to be discovered during a period of intensive familiarization with the situation being studied. A number of questions will help.

- What issues are present?
- Who says so; what is their status, expertise and motive in saying so?
- What significance do these issues have for people?
- Which other people, beyond the immediate field of investigation, are also affected and how?
- What other issues present a context in which the former issues can be understood?
- What concepts are you prepared to add to the mix, which your studies suggest are likely to be relevant to this situation? Here's one place for formal theories and their variables.
- What judgements are you prepared to make about the significance of all these issues, both as a result of your studies, and as a result of your growing familiarity with the situation? Here's another place for formal theories and variables.
- What evidence and rationale do you have for these judgements? Here's a place for empirical findings, as reported in the academic literature, and a place for empirical findings of your own.

In other words, you use the situation itself from which to build a theory which you can espouse, and which reflects the concerns of the people involved: though you have the opportunity for building in any academic ideas which appear to fit the situation. You don't import a pre-formed theory in most cases. The situation provides the theory, and the relevant issues – not variables – are used as the components whose relationship you will assess and explore.

There is no easily identifiable absolute 'reality' or 'truth', as the hypothetico-deductive method would require; instead, the first five questions explore the various perspectives that go to make up people's understanding of the situation, while the last three provide concepts and ideas to give an academic, but relevant, underpinning to the issues, and begin to address the matter of evidence and its validity: your own, and the academic community's, understanding of what is involved. You will find more on this approach, which is taken from a technique in educational research called 'illuminative evaluation', in Parlett (1981).

Crossing disciplinary boundaries

This is a search for coherence, and it offers you the same choice as before. Either refuse battle, by finding a neat and well-defined problem within the boundaries of one academic discipline (which is certainly possible at undergraduate level, and with the few professional projects which focus primarily on a technique); or accept the messiness, abandon any attempt at integrating academic disciplines into a single framework, and build a framework by consensus. The only way of integrating ideas across disciplines, and staying true to the situation you're researching, is to involve other people in a collaborative enterprise. The questions to pose are as follows:

- Who are the key people who admit to 'owning' the problem or issues covered by the topic of your project? Who else is actually involved, but doesn't feel involved or affected?
- Can these people, or anyone else in addition, help you to design the research: to identify the significant issues, and to shape the questions which you should ask? Do they have a role in interpreting the results?
- What are their points of view, what stories do they create about the issues in question (Mair, 1990; Read *et al.*, 1989), what is their interest in maintaining them, and their motives for doing so: who are the 'stakeholders'? How do you preserve the integrity of your own ideas, and the validity of all these points of view?
- As your project develops, how will they be affected by your understanding of the issues, your findings, and your recommendations?

We're making the assumption that knowledge does not come from the application of theory to practice, but rather that it can be achieved by the recognition of theories which already exist in the practitioner field. Some are explicit, in the form of personal theories that practitioners use for addressing their problems; some are implicit, in the form of the activities in which they engage. This distinction isn't as mysterious as it may appear. When you say to yourself, 'It's no use rushing to catch the bus, it's Monday, and on Mondays the buses always run late', you're stating an explicit personal theory based on your experience of bus frequencies, Monday morning feelings, and the propensity of bus drivers to wait for passengers. But you mightn't consciously put it into words. When you set your alarm and walk to the bus-stop for a particular bus, the time you set on the clock, and the speed at which you walk, express an implicit theory. Your actions **are** the theory. If your behavioural taught courses have dealt with the work of George Kelly, you'll recognize his approach in this statement. See Bannister and Fransella (1985).

If theories are embodied in practice, then it is essential for you to involve practitioners in shaping your project and designing the questions to ask, not merely in answering your questions. Research should be collaborative, rather than something which you bring in from outside. Clearly, the project you will submit has to be your own work, and you will be responsible for its shape and its outcomes. But 'your own work' consists of making the project come about by asking the questions listed above; it doesn't, surely, consist of bringing in a theory from outside, a pre-set framework which tells you in advance what is significant, and what variables you will be measuring. To quote Stewart and Stewart (1982: 6), 'Many managers are fed up with experts offering them ready-made solutions', and Hunt (1987: 109), 'Unless theories come from practice, they will not apply to practice'. The latter is a book worth looking at, especially if your topic involves anything to do with employee training and development, while the former relates to a particular technique designed to resolve some of these problems, outlined in section 13.1.

Handling non-technical problems

Again, your choice of topic will largely determine the approach to adopt. If your topic is narrowly technical, the problems of values, social consequence and policy may be minimal. Deploy the big battalions. On the other hand, you may have chosen your topic precisely because these problems exist, in which case guerrilla tactics are essential. This will become apparent in the methods you use to gather your data, and in the way in which you interpret and discuss these data.

- Are the meaning and significance of the issues you're studying determined largely by the situation? If so, the case study is a very good way of structuring your data-gathering and reporting the results (section 10.2). A linked series of cases, each exploring an issue and its situational determinants, can be very illuminating.
- Do the varying views of significant individuals give rise to the issues and problems you're dealing with? If so, key informant interviews will be useful (section 11.3).
- Does the complexity arise because of the divergent views of different interest groups and pressure groups? Conversational techniques (section 11.1) coupled with semi-structured interviews (section 11.1) and/or structured interviews (section 12.2) will be useful, in which you'll cross-tabulate results round the interests, conflicting views, and political or motivational stances of the groups, rather than round any 'variables' that might in theory be involved. This may involve going outside the department, or outside the organization, for some of the data.
- Do views change, or does the significance of results alter, as events happen over time? It may be worth structuring part of your empirical work in the form of a historical review and analysis (section 10.2): an account of change over time. This focuses on events, and on a presentation of the current state of the issues and pressures giving rise to those events, at different time-periods. It's well-suited, for example, to projects in which the evolution of strategy is more important than the application of strategy.

Details of these methods and techniques, both quantitative and qualitative, are given in Part Three. For the moment, you need to remember the implication of this approach for your discussion and interpretation of results. With this kind of topic, you're not looking for a 'right answer' which counts as an explanation to report to your sponsor and tutor. Instead, you're seeking to bring understanding by providing a description of a state of events and the situation which enfolds them: meaning arises from the situation. If the description is a good one, it will explain why certain things have happened, and might predict what is likely to happen. To the extent that the issues you have explored are general, and not limited to the department or company in which you're working, your interpretation will have the generality associated with effective theories. You might like to take a quick glance at Table 8.7 for some definitions that are relevant to this account. You might also want to make arrangements to obtain a copy of Miles and Huberman (1994); many of the techniques outlined therein will be very useful in your empirical work; but, for the moment, their account in Chapters 1 and 2, and a brief glance at pages 143–8 in particular, would be particularly relevant to the points I've just made.

Your discussion must therefore pay particular attention to two things: the evidence you supply in describing the events and situations; and the evidence you provide which demonstrates how typical and how generalizable your assertions may be.

The contingency of problems on the people who perceive them

Were you in agreement with your sponsor and tutor in advance on the nature of the problem you chose for your topic? Are all your informants likely to see your topic in the same terms? If so, well and good – bring out the big battalions. Alternatively, if you're working with a topic in which knowledge arises from explicit statements of values, biases, and political stances, or in which the significance of events must be recognized and the judgement of practitioners used to determine their significance, then it's back to guerrilla tactics. Your job is to make the values, biases and stances explicit in the first place, and, most importantly, to devise ways of validating the findings. Some useful questions to consider are as follows:

■ Are they right? However expert the judgement and extensive the experience of informants, there will be occasions when they're wrong. It helps to know about some of the biases to which expert decision-makers are vulnerable, and to guard against them by taking other informants' opinions. Some of the more common biases are shown in Table 6.1; an interesting account in less formal terms is provided by Gilovich (1991).

■ Are people agreed on what needs attending to, and on its significance? This may well be evidence of its validity. Alternatively, a stereotype may be operating (see Table 14.2), the truth of which should be independently established, by drawing on what you know from your programme of study, by asking questions of a wider group of people, or by arguing from first principles. (For example, by exploring the links between organizational objectives, as expressed in corporate policy and primary task statements, and the ways in which people's behaviour gives expression to the objectives. Do their beliefs and actions follow logically from the objectives?)

■ If beliefs and action are value-laden, what are the values, which people share them and which people don't? How are conflicts resolved in decision-taking, and what are the implications for action? What are your own values for the issue involved, and how can you resolve any disparities?

■ How important are intuitions and gut feelings for the decisions being taken, and on what grounds are they based? Do they reflect a consistent position from occasion to occasion; how far are they based on experience, and how far on personal whim?

■ Is it possible for you to cross-check any of the findings that depend particularly on values, beliefs and intuitions? There is a number of possible methods: by feeding them back to informants and taking their reaction; by repeating the cycle of data-gathering, interpretation, checking impressions with more data and feedback to informants several times over; by using different data-gathering methods with the same informants and looking for consistency; by checking the extent of agreement between what people appear to believe, what they say they believe, and what they actually do.

6.4 THE ART OF GUERRILLA WARFARE

As you can see, effective project work depends on making an appropriate match between your methods, and the issues which you're researching. Most of the time, the nature of the practitioner problems which you address will require guerrilla tactics. Less frequently, there may be room for manoeuvre by the big battalions too.

Primarily, though, the nature of the battleground as I've described it calls for you to bring material from your reading and your own empirical work to bear on the issues which you have identified, by means of a **critical analysis** which ensures that your understanding, the story you have created, convinces your readers: your tutor and your examiners. It's helpful to think of critical analysis as involving two components: conceptual analysis, and evidence and argument.

Conceptual analysis

This involves you making a relevant selection of appropriate theoretical, conceptual and/or empirical findings, which you review to express your understanding of the issues with which your project deals. Chapter 8 describes the mechanics involved. You might find yourself developing a model of your own, incorporating an explicit or implicit thesis (see section 5.4); you might, alternatively, be using an existing analytic framework which you feel fits the issues which you have identified.

under-graduate

As I've said under each heading in section 6.3, there will be situations in which the hypothetico-deductive method, with its notion of testing of a single hypothesis, or a small number of small hypotheses, may apply, and it's my impression that this is most likely to happen with some undergraduate projects. It's difficult to give examples, since the suitability of the method depends so much on the existence of a particular, singular and well-defined issue, usually a technical problem, in a particular organization. However, Figure 4.1 is the structure which pre-eminently applies to topics of this kind, so you might proceed by asking yourself

Table 6.1 Some common biases in managers' thinking

In their task of making sense of the information available to them in making decisions, it is assumed that managers make judgements; that is, they use their experience to
(a) draw on pre-existing mental frameworks or personal theories
(b) apply these in order to interpret the significance of the information
(c) develop a plan for action which makes use of the information
In doing so, they may be led astray by the information available to them, into choosing an inappropriate mental framework:

Input biases
Biases in what is attended to, triggered off by:
• Availability of information: how easily certain data can be obtained, regardless of their relevance to the situation involved: personal preferences or values are often responsible
• Salience of information: perceived relevance of data to the issue at hand, due to the vividness of the data, regardless of relevance
• Anchoring effects: misinterpretation of the meaning of data, due to the impact of previous data; insufficient search for further data
• Perseverance effects: adherence to initial view regardless of further data

Output biases
Biases in the kinds of responses which are preferred, triggered off by:
• Functional fixedness: pre-existing orientation towards a category of responses found to be helpful in achieving the manager's goals
• Social desirability: responses reflecting colleagues', or the organization's, preferred way of doing things; an insidious form of political correctness
• Reasoning by analogy: responses chosen due to apparent similarity of present situation to other situations

Operational biases
Biases due to inaccurate inferences in making decisions, triggered off by:
• Inappropriate sampling: use of data which don't represent the situation adequately
• Absence of information: missing out data that are essential to the type of decision being taken
• Attribution errors: confusion between personal and situational influences on behaviour
• Illusory correlation: seeing patterns and links in different kinds of data where no such association exists

There is some evidence that personality may predispose a manager to particular idiosyncratic biases: Haley and Stumpf (1989). The main reference is Tversky and Kahneman (1982).

whether your topic, as it shapes up, seems to fit this structure particularly well, checking with your tutor to see if s/he agrees. Is it, in other words, possible to find a single body of literature which you can narrow down to a single issue, which you can address with a single method?

in-company

In your case, the pre-existing analytic framework is likely to be a concept or approach commonly used in the literature. Such analytic frameworks as the value chain, strategic drivers, the Ansoff matrix, portfolio analysis, the Dunphy-Stace organizational change matrix (Dunphy and Stace, 1988) are just some of the many conceptual models available in projects on strategic management and change, for example. All would involve you in describing the model, exemplifying its uses in similar situations in the literature, and applying it to your own organization: in other words, in showing how the issues with which you are dealing fit the model, and justifying this assertion.

In each case, you would need to recognize the limitations of the conceptual framework (no model is perfect in itself, or in its application to a particular situation); you'd need to make an argument for any extra factors which you decided to take into account; and you would review alternative conceptual frameworks which other workers in the same field have used, justifying your own choice.

To give an example. A student of mine decided to use the Zeithaml approach to quality of service (Zeithaml, 1990) to describe and evaluate the relationship between what his organization (the local police constabulary) provided by way of service to two client groups: the general public, and a variety of groups internal to the criminal justice service. He justified this model for quality, rather than alternatives he reviewed, since Zeithaml's approach defines quality of service in itself in terms of the mismatch between client wants and provider capability, rather than in absolute terms; and he altered some of the provider–client relationships in the model to reflect the two different client groups involved, justifying the alterations by looking at what other authors had done in related circumstances and by means of a review of recent shifts in strategic orientation within his constabulary which he conducted collaboratively with some of his colleagues in provider and client departments.

In all cases, the end-point of a conceptual analysis is a working model, applied to your own organization and expressed in just such terms that the empirical questions which you will address in your own data-gathering are obvious to the reader: as obvious as the hypothesis-to-be-tested in the undergraduate situation described above. It is an argument, with justifications, which results in questions to be asked and, often, a single strong thesis to be justified.

MBA

With some MBA topics, it is possible to adopt an approach which provides you with a formal scheme for combining both New Paradigm and hypothetico-deductive approaches – for progressing from guerrilla skirmishes to conflict at army level, as it were. It's called 'Grounded Theory' and, technically, is neither a hypothetico-deductive method nor a New Paradigm method, but a process of analytic induction (Burgess, 1982a). The approach merits longer discussion than I want to give it here (it doesn't entirely resolve the criticisms I've levelled at the hypothetico-deductive method, for example, as Burgess (1982a: 211) points out); but you may find it useful if you have the time for it, so the following thumbnail sketch may be helpful.

Grounded Theory works by collecting data, generalizing findings into statements about the possible relationships involved, and checking out these statements by further data-collection to a point at which you can categorize types of result. (This part of the procedure should be very familiar: as Filley (1989) suggests, many business planning situations involve just such a process of collective judgement, though he emphasizes the interpersonal basis on which this happens.) Further data are collected to check the plausibility of these categories, to enable you to posit variables which may be involved, and the relationships between them. At this point, your conceptual analysis results in a small theory, which you proceed to extend with further data-collection, until you have the beginnings of an explanation for what's going on in the situation which you've been investigating. As you can see, the theory is said to emerge by induction from the realities of the situation, rather than being 'brought in from outside' in the way, illustrated in Figure 6.1, which is claimed for hypothetico-deductive approaches. Glaser (1978) and Glaser and Strauss (1967) are the main texts to look at. There are some brief comments on this approach as applied to the development of a scheme for structured observation in section 13.3.

Evidence and argument

This is the part of your project which is most your own, in which you report on the secondary data which you have collected, develop your story with data which provide convincing support for your point of view and compels acceptance by your reader: the actual battle, as it were, rather than the plan of campaign. Parts Three and Four provides you with the weapons to use; for the moment, it is sufficient to summarize the procedure involved.

all

Your argument will include a methodological discussion justifying the approach you took to the data you gathered; it will also present the data themselves, analysed and digested, presented in an informative way to illuminate the conceptual analysis, to give evidence concerning any thesis or theses which you are seeking to establish, to justify your assertions, and to move your whole argument forward. It will involve you in discussing the significance of the findings you have obtained, both for your organization and for the wider realm of organizations in general, or at least, those organizations which find themselves dealing with similar issues to your own; it will also lead to recommendations for action.

in-company

The most compelling argument of all is made if you have the opportunity to implement and evaluate your recommendations as part of your project work. While this is rarely possible, since most people in your position do not have sufficient time to take action and follow the results through in order to evaluate them prior to graduation, partial implementation of interim recommendations is sometimes possible within a one-year final year project framework. The name for this approach is 'action research'. If you want a good practical example (albeit in a project with greater scope than any which you are likely to have time for!), try Brown and Kaplan (1981).

6.5 PROJECT WORK AS INTELLIGENCE WORK

all

In all of this, whatever you do and however you conduct your campaign, your primary concern should be to answer the three questions: 'What's happening?', 'How can I prove it?' and 'How do I know?' You have to convince your readers that what you're saying is believable, and, while the New Paradigm methods are plausible because they beg fewer questions than the hypothetico-deductive approach, you're not absolved from the burden of proof when you're using them. Cold steel, remember?

Two authors are particularly helpful, if you want to know more about this issue of proof. Reason and Rowan (1981b) provide further examples of methods for ensuring validity, and could be read by anyone, at any level from undergraduate to Masters. Heron (1981) provides some more detailed conceptual underpinnings for the New Paradigm approach, being very appropriate background reading if you're working at Masters level.

Confidentiality

Regardless of your approach, you will of course need to be careful about the confidentiality of information which you receive from your respondents. Confidentiality has a peculiar importance in the New Paradigm approach, however, since you no longer believe you're gathering 'objective', hence neutral, evidence on the 'reality out there'. You have come to terms with the messiness of phenomena and events, and are aware that you're dealing with a fallible world in which truth is discovered, or, if you will, created, by fallible human beings, yourself and the people you're studying included. You deal in information which is value-laden, personal, judgemental, and frequently, politically sensitive.

As with any approach, you'll need to obtain permission to quote; conceal the provenance of particular viewpoints when you're particularly requested to do so (see the Confidentiality heading in section 12.1); keep data in a secure place; and, (where projects involve commercially sensitive data), make special arrangements for restricting the circulation of your project report. Your tutor is your guide here.

However, you are likely to find that these usual arrangements are insufficient. In involving your informants in the design of your investigation, in asking them to share their intuitions and judgements, and in involving them in helping you evaluate the validity of statements other people have made, you're already encountering situations in which confidentiality is an issue, well before the need to preserve confidentiality in writing your project report presents itself. You'll find that you make very little progress at all unless you confront the issue early, and the way to do this is by negotiation. It is your special responsibility to draw this issue to the attention of your informants, and, in creating a situation in which they will take a part in your project in the various ways I defined in section 6.3, create a 'safe space' in which you can fruitfully work together.

Some of this will involve you in jointly agreeing an acceptable procedure; other aspects are dealt with in Chapter 7, where the issue becomes one of the role which you're expressing in doing your project. But, notice, the word I used is 'negotiate': you must develop a method of working which assures your informants, while avoiding a situation in which they 'censor' your work. At times, this will involve you in an 'agreement to differ' on what the important issues are, and you'll need particular care in deciding what to report.

Truth or understanding?

Actually, the same problem faces people who work with the hypothetico-deductive method, though my impression is that it often remains latent and unrecognized. On the one hand, informants respond to research questions by playing the role of 'subject in a scientific investigation', being prepared to share confidences which they wouldn't share in a casual conversation. On the other hand, I'm sure that there are many things they don't mention, or which they sanitize by evasion or trivialization, when they feel that questions are getting too personal. Yet the hypothetico-deductive method is relatively insensitive to the problem.

This is partly because it rests on the positivist assumption (see section 6.1) that there is a 'truth out there' which we can discover if only we try hard enough; at some level, the inconveniences of human fallibility, evasion and motivation are ignored. Our own epistemology takes fallibility as a fundamental, and, rather than searching for 'truth', seeks **understanding**: the development of an account or story of real events out there, which makes sense to the wider community of collaborators and scholars, whose assumptions are made explicit and whose viability is established through action – when it seems to all of us to work in predicting the consequences of action.

The arguments which I outlined in section 6.3, in other words, don't apply simply to qualitative problems in management research or social research: they reflect an epistemology for **all** management and social science research, with no special status being granted to the quantitative approach (Henwood and Pidgeon, 1992). As Gill and Johnson (1991) point out, this is a radical view (especially to people trained in physics, science or engineering, prior to their study of management!), and I can only refer you to authors who reflect what is currently known as the postmodern paradigm of research. Perhaps the most accessible are Miles and Huberman (1994) – see their Chapter 1 for a useful summary, and Cassell and Symon (1994); Reason and Rowan (1981a) makes a good reader covering many related issues. You might also find the forum on theory building in the October 1989 issue of the *Academy of Management Review* (vol. 14, no. 4) useful in this respect, and the special issue of *Management Education and Development* (1990, vol. 21, part 3) devoted to postmodern approaches to management; Clegg (1992) has a good discussion of the pros and cons of the postmodernist view for management work in general.

If you want an account of why the postmodern approach matters, and if you can cope with pessimistic conclusions, read Boje (1994).

In conclusion, let me offer you a new term. For all the reasons outlined in section 6.3, it would seem sensible to avoid the word 'research' as a description of what you're doing, because of its connotations with a very specialized and, some would say, specious, approach. The point is, it's an approach which is rarely going to be applicable. 'Scholarship' is not a bad substitute, or, if you find it more comfortable, simply 'project work'. That's the sense in which I've used the word 'project' in the early chapters (you'll note that, except for the title page of the book, 'research' rarely appears), and that's the spirit in which Figure 6.1(c) stands as a model for what we're about.

The role you're in | 7

As you can see from the preceding chapter, project work is based on assumptions which differ substantially from those which underlie scientific research. Unfortunately, there is a tendency for many informal discussions between tutors and students, and most formal accounts in the textbooks to which you will be referred, to adhere to the hypothetico-deductive model, if only implicitly. This is particularly true of the role ascribed to you. This results in a vagueness about how you are to be seen: are you an academic taking concepts and techniques into the field of practice (see Figure 6.1); a scientist about to investigate a hypothesis which seems to apply to the practitioner field; a practitioner/employee puzzling out the relevance of academic ideas to his or her own situation; or simply someone doing their best in an underspecified role?

The purpose of this chapter is to examine this issue of role. (A role, for the record, is a set of expectations of the behaviour which is felt to be appropriate for a person in any social position.) It's an important matter, because how you are seen will make a difference to how you are treated; furthermore, how you see yourself will make a difference to how you treat other people. And in an enterprise which is so dependent on social interaction (see section 6.3!), you have to be crystal clear on your role if you're to be successful.

All investigative work involves four main stages: gaining entry to the field, defining your role, doing work under some form of supervision, and leaving the field of work. These stages form the main sections of this chapter.

7.1 GAINING ENTRY

This phrase actually has two meanings. Taken literally, it concerns the ways in which your arrival in the project organization comes about, whether this is arranged for you, or contrived by yourself. The meta-phorical meaning is probably more important, and relates to the ways in which you establish yourself, and gain access to data, through the development of appropriate relationships with people who can help you. The latter is a matter of role, and is dealt with in section 7.2.

Arranging a placement with a local company

In most projects, the placement with a company will either be automatic, because you're there already, or it will be arranged for you. Occasionally, however, this doesn't happen, or you may choose to make an arrangement for yourself despite the existence of an arranged scheme: see Table 7.1. Your efforts in the latter case will be appreciated by your course tutors, provided – and this is an important proviso – that you go about it the right way. The main steps and issues in arranging a project placement for yourself are as follows.

Table 7.1 Gaining entry into an organization

- **Be opportunistic**
  Base your approach on doing what's possible, feasible, and relevant to the organization, rather than something excessively wedded to the 'scientific method'.

- **Allow plenty of time**
  Arranging a project usually takes longer than you expected.

- **Use existing contacts**
  Be shameless in the use of friends, relatives, or previous acquaintances to assist you in gaining entry.

- **Use non-threatening language**
  Plan your approach carefully: words like 'research', 'investigation', 'publishing results' may carry unacceptable connotations, in contrast to words like 'learning from your experience', 'discussion', and 'writing it up'.

- **Be positive about practicalities**
  Worries about the time demands of employee involvement can be countered by showing your flexibility; worries about confidentiality, by discussing a general approach in advance, and specific mechanisms after entry.

- **Offer a report of the outcomes**
  This would be specially written in a form most useful to the organization; a good project report, especially when written in 'management report' style (see section 4.4, Structure), is good, while a synopsis of a quarter the length is better.

After Buchanan *et al.* (1988)

■ Discuss the placement you have in mind with your course tutor or project tutor, take heed of his or her suggestions regarding which organizations are approachable, and remain in contact while you're making the arrangements. Don't ever proceed independently: your attempts at entry may clash with other people's, and organizations dislike dealing with several people from a single academic institution who appear to be unaware of each other's existence. Identify the groundrules regarding salary, if any, with your tutor.

■ Telephone the organization in the first instance, to establish the appropriate person to approach. If your entry is by personal acquaintance, establish with that person whether you shouldn't also be dealing with someone else.

■ Your next step is to write, even if you have a good contact and a firm verbal promise. Your course tutor or project tutor should be able to provide you with a pro-forma, or a letter of their own which explains the programme and backs up your approach, and may supply you with background brochures and the like. Allow plenty of lead-time. Provided you word your letter appropriately, there's no harm in approaching several organizations at once, to maximize your chances of a favourable reply.

■ Attend whatever interviews may be involved, following the usual procedures for preparation and self-presentation. One of your purposes will be to discuss the topic (ideally, involving the organization in the initial stages of choice and definition of the topic), to clarify how it can best be useful and relevant to them, and to identify the balance of project-related and other work which you will be doing for them. The organization may wish to state the terms of reference to which you will be working: completion dates, objectives and scope of the work you do for them, and so on. This may also be an opportunity to establish/confirm if and how much the organization will be paying you.

■ Don't make any further moves until you have a response in writing. I once had a full-time student who spent all of his grant on an air-ticket to Kenya, on the firm assurances of his girlfriend who had just been appointed to something quite senior in an accountant's office in Nairobi. Alas, when it finally arrived, the formal letter expressed regrets rather than a confirmation of the informal arrangements, and the student lost most of the money he'd spent on the fare.

■ Confirm your acceptance of the offer in writing, confirm the arrangements for starting, and report the details to your course tutor. If you received offers from more than one organization, make sure the tutor knows: he or she will be delighted, as this increases the pool of employers for future projects. And make sure you reply personally to the organization whose offer you turn down, regardless of the action your tutor takes.

■ On arrival, establish who is going to be your line manager (direct boss) and who is going to be your sponsor, if more than one person is involved.

How do you establish a pool of potential organizations to approach? I'd be surprised if you were entirely on your own, but if this is the case, try the Chamber of Commerce and ask for their list of local companies. Failing that, the County Council's Economic Development Unit should be able to provide you with details of local employer networks or perhaps a directory of local companies which they publish themselves. Your local TEC will publish booklets listing training opportunities for unemployed people; while you would be ineligible for the schemes in question, you could still build up a list of local companies whom you could approach with your own query.

It's probably best to ring the switchboard of any company in which you're interested, ask for the name of their training manager, and write to him or her by name, rather than sending a letter addressed impersonally.

You might find it useful to adopt some of the rules of thumb used by your tutors, and other qualified academic researchers, when they seek entry into an organization with their own research questions in mind. Table 7.1 presents some guidelines. I've dealt with many of these in detail already; so, for example, if you follow the suggestions of Chapter 6, your work should be feasible and relevant, and if you plan to write your project in the style I've suggested in section 4.4, it'll be easy to derive a synopsis to offer your putative employer. The table is based on Buchanan *et al.* (1988), a reference which is well worth reading in full. Another reference from the same book, Beynon (1988), is a sobering account of the defensiveness of, and pressures on, employers when they're approached with requests for project involvement, together with the ways (only some of which apply to yourself!) for coping with the ensuing situation.

In passing, I can't resist the comment that Buchanan's view of the research process being much 'messier' than formal accounts of completed research bears out much of what I was saying in Chapter 6: though I don't know whether he'd find the postmodern epistemology as convincing as I do.

Arranging a placement with an overseas company

It is highly unlikely that you would have to make your own arrangements: where they exist, projects based overseas are almost exclusively an integral part of a taught course and formal arrangements will be made for you.

However, if you aren't on that kind of programme, and your institution gives you the freedom to try and make your own arrangements overseas, your first step, as before, would be to obtain addresses.

Your academic library should have a copy of *Kompass Europe*, which lists companies by country; alternatively, try the commercial section of your public library. The latter should also stock *Chambers of Commerce Worldwide*, which lists chambers of commerce by country. The commercial section of the information service of the embassy for the country in question is another source. Finally, if you're interested in central and eastern Europe, and your institution is involved in one of the TEMPUS-Phare or British Council-sponsored programmes in this part of the world, you might care to explore the possibilities with the lecturer in charge. His or her budget will probably be too tight to take on an extra student, but he or she may be able to provide you with company details or other contacts in the country in question. You would then develop your contacts with the overseas company following the steps that apply to local companies, given above.

7.2 DEFINING YOUR ROLE, AT HOME AND ABROAD

Regardless of its location and basis, your project will demand that you define your role. There are six reasons for doing so:

- to build trust, and a series of working relationships;
- to gain access to informants and information;
- to help define each other's stance on what is important and significant;
- to gain support in approaching other people;
- possibly, to gain support for implementation proposals;
- to gain permission to report the findings externally.

In some cases, as Table 7.2 suggests, you will step into a predefined role; in others, you find yourself having to develop your role from scratch, overcoming, at times, some strange preconceptions on the part of your sponsor in doing so. It helps if you see yourself as engaged in a negotiation in the development of a contract. That is, you can't pre-empt the other person, or insist on your own point of view regardless of the other person's views; at the same time, you have a job to do which involves rules and constraints, which the other person must be persuaded to respect. You have to be prepared to meet half-way or thereabouts; and you may have to examine your own preconceptions about the organizational setting, being prepared to alter some and defend others, through a two-way process in which both you and your sponsor are engaged.

Table 7.2 Project entry arrangements

Type of project	Example	The main issues facing you
Integrated	Teaching Company Scheme Competency-based In-company taught	Interpreting your role within guidelines already laid down; handling the development of a relationship with a sponsor who may also be your line manager; often, working with a series of linked assignments rather than a single project, hence, a series of people.
Part-time	Diploma, MBA, professional programmes in which the project is done for your employer, but academic input is by and in the teaching institution	Developing your role, usually within expectations on the part of the teaching institution, but with under-specified expectations on the part of your employer; occasionally, employer expectations have been set, for good or ill, by previous projects done in the company; finding a mentor anywhere that's appropriate.
Full-time, entry arranged (also some distance-learning programmes)	Any programme in which a course or project tutor works from a list of previously participating companies, to which he or she keeps adding new companies	Developing your role in a situation where support and goodwill exist in principle, but where the previous projects done will have a strong bearing on how you're received; making your line manager into a sponsor; improving links with the in-company contact person for the scheme; building new project opportunities for the future.
Part-time, entry not arranged	Some distance-learning programmes; some Diploma-level programmes	Arranging a project in the first place; mustering teaching institution support
Any group-based project	Some Diploma programmes; some integrated programmes	Add to the relevant items above, the development of group working relationships, and careful reporting/liaison arrangements with tutor and sponsor.

Table 7.3 The project student's role: stances and responses

Project type	Your role as you intend to be perceived	The response it engenders
Undergraduate, full-time	A subject-matter expert	Someone with many corners to be knocked off
	A supplicant who needs help	A nuisance
	An enquiring mind	A bit exhausting, but bright-eyed and bushy-tailed
	An informed assistant	Someone potentially useful
	An intelligent apprentice	Good: give him/her something useful to do, help as much as there's time for
Diploma, MBA, in-company	An academic employee	A curiosity, possibly resented
	Someone who's learning all the answers	A bit of an irrelevance, or even a threat
	An employee who's making him/ herself more marketable	A potential competitor or deserter
	An employee improving him/herself for the good of the firm	A useful source of ideas and techniques; we admire the energy involved
Professional	A technical expert	Boss: Fine if I can use the expertise, otherwise I'm a bit indifferent Colleague already in profession: Join the club Colleague not in profession: I feel a bit guilty
	A person working hard at joining the profession	Deserving of sympathy, respect and help
All	A scientist engaged in research	A wild-eyed idealist
	A person who knows more than they	A pointy-headed intellectual
	Someone doing a project for mutual benefit	A realist, to be assisted and helped to the extent that mutual self-interests are served

Arranging time for your project

One of the earliest things which you'll have to establish with your sponsor is the nature and amount of other work, unrelated to your project, which you are expected to do for your host organization. If your project is 'integrated', as I've described it in Table 7.2, the expectation will be that you do little else; although there may be occasions, when there's a 'panic' on in your department, that you help out to the extent that you're qualified to do so.

under-graduate

You will almost certainly be placed as a full-time employee for the duration of your project, and will be given other work to do. Hopefully, the work will be in the broad area or field of your topic, at a level suited to your abilities and skills, and you find that you learn a lot from your general work that is useful to your project. If that isn't the case, two things are important. Firstly, you must keep track of how much time you've been able to devote to your project (your project diary is a useful *aide-mémoire*), ensuring you talk to your sponsor, and/or your line manager, if you feel that it isn't sufficient. You might want to check with your tutor as part of this process.

Secondly, and assuming that you've done the first , why not accept the apparent irrelevancy as potentially useful in the long run? If you feel that the level of work is somewhat trivial (and this seems more common than work which is too difficult: Saxton and Ashworth (1990)), all the more energy available for your project! In any case, anyone aiming at some form of management career can learn a lot which is personally useful even if it contributes little to the project. One of my undergraduates interested in computer-assisted learning and training was very despondent with the work he was asked to do (sandblasting and degreasing bridge bearings on the shopfloor of a heavy manufacturing company); in the end, he managed to negotiate one day off in five in which he could progress his project. Five years later, as a training officer, he remarked on the insights the experience had given him into informal norms, unofficial leadership, and the power of shopfloor culture, which his academic courses in behavioural studies could only handle in conceptual terms, and which, given his current position in the management structure, he could no longer be party to.

in-company

If you're already an employee, it's particularly important to sort this issue out quickly. The temptation to do little else but 'think about' the project, for weeks that turn into months, will be severe, given the day-to-day work which creates pressures on your time. Much will depend on the amount of support which exists for your involvement in the programme in the first place. At one extreme, you may be forced into doing all your project work at home, at weekends; at the other, you may be lucky, and find yourself with a project topic which is an integral part of your normal work. All you have to do in this case is to negotiate additional time off for any data-gathering and analysis which need to occur outside company premises.

Managing perceptions

At home. Whatever your level of study, the process of negotiation doesn't end when you come to an agreement on time. Your role depends on perceptions and impressions formed throughout the period in which you're doing project work, and, while first impressions are important, so are enduring perceptions of yourself in the job. This is important if you're an undergraduate, since it will affect the degree of cooperation you get for the project; it's even more important if you're in-company based, since you're unlikely to be walking away from the firm when your project is complete.

all

It helps to anticipate some of the roles which are open to you, and some of the expectations and responses which these might engender. Table 7.3 presents a number of possible combinations: some of these are viable and would be likely to lead to fruitful cooperation; others will result in a dissipation of energies and, if persevered in, can be terminal to the success of your project. Admittedly, parts of the table are a little burlesqued, and I'm not quoting a reference to an empirical study; but I have encountered all these combinations as a project tutor, and would suggest that there are some obvious kamikaze roles which it's wise to avoid.

The roles of 'informed assistant' and 'intelligent apprentice' would seem to fit best if you're an undergraduate; coming across as a 'self-and-company-improver', handled with due modesty, should work if you're in-company based; and 'professional aspirant' ought to increase your support if you're in a professionalized department and are following a professional programme. In all cases, the notion of negotiated contract is helpful. Once agreed, a contract is a bargain from which both parties expect to gain: so, the better your contract, the more people will help you because in doing so, they also help themselves. This is the role of 'someone doing a project for mutual benefit'.

While on the subject of burlesques, if you want some light relief from your project work, try Lodge (1988). It's a novel which illustrates how not to go about building in-company relationships. The descriptions of attitudes in the manufacturing environment, at both shopfloor and management level, are a little stereotyped and, at times, awkwardly expressed, but quite informative if you've never been in a metal-bashing industrial environment before.

Overseas. Much of what you take for granted about working relationships will be different when you're abroad; of course, you know this, since the resulting personal development challenges are probably part of your reason for seeking an overseas placement. This is an argument for greater sensitivity and more tentative exploration of the role expected of you. If you have management experience as a member of a part-time DMS or MBA programme, you might be regarded as a foreign 'expert' in some cultures; if an undergraduate, you are likely to be construed according to the norms which apply to students, rather than employees, in the country in question.

Norms vary dramatically, and you should take advice on how to prepare yourself for the culture before you leave. The student role in much of central and eastern Europe is that of 'consumer of the academic expert's wisdom' (Jankowicz, 1994), and the role of in-company management trainee involves somewhat more passive exposure to an authoritative trainer or supervisory style (Holden and Cooper, 1994; Millman, 1993; Woodall, 1992; Jankowicz, 1993) than is the case in the UK. Your own reading of such texts as Hofstede (1991), Smith *et al.* (1989) and Tayeb (1988) will prepare you in general terms for the interactions involved in being supervised by an overseas manager in his or her own culture. However, if you haven't already encountered them as part of your lectures in the behavioural subjects and are preparing from scratch, you would probably be better served by the Butterworth-Heinemann *Cultural Guides* series, choosing the book which covers your country of interest, and perhaps reading Randlesome *et al.* (1993) for an overview of western Europe, or Moran and Johnson (1992) which covers more western European countries but also deals with central and eastern Europe. In conclusion, and at the risk of being tiresome, I must add that Boisot (1994) is particularly good on issues in the post-command economies and will give you useful information on China, should your journey be in that direction.

The basis of your expertise

Even your most expert activity depends on negotiation. Your project may involve you in gathering data using techniques which nobody else in your organization understands. But, to the extent that the outcomes of your project will inform the decisions which people in the organization make, this expertise should be shared through negotiation. People who take decisions operate in idiosyncratic personal worlds for much of the time (Eden *et al.*, 1979; Isenberg, 1984); intuition and judgement are very personal things, as you'll remember from section 6.2. To be useful, your use of expertise will be most effective if you've negotiated the questions and approach with the people involved.

You may find a succinct statement of Eden's ideas helpful in this respect. He talks about three possible roles: those of Expert, Empathizer and Negotiator (Eden and Sims, 1979). The **Expert** has coercive power, a power that comes from the techniques he or she deploys:

> If the peddler of science and reason suggests a formulation for a problem and a solution to it, the client who ignores such advice and help may be seen by himself and his colleagues as a backwoodsman, kicking in the face of rationality.
>
> Eden and Sims (1979: 123)

The **Empathizer** operates by offering his or her services as a sympathetic problem-solver to the individual who's closest to the project (your sponsor, in most cases). The **Negotiator** focuses on the perceptions of the issues and problems being investigated in the project, and handles the task of problem definition and resolution cooperatively (since, as I've said above, the definition is often part of the problem being researched in your project). In their account, which deals with the roles available to operational research consultants, Eden and Sims argue in favour of the role of Negotiator, and I'm inclined to agree.

As someone rather different, not a consultant but a person who's working on a project, the role of 'technical expert' isn't available to you, (unless you're in certain foreign companies, and even then excessive reliance would be undesirable). Remember the definition of role? It's partly a matter of how others see you; whether you're an undergraduate or an in-company colleague, the people you work with won't see you in the way they view an outside consultant, as a person with substantial power and expertise.

You could conceivably be seen as an Empathizer, but there are dangers. To empathize is to share in the concerns of the last person who's spoken to you, and to get tangled up in potential conflicts of loyalty. Though personal involvement is an integral part of the research process (the argument expressed in section 6.2), excessive empathy would remove whatever basis you have for ensuring the validity of your findings, which (you'll recall from section 6.3) requires you to work with many views, without subscribing blindly to one.

You're left with the role of Negotiator as a basis for your expertise. What is involved? Briefly, the definition and redefinition of issues and problems with the people involved in, and affected by, the issues which your project explores; in more detail, the adherence to the mode of operation I outlined in section 6.3, which I wrote with this role especially in mind. Moreover, this is exactly the role to adopt if you're in a placement overseas.

In the role of Negotiatior, your work becomes explicit, because others have shared in its planning; many of your assumptions are shared by other people; and your goals have been discussed and argued over in detail. The kind of debate on the legitimacy of secrecy and concealment of objectives which characterizes accounts of sociological and anthropological field projects (Burgess, 1982b) shouldn't be required in management project work. In discussing overt participant observation methods, Burgess provides you with two additional role descriptions which you might care to try on for size when you're gathering your data: if you're a part-time student based in the organization, you might consider the implications of considering yourself as a 'participant-as-observer'; whereas, if you're an undergraduate, what about the 'observer-as-participant'?

Burgess also has some interesting findings to report on the matter of sex-roles, specifically, on the degree of cooperation which male and female researchers get from the people with whom they're working. Males who hold a conventional stereotype of females are still likely to see the female researcher as somewhat vulnerable and requiring particular help and assistance (Golde, 1970), a matter which you may feel is relevant if you're a female, in certain types of organization. The management role itself is currently defined largely according to a masculine stereotype, possibly because males make up the majority of managers (Hunt , 1975). While the stereotype may be changing (Rothwell, 1985), it is sufficiently marked for it to affect the way in which people will relate to you. Several of the articles in the compilation of which Rothwell forms a part, would be well worth your attention, Marshall (1985) and Chambers (1985) in particular. There is also a good article on role problems for female researchers by Easterday *et al.* (1982).

7.3 WORKING UNDER SUPERVISION

All investigative work is done under some form of supervision. Academics working with grant aid will have a person in the funding agency to report to periodically, while those without grants will occasionally be asked how things are going by their heads of department. So the fact that you have to report to someone else isn't unusual. What is different about project work is that the people you report to will have an involvement in your assessment – your tutor, almost invariably, and your sponsor, frequently. The obvious implication is that the relationship you have with them is important, and needs to be maintained.

You need to talk with them sufficiently to know what they'll be looking for in the assessment of your completed work. The details were dealt with in Chapter 4. Similarly, the role of your tutor in helping you to choose a topic was dealt with in Chapter 3. However, to leave it at that would be to ignore a very important part of the role relationship: the potential for assistance during the project, and the potential for improving your work, which regular contact provides.

Your tutor

With one exception, the worst project I've seen was one in which the student never met me, and ignored all attempts to make contact. Somewhat more satisfactory, but still leading to very weak work, were the projects in which the student met me once, at the start, and never appeared again. Thinking back on where the weaknesses arose, it would seem particularly necessary to make contact with your tutor at least at the following times:

1. When you first start and are considering possible topics; indeed, you'll introduce yourself to several potential tutors at this stage. At this point, you're looking for general guidance, judging the kind of relationship you are likely to have, and estimating the interest each tutor has for your topic ideas. You should expect some initial suggestions on the reading which would help you confirm the topic. Think of yourself as choosing the tutor, as much as of the tutor advising you, and consider changing topic or tutor diplomatically if you don't like what you see.
2. When you're confirming your choice of topic, the terms of reference which your sponsor has offered you, and the approach you're to adopt. Some help with the structuring of your project, advice on the terms of reference, and an initial, fairly focused reading list are the things to expect.
3. When you've done some substantial reading and are looking for feedback on your early ideas. You might wish to combine this with advice on your theme, discussion of the issues you're going to investigate, and guidance on the project methods and analysis techniques which you're planning to use. If you've begun writing at this stage, you might like to send it all, or a sample, to the tutor in advance of your meeting. You might be referred to more specialist texts at this stage. This is also probably the latest time for discussion of the form which your project document should take.
4. When you have the results of your pilot study, or the findings on the first issues you investigated, and are looking for a friendly and informed brain with which to mull over the results, and fine-tune the main empirical stage. Have something on each of these in writing, and send it in advance if you can. This might be a useful time to offer any further material which you've written, for the tutor's comments.
5. When the main data on most of the main issues are in and analysed, and you have some conclusions to discuss. This may be an opportunity

to discuss the need for further investigation or implementation and evaluation, reading, or writing, in the case of projects structured more on a Masters, rather than on an undergraduate basis.

6. When the bulk of your project document is ready, and you're looking for the results of an informal assessment of what you're about to complete.

7. After completion, around the time of your assessment, and certainly just before your oral assessment, if there is one.

If you have been showing your tutor your written work as you produce it, there may be no need for Stage 6. Indeed, some tutors would be unwilling to read a draft in this way, but if you can get their help, it could make a difference to the assessment you finally receive – provided you act on the tutor's advice.

Seven contact occasions works out at one every month or six weeks in a long project, and one every week in a short, professional project. In the latter case, you'll find yourself talking on the phone rather than meeting face to face, and certainly doing what commonly happens in either case: combining stages 1 and 2, 3 and 4, and 6 and 7. I suspect that some tutors may see the full number of meetings as excessive spoonfeeding, and curse me for raising your expectations. Certainly, if every student they're supervising followed this schedule, some tutors (shall we say, **all** in the ex-polytechnics?) would find life impossible. However, it's your project, and you're entitled to the tutor's advice. They should respond to your enthusiasm.

Quite apart from the times described in these stages, your tutor can be helpful on an unscheduled basis. Tutors are particularly useful in backing you up when you need to approach informants outside your organization, and in helping you negotiate for special equipment, expenses and the like; but in these cases, make sure that you've discussed the issue with your sponsor first.

> **under-graduate**

It's common in your case for the tutor to be involved in a visit to the organization in which you've been placed for your project. Follow whatever guidelines your programme provides, while seizing on the visit as a major opportunity to deal with one or more of the stages I've outlined above. A lot will depend on the timing of the visit, which is likely to be beyond your control, as your tutor may have a number of students to get round. Occasionally, a single placement tutor does all the visits to all the students following a particular programme, and you may not meet with your own project tutor. Nevertheless, you'll find that the placement tutor is interested and helpful, and at the very least he or she will be willing to act as a messenger on your behalf. You'll find this is a particularly essential service if your placement is overseas.

Table 7.4 Roles and relationships between student, tutor, and sponsor

---

In the tutor–student relationship:*

Tutors expect their students to:
1. Be more independent than the students expect.
2. Produce regular written work, ideally, typewritten.
3. Seek help from other people as well as the tutor (e.g., the sponsor or mentor!).
4. Attend meetings regularly, organized at their own initiative without needing to be chased.
5. Report their progress honestly.
6. Follow the advice they're given.
7. Be enthusiastic about their projects.
8. Surprise them: come up with findings, ideas etc. that hadn't occurred to them.
9. Be part of a mutually enjoyable relationship.

Students expect their tutors to:
1. Actively supervise them.
2. Read and understand written project extracts submitted by them.
3. Be available when they're needed.
4. Be friendly, open and supportive.
5. Be constructively critical.
6. Have a good knowledge of the topic of the project.
7. Make arrangements so they can give their full attention to the student during tutorials.
8. Add to the information available to them by recommending appropriate reading.
9. Exert their influence on the student's behalf.

In the sponsor–student relationship:†

Your sponsor may adopt one or more of the following roles towards you:
1. Negotiator
2. Mother
3. Pressurizer and reminder
4. Colleague and equal
5. Protector
6. Confidence builder
7. *Laissez-faire* neglector, leaving you to just 'get on with it'

---

*Phillips and Pugh (1987)
†Saxton and Ashworth (1990)

all

You may be interested in some research findings on the relationship between Ph.D. tutors and students, reported by Phillips and Pugh (1987). Many of the items apply to business and management projects at our own level of concern, though perhaps some of them (e.g. item 8 in the first list and 9 in the second) probably don't; all are reported in Table 7.4. The discussion by Phillips and Pugh reinforces the importance of good role relationships.

Your sponsor

This relationship is often neglected. It shouldn't be, since the sponsor plays an important part in your project, quite apart from any role he or she might have in assessment (though the latter is usually rare).

In principle, your sponsor should have a well-defined and formal relationship with you, having agreed to act in the sponsoring role. In practice, this relationship may not be so straightforward. Sometimes, the agreement has been made directly between the two of you, in the case of in-company-based projects, or between the sponsor and your institution, in the case of undergraduates, and many issues will have been ironed out in advance. In other cases, the arrangement has been made by someone else in the organization, and your sponsor becomes involved on the day you arrive in the department. It's wise to establish which, in advance of your arrival.

The sponsor's primary and overriding concern will be to manage your presence, your work, and its outcomes, as a contribution to the work of his or her department. Any concern with your training and development is, in this case, secondary from the sponsor's point of view, and you should expect any early negotiations which establish your role, and the entire period during which you'll be under supervision, to be conducted on this basis. Having said that, the help which sponsors give is rarely negligible, and often contributes substantially to the success of your work, as mentor and friend.

under-
graduate

It helps if you remember that your sponsor has other management responsibilities as well as looking after yourself, so you should determine what kind of assistance and involvement your sponsor is prepared to provide, as early as possible. Quite apart from the informal contacts which you may have on a day-to-day basis, it will be useful for you to arrange a regular progress meeting with him/her, every week or fortnight. You'll find that this is best negotiated a week or so after your arrival, rather than immediately. Give yourselves time to get used to each other.

Sponsors differ in the styles they adopt towards their placement students; Saxton and Ashworth (1990) suggest that different sponsors adopt different roles, and the really good ones vary the role according to your needs. The roles they encountered in their research on this topic are shown in Table 7.4. Clearly, someone who adopts the Negotiating style is, as my comments in previous sections suggest, most likely to respond to the particular needs arising from your project work, and to your own adoption of the negotiating style which I advocate.

As a general resource, your sponsor can be very helpful in:

■ providing information about the organization;
■ arranging access to other people, and advising who is likely to be helpful;
■ advising you on how best to approach them;
■ acting as a sounding-board for your ideas;
■ informing you of the ways in which the concepts, procedures and techniques which you've learnt in your programme translate into practice;
■ advising on the realism of your developing project ideas;
■ informally evaluating your results and conclusions;
■ advising on the feasibility of implementation of any of your recommendations – the sponsor of an overseas project should, if approached appropriately, be a particularly helpful source of information about local customs and mores.

all

The sponsor's role of sounding-board, evaluator, and 'reality-monitor' is especially helpful in your own case. Particularly when you're analysing your early results, your own concern, very properly, will be with the accurate extraction of information from data; you'll be so close to the figures that the implications may escape you. Yet, as I've said in section 6.3, there is an interplay between the technical meaning of data, and their practical implications, so that the meaning of the former is determined by the latter. Your sponsor is well placed to ask apparently naive 'non-academic' questions, which will contribute to the technical accuracy of what you're doing, as well as suggesting practical implications.

under-graduate

As a student doing my first project, I remember collecting data on the ways in which managers made forecasts, and showing the results to my sponsor. I'd expected him to be interested in the issue of the managers' accuracy, but his question was somewhat different: 'I don't really follow the details, and in any case, what they're doing is difficult, so I wouldn't expect them to be very accurate. But tell me: is this a way of identifying who's more ready to take risks, and who isn't?'

He was interested in their style and their personalities, as people he knew very well; but the question served to focus my attention on the extremity of managers' forecasts, irrespective of their accuracy, and forced me to establish something which I should have addressed anyway, namely, to discover what counts as a non-extreme forecast or, in statistical jargon, the 'expected value of scores'. I had to know this before I could get much further with my own, technical question, which concerned the development of a method for measuring forecasting accuracy, but the issue hadn't occurred to me.

Finally, there's a form of help which is often under-utilized, but which is particularly important because it helps to determine the practical scope, relevance, and applicability of your ideas. You'll find that it helps to view your sponsor as a repository of the current practices and conventional wisdoms of the industry, product range, or market in which the organization operates. The way in which this knowledge is expressed is often implicit in the advice he or she gives you, and it will be up to you to make it explicit, by asking the question 'why?', and by making inferences for yourself.

in-company

If your topic is one which deals with strategic issues, or one in which you're working on an issue directly related to the work of your Department, your sponsor will show keen interest in your activities, and may have a role as the member of a team of supporters with whom you meet regularly. A recent project with which I was connected concerned the review and development of various forms of strategic partnership between the student's company and some of its overseas clients, with a view to the development of the company's strategy on a global scale. As you can imagine, the sponsor showed keen interest and was particularly involved in supporting the work, as he would have the responsibility for managing and monitoring implementation!

Your mentor

all

Sometimes, a sponsor remains fairly distant from your project, simply being there as a line manager to whom you report. Many of the activities which I've outlined above then fall to someone else: a person you've chosen as mentor. He or she'll do everything which your sponsor could do for you, as I've described above, and will be a key figure among your network of helpers (see section 5.1). The difference is that you'll have chosen the individual concerned, he or she won't have line management responsibility for you, may be a colleague, and is more likely to help you purely as a friend. After all, mentoring is becoming increasingly popular for management development in general, whether as part of personal development, for assistance in non-college-based project work (Smith, 1990) or collaborative research in general (Whitehead, 1994). You may as well take advantage of the trend, and look for a mentor for yourself! As you'll recall from section 3.1, the most useful mentor you can have is someone who has already completed a project, having been a student registered on the same programme as yourself, if you can find such a person. He or she will be particularly helpful in the role of a coach.

Coaching is a skill in which tasks are set in such a way that two things are achieved: the task itself is completed, and the person carrying out the task learns something new in the process of task completion. How much care and attention your mentor will give you, and whether their interest in your work will stretch to an explicit setting of tasks which have this effect, will depend very much on the relationship you develop, and on the insight which your mentor developed into his or her own project activities.

Some tasks he or she will set you are no more than questions, reflected back at you to encourage you to think the answers through for yourself, and followed by appropriate feedback. If you think your own queries through in this way, you may find that you can act as your own mentor for much of the time! Certainly, this form of coaching is an acquired skill. Many tutors have it, and some sponsors. In setting up your network of helpers, you might like to look for people who are useful because they have this knack of helping you to think things through, without simply 'giving you the answers'.

7.4 LETTING GO AND SAYING GOODBYE

It may seem strange to be considering this issue soon after you've begun. However, there is a good reason for doing so. In one sense, project work (like research work in general) never finishes. Initial findings expand the scope of your interests, your investigation raises issues which demand further exploration, and (especially if your topic wasn't thought through sufficiently at the outset), you arrive at the realization that you're only getting to grips with the real issues when your initially planned data-gathering and analysis are nearing completion. There is every temptation to go on for too long: but the deadline for submission is rapidly approaching, and the process of writing up and submitting your project report will, as I've described in section 5.2, take longer than you initially estimated. If you decide on a firm date for completion well in advance and stick to it, you'll find that you're able to structure and progress your work effectively throughout.

Sticking to the completion date is only a part of the disengagement process: a number of other activities should be anticipated and planned for.

The employer's report

Quite apart from producing the project report, which your sponsor may be interested in reading, it's possible that you will be asked to provide a briefer, practitioner-orientated summary by your sponsor. (If you promised a synopsis as a condition of entry, then of course it's mandatory that you produce it in any case.)

under-graduate

It makes for appropriate termination and disengagement if you ask your sponsor for the form this should take. One useful form is to provide a brief, non-academic, non-critical account of the main points which you wish to bring to the organization's attention. For example, the five major conclusions arising from your work which you feel will be most helpful to the organization, together with your supporting evidence for them (Buchanan *et al.*, 1988: 64). An oral presentation to your sponsor and a small group of colleagues whom he or she may wish to invite will act as a demonstration of your sincere interest in the company who've given you their time, thank them for their efforts, and provide you with the opportunity of influencing the company in a small way. So many undergraduate projects end with the quiet disappearance of the student; with a whimper rather than a bang.

in-company

MBA

This report may form a basis for the future implementation of your findings, and influence the scope of your own subsequent activities. In the case of topics of major corporate importance, it may affect the nature of your job and its responsibilities, especially if you're the person who is asked to be responsible for implementation. Viewed from this perspective, a successful in-company project may be the means by which you reposition yourself within the organization and, in effect, rewrite your job description. This is worth thinking through in advance!

Agreeing confidentiality

all

This, too is an issue which matters very much at the end of your project, but which should be thought through, raised with your sponsor and agreed, well in advance. Who is to see your project report? Three people at least will be involved: your sponsor, your tutor as internal examiner, and the external examiner, should he or she choose to do so. An employer who objects to the latter two people is simply not a viable project proposition, and you must know this from the very start.

But there may well be a wider audience: you may have to make a presentation in your teaching institution to more than one internal examiner, or to an audience of students and staff. You will certainly be expected to deposit a copy of the project report in the library.

Where your report contains sensitive information, the concern of employers is usually to ensure that what you have to say is accurate, regardless of whether it's favourable or unfavourable to the organization or some interest group within it. My impression is that in the overwhelming majority of cases you won't have to worry about any form of 'censorship'. If you have followed the negotiating strategy outlined in section 7.2, and have engaged in a process of cross-checking as an inherent part of your approach to the research process (see section 6.3), you should already have ensured the accuracy of your report, and tackled the issues arising from conflicting perspectives on the interpretation of your work, well before the time comes for you to submit your report.

Occasionally, however, your project will have involved you in commercially sensitive issues, and your company may wish to prevent their competitors from learning the details of your findings. While this event would be unlikely, their concern for the possibility must be respected, and you will find that your institution has arrangements for putting your report under an embargo for a number of years, restricting or indeed preventing access to library copies. You should contact your tutor, explore the arrangements with your librarian, and make sure that your sponsor receives details of the arrangements in writing from your institution.

The impression you create

Whether you're an undergraduate or an in-company employee, the impression you create when you depart will affect the chances of other students doing projects with the organization in the future.

Reviewing and using the literature | 8

A project is an exercise in which you construct an argument, drawing on your own ideas and on various data used to support these ideas. As you might recall from section 4.2, these data fall into two types: **primary**, being the material you gather yourself in the empirical stages of your project work and **secondary**, the material gathered by other people before you, made available to you in a variety of locations. The whole of Part Three will deal with how to marshal primary data; the purpose of this present chapter is to help you to handle secondary data, or what is often known as 'the literature'. You'll find yourself using the published literature in two ways: for review, and for referencing; the first part of this chapter outlines what is involved in both. In each case, you will need to know what subjects and authors to look for, where and how to look for them, and how to use them when you've found them. These issues provide the remaining sections of this chapter.

8.1 USING LITERATURE FOR REVIEW AND FOR REFERENCING

Review

You will be reviewing the literature at the outset of your work, when your choose a topic for your project, and throughout your work, when you present other writings more thoroughly and systematically to your readers as you build your conceptual analysis (see section 6.4). The former activity is self-evident, being one of the methods open to you in choosing and identifying a topic, as outlined in Chapter 3. The latter – the need for some detailed library time, in order to brief yourself and familiarize yourself with the literature rather more thoroughly – is perhaps less obvious. Knowledge doesn't exist in a vacuum, and your work only has value in relation to other people's. Your work and your findings will be significant only to the extent that they're the same as, or different from, other people's work and findings.

The result of this more detailed reading is twofold. You become more informed and you put yourself in a position to inform other people, your readers, by means of a literature review presented in your project document. This is a description and critical analysis of what other authors have said on material relating to your topic. It's usual to subdivide this material into different subjects, starting with the more general statements of broad scope, and going on to consider the different subjects in more detail, so that you end up narrowing down to a consideration of a small number of authors whose ideas and results are directly relevant to the precise subject-matter of your topic. (Glance back at the discussion in section 4.5, and Figures 4.1 and 4.2, on this issue.)

Many undergraduate project documents handle the literature review as a single, connected account presented shortly after the introduction, and before the empirical section begins. This is particularly appropriate where a single, fairly technical issue forms the basis of the project. (See Figure 4.1.)

under-graduate

This is less likely in other kinds of project. You may be dealing with a number of related themes, and it may be more convenient to present the literature in different stages (perhaps in different sections or chapters) as you tackle various aspects and issues throughout the project document (see Figure 4.2), building your argument issue by issue.

in-company

diploma

In either case, though, you would also expect to return to the literature during the discussion and conclusions sections of your project report. You will want to present the significance of your empirical findings in the light of other people's work, and you will want to draw on other authors in arguing for the recommendations which you wish to make in the light of your findings. This is the 'broadening out' stage of the project document, as shown in Figures 4.1 and 4.2.

MBA

all

An example of literature reviewing is shown in Table 8.1. It's only a brief outline, to show what I mean by presenting other people's work, and to demonstrate the way in which you progress from the general to the more specific in the course of the review. The ellipses (...) indicate positions in the review where you would wish to expand the preceding point in more detail than I have. I'm limited to just a page, whereas literature reviews in business and management projects tend to run between 4 and 20 or so pages in total! It's difficult to be more precise than that; it's my impression that projects based in the more numerate subjects (finance, accounting, quantitative methods) would tend to have briefer reviews, or to concentrate in greater detail on a smaller number of authors than my example.

Table 8.1 Using the literature: for purposes of review

In a DMS or MBA project on leadership, in which the thesis is that 'Negotiation skills training can be used to develop managers as leaders', the bare bones of the argument might run as follows:

The early work on leadership in management can be divided into three phases. At first, leadership was viewed as a property of the person, the 'trait theories' being reviewed by Stogdill (1948), and Mann (1959).	Starting at a general level
The main findings were that . . .	A few sentences
However, the main difficulty from the manager's point of view was that none of these theories indicated what s/he should do in order to be effective. It might be more helpful to ask what skills were involved in leadership: skills which anyone might learn to become a more effective manager. The emphasis shifted to a focus on behaviour, largely as a result of the Ohio studies (Stogdill and Coons 1957) on . . . ,	Brief summary
and the Michigan studies of supervisors (Likert, 1961)	Brief summary
Bales' work on leaderless groups (Parsons *et al.*, 1953) was also influential, since it demonstrated that . . . ;	Brief summary Brief overview
The general thrust was that . . . ;	
the difficulty was, as Fiedler first indicated, that the behavioural style which a manager adopts is unlikely to be effective in all situations: (Fiedler, 1967)	Brief summary
Indeed, style is contingent on situation, and various aspects of this view have been presented in recent years, e.g.	Examples most relevant to project
Most recently, however, there has been a shift of emphasis, away from the behaviourally explicit, to an exploration of the ways in which managers perceive, interpret and understand the situations in which they exercise leadership. Smith and Peterson (1988) present a detailed exposition, in which their observation that leadership involves the management of events is particularly important to the work reported in this project . . .	More detailed account
Specifically, events must be recognized as significant in the organizational culture (Misumi, 1985) . . .	Brief summary
by an active process on the part of the manager (Bannister and Fransella, 1985) . . . ; leadership arises as the supervisor actively manages the understandings and meanings of his/her subordinates (Pfeffer, 1981) . . . ; and this involves a process of negotiation with others (Hosking and Morley, 1988). . . .	More detailed account . . . much fine detail: the issues to be explored in the empirical section will shortly be presented and must follow on seamlessly as a continuation of the argument.

Referencing

A reference consists of three parts: the text being referenced, the reference itself, and the corresponding bibliographic entry. The first two, text and reference, will appear in the main body of your project report, while the third appears in a bibliography presented at the end of your project report.

You should find yourself using references throughout your project, for a number of different purposes outlined in Table 8.2. What you're doing, essentially, is twofold. You're justifying the statements you make, in a way which demonstrates your knowledge, and you're referring the reader to the original secondary source, specifically enough so that he or she could, in principle, look up the original author for him- or herself. You'll notice that I've been doing it throughout this book.

A number of conventions govern the form taken by the reference itself. There are in fact two main conventions for referencing, the name-date reference and the numbered reference, and you shouldn't mix the two: decide on one kind and stick to it throughout. One of these, the name-date format, is shown in Table 8.3. This itself has a number of variations, and you should check to see whether your tutor or your librarian recommend a particular variation before proceeding with the form I've provided. If you use the name-date convention, one very useful bit of fine-tuning is to include the number of the page where you obtained the quotation, immediately after the name and date in the body of your text, as I've done in the first example in Table 8.2.

Numbered references take much the same form in the bibliography as the name-date reference; however, instead of providing a name and date in the body of the text, all that appears is a number, which refers the reader to the full name and date details given in the bibliography. These are listed sequentially in the order in which they occur in the main body of the text.

The numbered reference convention is useful because it allows you to include marginal comments and 'footnotes' in the numbered sequence, as well as references themselves. When you find yourself referring to the same item as one referred to earlier, you don't repeat the full details in the bibliography each time, but simply write the abbreviation 'op. cit.' ('in the work quoted') after the sequence number and author name. If you refer to the same item as before in immediate succession, use the abbreviation 'ibid.' ('in the same place') instead. Finally , if you are using this convention, the list of items at the end of your project report should be headed 'References' rather than 'Bibliography'.

Tables 8.1 and 8.2 look quite impressive. And so they should: they represent the knowledge which you will have developed by the end of your

Table 8.2 Using the literature: for purposes of referencing

- **To attribute a quotation**
  You may be making the point that senior executives often hold very firm ideas, being people who believe strongly in what they are doing. You might wish to include the following quotation: 'A rude awakening, such as when Iacocca was fired by Ford, may be required for the leader to make a meaningful change in personal and corporate direction' (London, 1988: 53). Quotations are always enclosed within inverted commas, and must always have a reference; a page reference is valuable too.

- **To provide justification for a strong statement**
  For example, your text might be making the firm statement that 'a single event may have an enormous impact on national policymaking'. You might continue with the example of the impact which the Soviet launch of the Sputnik satellite had on US government policy on science, technology, and the professions, ending your text with '(Schön, 1983)', where just this point is made.

- **To tell your reader where an idea comes from**
  Take the idea that Japanese chief executives avoid stating corporate objectives very explicitly, because, unlike their American counterparts, they prefer to assume that their managers understand corporate philosophy and organizational environment sufficiently well that their intuitions will tell them the precise objective to set in any particular situation. If your text made this assertion, the reference would be Ouchi (1981). He said it first.

- **To argue for the reasonableness of your methods, since they are as used by other people working in the field**
  You might find you have to justify your use of semi-structured interviews with some departmental managers to check the results of interviews with other managers, by pointing out that this is an example of 'historical' or 'anthropological' technique, commonly used in such situations. You'd quote a number of authors who advocate it, thus: (Barzun and Graff, 1985; Parlett, 1981); or who have used it in similar circumstances to your own, say (Snyder, 1988).

And also:

- **To help interpret your results**
  You'd quote any similar findings obtained by other people (and also any contradictory ones!).

- **To help you to build your argument**
  Who agrees with you, who disagrees with you, who suggests that under certain circumstances, things might look this way, whereas, (according to someone else), if other issues were taken into consideration, the opposite might follow. 'Therefore, on balance, the following seems sensible . . .'.

Table 8.3 The name-date referencing convention

In the body of the text
- Just after the material which you want to reference:
  Open bracket, author surname, year of publication, close bracket
  In the case of two authors, give both surnames separated by 'and'.
  In the case of more than two authors, give the first surname followed by '*et al.*'

In the bibliography
- Where the item is a book:
  Author surname, initials (of each author involved, the last one, if more than one, being preceded by 'and', all but the last separated by commas); open brackets, year of publication, close brackets; title of book, each word beginning with a capital letter, the whole title underlined; place of publication, colon, name of publisher. For example:
  Eden C., Jones S. and Sims D. (1979) <u>Thinking in Organisations</u> London: Macmillan.
- Where the item is a journal article:
  Author surname, initials (of each author involved, the last one, if more than one, being preceded by 'and', all but the last separated by commas); open brackets, year of publication, close brackets; open inverted commas; title of the article, only the first word beginning with a capital letter; close inverted commas; title of the journal, each word beginning with a capital letter, the whole title underlined; volume number also underlined, comma, issue number, comma, inclusive page numbers. For example:
  Stoeckeler H.S. and Hasegawa M. (1974) 'A technique for identifying values as behavioural potentials in making consumer housing decisions' <u>Home Economics Research Journal</u> 2, 4, 268–280.
- Where the item is in a collection of items with an editor:
  Author surname, initials (of each author involved, the last one, if more than one, being preceded by 'and', all but the last separated by commas); open brackets, year of publication, close brackets; open inverted commas; title of the item, only the first word beginning with a capital letter; close inverted commas, comma; the word 'in', editor's surname, initials (of each editor involved, the last one, if more than one, being preceded by 'and', all but the last separated by commas); open brackets, the abbreviation 'ed.', or 'eds' if several editors are involved, close brackets; title of the book, each word beginning with a capital letter, the whole title underlined; place of publication, colon, name of publisher. For example:
  Brown L.D.and Kaplan R.E. (1981) 'Participative research in a factory' in Reason P. and Rowan J. (eds) <u>Human Inquiry: a Sourcebook of New Paradigm Research</u> Chichester: John Wiley & Sons.

Note that after the first line, the left-hand margin of a reference running over more than one line is indented by a few characters to help the reader pick out each separate reference.

Underlinings under journal and book titles are a hangover from the days of non-italic typewriter fonts: underlining is a printer's convention indicating that the words should be set in italic. If you're using a word processor, you might just as well do what the printer used to do and use italic instead of underlinings where indicated above. If you're using a typewriter, just use underlining.

The abbreviation '*et al.*' (meaning 'and others') is often put in italic, to indicate its foreign (Latin!) origin.

project, and the scholarly skills which you will have learnt. They're the very best you can do! But how do you get to this point? How do you find all this out in the first place?

8.2 WHAT TO LOOK FOR

Knowing what to look for is the chief problem when you wish to use the literature for review purposes. You know that there's information out there somewhere, which will help you choose a particular topic for your project in the first place, or allow you to present the work of other people in a systematic way once you get going, but – what work? In which fields? Done by which authors? Moreover, you know something about the literature already, from your taught courses and from your reading – but this isn't sufficient, is it? How much more is needed? What kind of material is lacking?

Answering these questions involves a two-stage process:

1. identifying subject-matter relevant to your topic;
2. finding references to authors who have published on these subjects, and getting hold of the publication itself.

Identifying subject-matter: initial steps

If you know what subject-matter is relevant to your topic, all is well: you look for references to authors who have covered precisely this subject. If you don't, you will need to discover the subject-matter, starting with some feeling or hunch that certain types of material may be involved. How do you develop this hunch?

Firstly, by talking to your tutor. At the beginning of your project, as soon as you are clear enough about your Aspect and topic to discuss them with your tutor, you can expect to be given an initial reading list at the end of the tutorial. This is likely to consist of enough items to give you a breadth of coverage, involving subject-matter which the tutor anticipates will be directly relevant to your topic as it develops, but also related material. The items will most likely be a mixture of subject headings, and author references; the list will most likely contain one or two key references, essential reading because the work done by the authors is definitive and has set the terms of debate for any project work in the particular field involved. If he or she doesn't offer you such a list, you must insist. Needless to say, you must then get hold of all the items on the list! Scan all of them, and read some of them in detail, immediately.

A second source of ideas is your set of lecture notes on the field in question. Jot down a list of the subjects which occur to you as you read over the notes most relevant to your topic and copy out the names of any authors who sound relevant.

Identifying subject-matter: developing a systematic list

As you think about the subjects and their different aspects, fresh ideas will begin to occur to you. (Also, as you find references and begin your reading, you'll find that the initial authors refer to subject-matter and other authors who, you feel, you must read in their turn, and you'll want to add them to your growing list.) Very soon, you'll discover that the list begins to get messy: to sprawl out over many fields, sub-fields, people, dates and places. You need to bring some structure to it, in order to guide your literature searching and reading more systematically, and so that you can work out, for each subject, where and when to stop reading!

Howard and Sharp (1983: 70) suggest that you construct a relevance tree. You'll remember what this is from section 3.3, where the relevance tree was introduced as one of the techniques for choosing a topic in cases of emergency. A tree for systematizing your reading is very similar, being a directed graph of headings and subheadings standing for the different subjects, and their subordinate aspects, which you feel you should read. An example is given as Figure 8.1. The advantage of the tree is that it helps you to decide on the following.

■ Which subjects are directly relevant to your topic, as opposed to those which are less relevant and therefore probably not worth spending further time locating, reading, and writing up in your literature review. This decision is a pure judgement on your part, but, if you're in doubt, show the tree to your tutor and discuss the issue with him or her.
■ Which subjects you will locate and read now, as opposed to those which you'll need to locate later on in your project work. Again, this is a judgement which you must make yourself, with help if necessary.
■ Which subject is more important, and which is less important. While your own judgement is involved here, you do have some direct clues from the shape taken by the tree as it develops. You'll notice, for example, that the more important subjects tend to have more branches 'pointing to' them in the tree.

Thus, in Figure 8.1, the student has decided to focus initial reading in three subject-areas: support for small businesses, particularly those involved in manufacturing, and with particular reference to funding available from venture capitalists. The student recognizes that the literature on non-entrepreneurial small businesses, and on State-funded information services, may be relevant to the topic (for example, before an entrepreneur can approach a funding agency, the entrepreneur needs

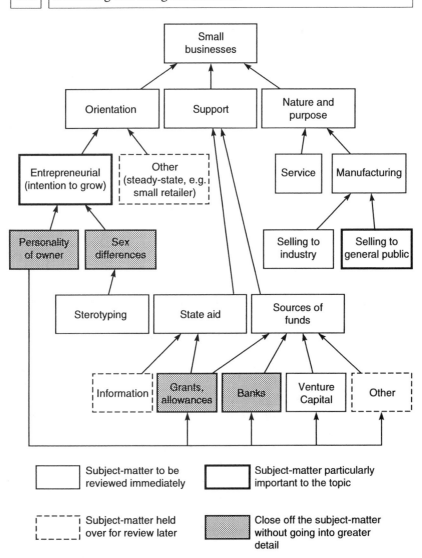

Figure 8.1 A sample relevance tree for literature searching. The student chooses the topic of 'Funding Entrepreneurial Start-ups' and decides to make a relevance tree of the subjects in which initial reading is to be done.

information on how to find one, and state information services can be particularly useful here); however, the student chooses to leave reading in these subject-areas till later. While intending to read all there is to know about venture capitalists, he or she will only focus on state allowance schemes, and on the banks, insofar as they help to fund entrepreneurial small businesses. Similarly, in the subject-areas of personality of owner, and sex differences, he or she will close off the potential amount of reading involved by focusing only on the ways in which personality and sex stereotypes affect the decision by the funding agency to lend money to the entrepreneur.

You may find the following rule of thumb helpful, when making judgements like these. It's taken from the field of task analysis for training purposes, where similar trees are often used (Annett and Duncan, 1967). If you're wondering whether to split up a branch further, or to stop at that point, ask yourself two questions.

■ What are the chances of not spotting relevant subject-matter if I stop here? (A question of how much material is left to be found.)
■ What are the costs, in terms of important subject-matter ignored, of stopping at this point? (A question of the standard of excellence which you wish to achieve in demonstrating your knowledge of the field.)

If you get the feeling that the chances of missing relevant subject-matter are high, and that the costs of ignoring important subject-matter are also high, then you should split up that item of subject-matter down further. If both of these factors are low, then there's probably no need to do so. If one of the factors is high but the other low, you have a judgement to make! Although there's no absolute answer to either of these questions, as your reading progresses and you become familiar with the literature around your topic, you'll find that your confidence in answering these questions will grow.

You would expect to read several books, articles, and other sources for each subject-area of the relevance tree, sequencing your reading, and concentrating your attention, as you planned when drawing it up. Each item read would merit its own filecard, as described in section 5.3. As time went on, you would certainly decide to go into greater depth than you'd originally anticipated with some of the subject-areas, as your initial reading indicated new subject-matter and aspects of the old that hadn't occurred to you. It would be best to add these into your original tree, so that whenever you use it you obtain an overview of the whole field, an indication of the balance of your reading across the field, and an indication of how much more you still have to do.

Start off the relevance tree on a double-page spread of your project diary, write small, and spread the items out with lots of space in between so that you can add items as your reading progresses!

All very well, you might say. But where do I locate all this information, how exactly do I look for it, and, particularly, how do I discover the names of the authors, and the titles of the publications in question?

8.3 WHERE AND HOW TO LOOK

This knowledge comes with practice, and is one of the skills involved in scholarship. If you're doing project work for the first time, then you need to know two things: what kinds of sources are available to you, and how to access them.

Where to look

Table 8.4 summarizes the variety of sources which you have at your disposal. The items are organized in descending order of detail and ascending order of organization, from top to bottom in the table. By which I mean that, lower down in the table are those data sources in which someone else has attempted to provide you with a guideline, or summary, of the data generated or presented by other people before them. Generally speaking, if you know exactly what you're looking for, you would approach a data source higher up the table; if, on the other hand, you're not quite sure but you wish to obtain an overview of the data that are available, you would approach a data source towards the bottom of the table.

As a general rule, when turning subject-matter into author references, try to enter Table 8.4 at as specific a level as possible: higher up rather than lower down. All of these data will be available either in your academic library, or through it (by means of inter-library loan, via a trade directory located in the library which you use as a source of the address of a company to which you must write, and so on). A list of the more important tertiary sources held by any academic library is shown in Table 8.5. Using them is quite straightforward.

- Normally, if you want to identify the different aspects of a broad subject, the chapter headings, section subheadings and index of a secondary source like a standard textbook, or book of readings, will provide you with an overview. If you want subject-matter at a less specific level than this, work within Segment A of Table 8.5. In other words, use the subject catalogue, looking at entries under the classification numbers which the library subject index tells you are relevant. Author's names will be the result. Other books by the same author held by your library can then be found in the author sequence catalogue.
- If you already have an author's name, and the publication is not held in your library, then move to Segment B of Table 8.5: the full reference can be obtained from one of the six tertiary sources listed here. Moreover, the last four provide items listed by subject, if you want to extend your subject search further. The publication can then be ordered through inter-library loan.

Table 8.4 Sources of information

Data generated by individuals and organizations
- Government bodies
- Private companies
- Trade associations
- Chambers of commerce
- Local employer networks
- Trade unions and employers' organizations
- Research organizations and professional bodies
- Patent Office
- Consumer organizations

Data recorded in primary sources
- Monographs (books on a single topic)
- Academic journal articles
- Conference papers
- Unpublished research reports (available from author)
- Newspapers and magazines (some features and news items)
- Company annual reports
- Company pricelists
- Company internal 'house magazines'

Data organized, collated and indexed in secondary sources
- Books of readings (collations of journal articles)
- Textbooks
- Encyclopaedias
- Bibliographies
- Dictionaries
- Academic journal review articles
- Academic journal annual index pages
- Annual review books (of topics in academic disciplines)
- Abstracts (periodic issues in many academic disciplines)
- 'Current Contents' (a collation of journal contents pages)

These are summarized and signposted in tertiary sources
- Subject guides
- Library catalogues and indexes
- On-line databases e.g. Management Contents, ABI Inform, on DIALOG
- Off-line databases on CD-ROM e.g. ABI Inform, ANBAR Abstracts, EXTEL, FAME
- Information services
- Librarians
- Your tutor

You turn these data into information by asking the right questions

---

After Hunter-Brown (1984), and Howard and Sharp (1983)

■ While you're still working at this broad level, you might wish to consult sources in Segments C and D of Table 8.5: research-oriented items, and journals respectively. While *Ulrich's Guide* is useful, since it lists journals by subject, your own library journal catalogue is likely to be a listing by journal name, which doesn't allow you to get to the author-name level but which will give you an idea of the general subject-matter to hand in the library.

■ Some more specialized tertiary sources are listed in Table 8.6.

As you become more knowledgeable about your field you might want to work at a very specific level indeed, contacting data sources directly, because you know the information isn't available in the library, or because you think you'll get what you want faster if you make a direct contact. Individual companies already known to you, chambers of commerce, and information services are often helpful in this respect. Other sources are listed in Table 8.6.

Finally, there is a tremendously useful tertiary source which enables you to get a feel for the development of ideas over time: the citation index. You'll notice, when you chase up the subjects in your relevance tree and read the authors whose work you have discovered, that they refer to other authors in their bibliographies, and you may need to find some of those items and read them in their turn. That's fine: it allows you to go backwards in time from the author in question. However, on occasion you'll get the feeling that you'd like to know what happened to the ideas which that author presented, and ask yourself 'I wonder who referenced this author in turn, subsequently to this particular publication?', working forwards in time, as it were.

A citation index allows you to do just that. You'll most likely want the Social Sciences Citation Index. It looks more complicated than it actually is, and wherever it's kept in your library you'll also find instructions on how to use it. Essentially, a citation index is a listing, by author, of everyone who has referred to that author's publications since they appeared. The finest creation of the librarian's craft, existing and purpose-built citation indexes are currently being misused by state agencies in an effort to evaluate higher education teaching institutions as a function of the number of people who have referred to the publications of staff employed by those institutions: a pernicious practice which confuses quantity with quality. You know better than that, and can use it for its proper purpose.

The items mentioned in Tables 8.5 and 8.6 represent a much wider range of sources, too numerous and specific to individual libraries to be listed in this book. Go into your library and talk to one of the staff! You'd be surprised to learn how much work they put into the compilation of

Table 8.5 Tertiary sources: general catalogues and indexes

A. Start off with
- *Library subject index*: lists all the subjects covered by your own library following a standard scheme, and provides the classification number of that subject, either Dewey or Library of Congress. Use this if you know the subject but not the author or title. Since the books are shelved in numbered sequence, allows you to locate the book on the shelf or to make a reservation. Use in conjunction with:
- *Subject or class catalogue*: lists all the books held by your library within each classification number, by author.
- *Author sequence catalogue*: lists all the books held by your library, alphabetically by author. Use this directly if you know the author's name.
- *Title sequence catalogue*: Lists all the books held by your library, alphabetically by title.
- *OPAC*: the Online Public Access Catalogue, a computerized database which has almost replaced the function of all four catalogues shown above; talks to its replicas in other libraries via JANET, the academic electronic network.

B. If it's not in your own library, try
- *British Library Catalogue, National Union Catalogue (Library of Congress)*: list all the books held in stock, since the fifteenth century to the recent present, by these two libraries (which are copyright libraries: that is, they receive a copy of every book published). Most items are referenced by author, not by title. The most important information is the classification number, Dewey or Library of Congress, and the ISBN number, a unique identifying code for the book in question. Use these to order older books via inter-library loan, if not held by your own library.
- *British National Bibliography, British Books in Print, Cumulative Book Index, Books in Print*: list all the books published and in print in the UK and USA respectively, from 1950 onwards. Use these for your general needs. Subject, author, and title sequences are included.

C. None of the above cover theses, so try in addition
- *ASLIB Index to Theses*: Biannual publication listing theses prepared for higher degrees by students in British universities.
- *Dissertation Abstracts*: provides a brief paragraph summarizing the content of each thesis prepared by Ph.D. students in the UK and USA.
- *CRIB (Current Research in British Universities and Colleges)*: Lists all research currently being carried out in the UK: useful for making direct contact with people in your field.

D. But few of the above include journals, so look at
- *Business Periodicals Index*: Alphabetic list of authors, titles and subjects of business journals.
- *ANBAR*: Lists management books and journals by author and subject.
- *Research Index*: Up-to-date listing by subject and company name; fortnightly.
- *Ulrich's Guide to International Periodicals*: annual three-volume catalogue of all journals published in most world languages, listed by title and by subject.
- *Journal catalogues*: in two forms – journals held by the library listed by classification number, and by title.

Table 8.6 Tertiary sources: some specialized indexes and services

- *HMSO Guide*: lists UK government publications. Useful since this information is not usually covered in the Table 8.5 tertiary sources. Your first means of accessing Command Papers, government statistical series, reports of state organizations.
- *Chadwick-Healey Catalogue of British Official Publications*: Microfilmed catalogue to non-HMSO publications of national bodies, e.g. Manpower Services Commission, Sports Council.
- *Index to the Statutes*: used to trace Acts of Parliament if the title and year are not known.
- *EEC Documentation Bulletin*: fortnightly listing of Economic Community documents, Instruments, publications and studies, international economic reviews; periodic index.
- *Index to Financial Times*: monthly index by subject/company name of all news and feature articles appearing in *Financial Times*; not to be confused with *Financial Times Index*, which is a generic term for various share performance indices.
- *Index to McCarthy Industry Files*: provides access to the *McCarthy Files*, a regular service of photocopied items on individual industrial and commercial sectors.
- *Index to Mintel Reports*: provides access to the Mintel market research reports series, covering market intelligence, personal finance, retail intelligence and leisure intelligence.
- *Kelly's Business Directory, Kompass*: two major commercial directories.

- *Companies Registration Offices*: these are locations, in Cardiff and Edinburgh, where publicly available company records can be obtained: your library should keep a stock of application forms.
- *The Information Bureau* (was the Daily Telegraph Information Bureau): answers individual queries – 5 mins £5.00, 15 mins £20, 30 mins £35, 1hr £65 Access/Visa paid; longer projects costed at hourly rate. Useful for a last-ditch enquiry or one-off topic, e.g. checking facts, company press profiles. Tel. 0171 924 4414, fax 0171 924 4456.
- *Institute of Management Library* (was the British Institute of Management Library): helpful series of initial reading lists on business and management topics; general holdings concentrate on business and management practice, procedures and techniques; free if you, your company, or your academic library is a corporate member; otherwise a small fee. Tel. 01536 204222, fax 01536 401013.
- *European Documentation Centres*: some 50-or-so libraries in this country receive all EU publications. If your library isn't one, staff will give you the location of the nearest.
- *Economist Intelligence Unit*: in case you wondered. Alas, this is a commercial service dealing only with corporate clients, charging hefty fees.

secondary and tertiary sources, writing guides to all sorts of subject-matter they hold. You never quite realize this while you're using the library for general lending or reference in support of your taught courses, until you start work on your project. Indeed, I suspect that the authors of many of the less successful projects I've dealt with never discovered this fact. A helpful librarian is a wondrous thing.

How to look

To return to Table 8.4. The more specific your relevance tree, the more likely it is that you'll look for publications located at the top of the table; however, when you're reading in order to decide on your topic, and, more generally, when you're in the early stages of your project, you're more likely to be concentrating on items towards the bottom.

There is one problem, however. All of the sources in Tables 8.4 to 8.6 allow you to access data, rather than information. (Data are **specific findings and assertions**, which may or may not be meaningful to any given person. They can swamp and confuse the individual who's unprepared. Information, by contrast, is made up of **data expressed in such a way that they remove some uncertainty** which that person has. Information provides an answer to a query the person had; it informs.) There are two simple ways of turning data into information. Firstly, by having a particular query in mind when you go to examine the data; and secondly, as I've already suggested, by approaching the data at the most specific level you can.

In point of fact, your work with the literature should always involve a set of questions with which you will interrogate the data available to you, as follows.

- ■ What do I need to know?' The items in your relevance tree, and the point you have reached in building your argument, will guide you in deciding what it is you're looking for, and the more specific items in the tree will be particularly helpful.
- ■ 'How will I know when I've found it?' Summarize what you know about the subject already, and be prepared to look for information which is consistent, complementary, or relevant. Does it make sense, taken with what you know?
- ■ 'How precise an answer do I require?' You are likely to need greater precision towards the end of your project, and less precision early on. Don't worry if, at the start, you can only think in generalities. As you read more, the specificity will come!
- ■ 'How important is it that I should find the answer?' There's no point in spending a long time on something which is trivial, or which represents a fine-tuning of your existing information.

Therefore,

- 'How long will I spend in looking for the answer?'
- 'How recent should the answer be?' Knowledge in some subject areas changes very rapidly (e.g. economic statistics, or information on the performance of a particular company), while knowledge in other areas is slower to change (e.g. theories about employee motivation). In the former case, you must look for recent publications. You have more freedom of choice in the latter case. Is your purpose to record the broad thrust of the ideas, or to summarize current thinking?

Finally,

- 'Is there anything I really must know?' This is a catch-all question, probably more important at the beginning of your reading, which refers to the existence of definitive publications. These are statements about your topic which are key publications, either because they contain the best wisdom available about some aspect of your topic which anyone working in the field is required to know, or because they're written by someone who was either wise or controversial in the past, or is currently being quoted by other people working in your field. Your tutor's initial reading list should be your best source here, or, failing that, a recent textbook.

Literature searching is most effective when you have done some preparatory work to think through how best to identify the information which you require. This is particularly so with computerized data sources: on-line and off-line databases.

On-line databases. These come to you in the form of a system consisting of two main components: a computer terminal and a librarian. The terminal gives you access to any one or more of hundreds of databases located anywhere in the world, while the librarian will assist you to frame a set of criteria, rather like the questions I've listed above, which are intended to establish, as specifically as possible, exactly the information you require. The databases consist of references to all manner of publications, classified by subject. Different databases deal with different groups of subjects. A typical query will scan anything between 500 and 10 000 references, to end up with a list of perhaps 5 to 20 which meet your criteria.

The chief characteristic of an on-line database is the flexibility with which you can search the data for the information you require. For example, you might vaguely remember that an article you once came across dealt with the factors increasing questionnaire response rate, and that the photocopy you saw seemed quite old. The librarian is an expert in expressing this in a quasi-logical form which the computer system can use as a formal search criterion. Inputting an instruction into the computer along the lines of 'questionnaire response rates AND (>1968 AND <1980)' would allow the system to find the article if the words 'questionnaire response rates' appeared in that order in the title of the original article held on the database, assuming the publication date was between 1969 and 1979 inclusive. However, only the criterion 'questionnaire AND response rate AND (>1968 AND <1980)' would find it if these words appeared in a different order in the title, e.g. 'Response rates for the social survey questionnaire'; again, assuming the date was within the range.

All on-line systems are accessed through a host system (DIALOG being the host for Management Contents, ABI Information, and Dissertation Abstracts, for example) with which the librarian will be familiar. That, and the knowledge of the logical search criteria, explains why you need the librarian's help, and why an extensive search can be very expensive (of the order of £85 at full cost). However, on-line searches can be very effective once you have an initial familiarity with the literature, and are quite feasible if you can persuade your organization to pay the fees involved.

Off-line databases. This expense has been one of the factors influencing the increase in popularity of CD-ROM-based databases: since you refer to them in your own, rather than the computer's, time, costs are negligible once the library have paid a general subscription for a particular set of CD-ROM-based services, and there is no cost to you other than your time. Being updated monthly or quarterly, the information on any one disc may not be as up-to-date as in an on-line database; however, as most journals also appear quarterly, you'll find that the refresh rate of the information is good enough for most purposes. You do the logical search yourself, following printed guidelines prepared by the library in most cases but relying on the user-friendliness of the CD-ROM search interface in others.

8.4 WHAT TO DO WITH IT ONCE YOU'VE GOT IT

All your efforts to familiarize yourself with the literature, and all your hard work in referencing your presentation in an appropriately scholarly way, may be irrelevant unless you present your knowledge in a sensible form. While your tutor and sponsor don't look for the fundamental wisdoms that redefine the boundaries of knowledge in your subject area, nevertheless they would like you to express yourself in a clear, logical, and self-consistent manner.

This comment applies as much to primary data (the use you make of the results you've gathered for yourself) as it does to the secondary data which you present in your literature review. In the former case, the rules governing your use of the methods and techniques with which your data are gathered will provide you with safeguards (see Part Three); in the latter, it's helpful if you're clear on the forms in which secondary data can be presented, and are aware of some pitfalls of thinking and presentation.

Table 8.7 summarizes some of the most common forms of discourse which you're likely to encounter in your reading and to utilize in your written project report. Perhaps the best way of using the table would be to acknowledge that your report will be a mixture of all of these forms; to understand each of them well enough so that you know when you're using each; and to refer to the table when you're writing, so that you can keep an eye on what you're doing.

So, for example, a report which is just one long description is not an acceptable outcome of your project, nor is a long literature review. It helps if you work to a pre-existing model you've encountered in the literature, or construct a model to guide your work, as outlined in section 6.4) and especially if you're explicitly aware that you're doing so. Indeed, your thesis (see section 5.4) is itself the beginnings of a model, and you may want to flesh this model out a little as you work within the terms of your thesis.

If your project report comprises conceptual analyses, evidence and critical argument as outlined earlier, it has be leavened by reference to principles, and will include an element of explanation for some of the issues which you have explored. Most regulations insist on some form of empirical content; clearly, if you're gathering and presenting data, you can do so only with some prior principles in mind, as an outcome of some theory which states that it's just these data which you should gather to justify the assertions which you wish to make.

At some stage or other, then, you'll be using each and every one of these forms of argument: make sure that you know which is which. Weak projects are often unsuccessful because the student thought he or she was explaining, when all that was presented was a description.

Chapter 14 contains further useful guidelines on what to do with your information once you've got it.

Table 8.7 Forms of argument and presentation

- **An assertion:** an utterance written down by yourself – a simple statement.
- **A description:** an account of whatever you see to be the case – a series of assertions which define something or some state of affairs. These assertions may or may not be accurate, detailed, or exact. Descriptions are always made from some point of view, or to some purpose; so alternative descriptions are always possible. The case studies which you're given in your lectures (especially at MBA level) are neither explanations, models, nor theories: they're descriptions.
- **A model:** sometimes used loosely to stand for a relatively inaccurate or underspecified theory, the word is properly used to stand for a systematic description which maps or represents some state of affairs. Another way of saying this is that it's a statement of what the state of affairs would look like if your description mapped them accurately or exactly. You design models as a starting-point, to enable yourself to experiment with, and understand, the state of affairs.
- **A principle:** a statement about the relationships between variables, issues or events, which has been previously researched and found to be accurate in general as well as in specific instances.
- **A theory:** A set of statements incorporating principles, using which it is possible to explain a particular occurrence as an instance of a wider set of affairs.
- **An explanation:** a description which provides reasons and thereby removes uncertainty or increases understanding, by means of assertions which say something about the relationships between two or more variables, issues or events, and which draw on previously established principles. You can't claim to have explained something if all you've done is describe it. A very detailed description is almost an explanation, except for one characteristic: an explanation provides sufficient understanding of principles for you to envisage an alternative, or improved state of affairs; a description need not. Explanations are expressed by means of theories, and a theory is more than description.
- **An analysis:** a critical account of the component parts or factors involved in some state of affairs – the variables, issues, or events making up the state of affairs. However carefully the parts are described, an analysis doesn't explain the state of affairs, just as a description doesn't explain: you require some reference to principles in order to explain.
- **So, for example:** a description of the lighting system in your room can be provided by a series of assertions about switches, lightbulbs, wiring, and power sources, enough for your reader to be able to put on the light. A model of the lighting system would be provided by an electrical circuit diagram, and an analysis provided by means of a list of electrical components involved. An explanation of the lighting system would be sufficiently detailed and refer to just those principles, for your reader to be able to fix the lighting system if it went wrong, or to be able to envisage a better system. The principles would be taken from a theory of electricity and, conceivably, materials.

PART 3

A Guide to Empirical Work

Planning empirical work

9

If you were to ask me to state the overriding theme of Part Two, I would answer in one phrase: 'the valid handling of complexity'. Much of the material hitherto has concerned the rationale whereby you can support the statements you wish to make with evidence to justify them, working in a complex management environment in which there are varying expectations of your role. The theme of Part Three concerns how best to put this rationale to work, so that you can establish and support the assertions you wish to make.

The account in section 6.3 raises many questions for you to bear in mind. In addressing the problems of the messy management environment in which you'll be gathering your data, I may have created an impression that the empirical stage will be similarly messy and disorganized – yet it needn't be, provided that you address the complexity which faces you in terms of five straightforward steps.

- You state the thesis which you think you can establish, or state the conceptual model which you seek to use, with its main implications; both, as clearly and succinctly as possible (see section 5.4).
- You list the major issues involved: organizational, departmental, and personal.
- You work out a data-gathering approach which will investigate the issues and help to establish/negate, the thesis you have in mind, or which will best help you build your argument.
- You decide on an appropriate method by which to do so.
- You make use of a number of techniques to gather the data themselves.

The first two steps are up to you, since the conceptual work is your own, and the issues are shared between yourself and anyone within the organization with whom you're cooperating. The approach you adopt is a matter of design, and forms the subject-matter of this chapter. Once you have a design, you can decide on a method and one or more techniques; these are outlined in the chapter which follows.

9.1 PLANNING A DESIGN

You leave the house in the morning, get in your car, turn the ignition key and your car won't go. No forward movement whatsoever. Life comes to a standstill, blood pressure rises, and the first of the day's six appointments is due in an hour's time! What to do?

You switch into Keystone Cops mode, rush into the garden shed, bring out the spare battery you just happen to have there, and fit it in place; you run round to the coalshed and bring out the can of petrol you always keep on hand for emergencies and pour it into the petrol tank. You put water into the radiator and oil into the bit of the engine with the filler cap on top; and you put some brake fluid into the brake fluid thingy down at the side. It's taken an hour and you have to rush back indoors to put on a new coat since you got oil all over the one you were wearing, but its done; now to try the key in the ignition again. After all, that's what cars go on, isn't it – electricity and petrol, water and oil?

Well, sort of. But really, no, not in this instance, and for a rather subtle reason. It's not necessarily that your conceptual model is oversimplified; it's not that you're using the wrong conceptual model (the one pertaining to regular weekly servicing, rather than one-off emergency start-ups), though that's part of the problem. It's that your approach is disorganized and inefficient. It's pure Laurel and Hardy; it lacks **design**.

Forget them for the moment. Make some observations first of all. Aha! Gather some data! But how? **Design** your approach so that you:

■ try various possibilities one by one in a controlled manner;
■ eliminate possible alternative explanations;
■ avoid tests which will tell you that two possible causes are at work but which make it impossible to decide on their relative importance;
■ use a conceptual model that's suited to the problem in hand.

Okay, turn the key in the ignition, listen, and look. Does the engine fire? Er, well, not really: so it's either the starter motor, the solenoid, or the battery. You've eliminated oil, water, petrol and brake fluid as the source of the problem: they're irrelevant to the problem you're dealing with at present. Do the headlights come on? Yes: so it can't be the battery. Turn the key in the ignition and listen again: actually, the engine doesn't even cough, let alone fire. Turn the key again: you hear a clicking noise. So the solenoid is doing its job, and, by elimination, it must be the starter motor that's wrong. Other factors could be involved (maybe even your wiring), but they aren't the immediate problem.

That took you just one minute, so there's time to call out the AA, ring your garage, or failing all else, order a taxi to take you to work. Yes, your knowledge of solenoids, starters and so on was relevant, but, much more important, it was the approach, the design you adopted, which solved the problem you faced.

Design has been defined as the deliberately planned 'arrangement of conditions for analysis and collection of data in a manner that aims to combine relevance to the research purpose with economy of procedure' (Selltiz *et al.*, 1981). The idea behind a design is that different kinds of issues logically demand different kinds of data-gathering arrangement so that the data will be:

- relevant to your thesis or to the argument you wish to present;
- an adequate test of your thesis (i.e., unbiased and reliable);
- accurate in establishing causality, in situations where you wish to go beyond description to provide explanations for whatever is happening around you;
- capable of providing findings that can be generalized to situations other than those of your immediate organization.

You have to have some knowledge in order to put together an appropriate design, and that is one purpose in doing a literature review; but knowledge without design leads to inefficient and inaccurate data collection.

It makes sense if you have problems starting your car in the morning: but why is it necessary when doing a project? After all, you know what questions to ask your respondents, so why not simply go out and get on with it? Well, because it's never that simple. The best way to get across this idea of design, of logical necessity, is by means of an extended example. Suppose you're exploring the strategic options available to your company in addressing overseas markets, and want to survey different companies to identify the options open to you. You may decide to examine a number of different options, varying from those which you anticipate will be the easiest to those which initial investigation suggests will be the most difficult, to identify the factors that make for ease as opposed to difficulty in the case of your company, in its market, with its particular constraints.

Making comparisons on the basis of ease-or-difficulty seems logically appropriate, given the risks and expenditures involved in overseas investment, and given that the issue presents itself as one of choosing one of a set of alternative actions. So, in your industry you may know that joint ventures could be placed at the difficult end of the range, while direct exporting might be seen as easier (unless there are import quotas in the overseas country); manufacture under licence could be one way of overcoming this form of trade barrier, and might be placed more towards the easy end of the range for your company; and so forth. Your choice of this approach, leading to the selection of companies which practise these forms of trade, which represent extreme positions on the range, and which are willing to give you the information you need, would represent a design decision – one of **examining contrasting modes of operation** – in what is a descriptive and analytic project. Once you've decided on this form of design, then you might decide that the comparative case study seems most appropriate as the method to use.

But this design, like one of Coyote's efforts in the 'Roadrunner' cartoons, would be *predestined* to fail if the main issues which you wanted to explore concerned the development and growth of a department and company over time: examining contrasts seems illogical and inappropriate, and it makes much more sense to try and track the change in some way. In order to do so, you'd have to be present during a significant proportion of the time in question, being involved in the systematic collection of data at various time intervals, or you'd have to arrange to have access to data which systematically represent that time. You'd choose what's known as a **time-sampling design**. Your project work at this point would be largely descriptive, and so your key design consideration would involve the accuracy and reliability of your sampling of what's happening or has happened. If you also intended to explain the development and growth, then you'd need to find out enough background information to show which factors have and haven't influenced the changes. Archival search and analysis, coupled with an appropriate survey, would seem most appropriate as the approach to adopt.

On the other hand, if the issues you've identified relate to a major, one-off change occurring in the organization, then in order to describe the change, you could arrange to gather data on some key indicators both before and after the change, in a **before–after design**. If you wanted to explain the change, you'd need to have checked that these indicators are the most relevant to the events involved, and that other factors which might have been responsible weren't involved. If conditions were right and appropriate data were to hand, it's just possible that you could choose a field experiment as your method; alternatively, some form of survey would be required.

And so on. What these examples have in common is that the shape of your data-collection, the factors and events which you decide to notice, and those which you decide to ignore – in a word, the **conditions** – are arranged and structured deliberately, in order to cast the brightest light possible on the issues you're investigating. Where you intend to explain as well as describe and analyse, you have to arrange things so that you can exclude competing explanations which are not involved, as well as being able to identify the plausible explanations.

With one exception, it is difficult to provide you with more detailed guidelines on the planning of the design of your empirical work at this point: it depends on your topic, and particularly, on your thesis, or on the model you're using. Indeed, if the purpose of a thesis is to state the conclusions which you believe your data will support, and to help identify the kind of data which would refute such conclusions (see section 5.4), a good thesis is one which clearly expresses your design, so that the design – what you have to do to establish the thesis – is obvious from the way in which your thesis has been stated. Having said that, I will be providing more detailed guidelines on design when I describe the range of different methods and techniques which are open to you.

The exception concerns the matter of sampling. A good design will involve a decision on which data sources to address, and how to address them in order for your conclusions to be both valid with respect to your thesis, and generalizable beyond the situation in which the addressing is done.

9.2 SAMPLING

Sampling can be defined as the deliberate choice of a number of people, the sample, who are to provide you with data from which you will draw conclusions about some larger group, the population, whom these people represent. In order to draw a sample, you have to know how many people are in the population, and how this total is made up from people falling into various subgroups in which you might be interested. This may already be available as a published staff list, for example, if your project focuses on employees; or as a directory list of companies for the market you're exploring, if your focus is at the company level; alternatively, you may have to draw it up yourself. Such a list is called a sampling frame. The size of your sample and the way in which you draw it are matters for design, and will affect the validity and generalizability of the conclusions you draw.

There are two ways in which you can draw a sample. **Nonprobability sampling** involves identifying and questioning informants because you are interested in their individual positions, roles, or background experience; it's likely that you'll want to pose different questions to them accordingly. The population they represent consists of all the varied members of the company, department, or section that falls within the scope of your topic, and they may represent the company, department or section somewhat loosely. In other words, you're interested in variety – in their idiosyncratic viewpoint – and have no particular wish or need to generalize their answers directly to other people. In this situation, the proportion of the population whom you choose to talk to (or the probability of being chosen as a respondent) has no particular significance, other than being manageable in the time available to you.

In contrast, **probability sampling** involves you in identifying and questioning people because they are members of some population (a section, department, organization and so forth) and you want to ensure that your assertions are valid for your respondents, and are directly generalizable, without further inference, to that population. You pose the same questions to each sample member. And so, for example, if 75% of your respondents reply in a particular way (e.g. that they're in favour of some course of action), you're willing to conclude **directly**, without further inference, that their section, department, or organization would have replied identically (e.g. 75% of them would also have been in favour) had you asked them. In this situation, the proportion of the population whom you choose to talk to (or the probability of being chosen as a respondent) has an important bearing on the validity of your conclusions and on their generalizability.

Most management projects deal in small samples; you are more likely to be using nonprobability sampling methods, and you can generalize your conclusions by means of inference and triangulation (see section 10.2). However, many undergraduate projects, and most of those which involve a questionnaire survey, have the potential for you to use probability sampling methods, and thereby to draw direct conclusions to your population as well.

Nonprobability sampling methods

A variety of strategies is possible, each following a different rationale, and each of them reflecting the constraints within which you must work.

Accidental sampling. Accidental sampling involves the choice of a sample from the population whose views you want to discover, on the basis of convenience only: for example, because you can get access to them, because you can't obtain the funds or other forms of support to cast your net more systematically, or because your sponsor is uncomfortable in having you talk to some more systematically representative sample of that population.

There are drawbacks. You might very well find yourself in a situation where organizational pressures prevent you from using any other method, but your sample results may be biased with respect to the population as a whole, and sampling theory provides you with no systematic means of estimating the size of the bias. Given the pressures, you may have no choice but to work with an accidental sample. What you can and should do is to report your judgement of the nature of the bias, as a matter of scholarship rather than sampling theory; that is, make a list of the possible sources of bias given your thesis, the issue you're investigating, and the related issues, and discuss them in your project report.

Purposive sampling. Purposive sampling involves choosing people whose views are relevant to an issue because you make a judgement, and/or your collaborators persuade you that their views are particularly worth obtaining and typify important varieties of viewpoint. Several arrangements are possible.

- Key informant technique (Tremblay, 1982) – see section 11.3 – by which people with specialized knowledge about the issue in question are selected for interview.
- Taking 'slices through the organization' (Reeves and Harper, 1981b) selects people because of the positions they occupy in the organization. You might choose a vertical chain of command from chief executive down to first line manager, working within one or more business functions; a horizontal line to include people in a colleague relationship at one particular level within the organization; or a diagonal slice down the chain of command and across functions
- 'Snowball sampling' (Reeves and Harper, 1981b), by which new respondents are selected following the recommendations of people to whom you've already put your questions; as you proceed, the number of respondents grows like a snowball.

The drawback with purposive sampling is that you're never quite sure whether the basis for seeing people as 'typical' isn't gradually changing as you work through your sample. While it's a useful sampling technique for many situations, it should be avoided when you're exploring issues arising from changes that happen over the duration of your empirical work, and the members of your sample are differentially involved in, or affected by, the changes. In these circumstances, some people will be less typical than others on some aspects you're investigating, equal on others, and more typical on others again!

When using this method, you should report the possible error sources in your discussion of results. You might particularly want to do this collaboratively, by asking your respondents their own views about how typical they are, and about the assumptions they're making in talking to you.

Quota sampling. Quota sampling involves a choice of respondents who represent the diversity in the population in the same proportions as the diversity itself. You need to know what this diversity looks like before you start; you then continue to select people into subgroups as they become available to you until the quota is achieved. For example, if you knew that

20% of your local government authority's managers had a private-sector job history, and 80% hadn't, and you thought this was relevant to a study of the decision to privatize cleansing department services being made by the local authority, you'd want to represent this diversity by ensuring that the sample you talked to consisted of people from these backgrounds in these proportions.

Alternatively, if you didn't achieve quite the quota required and your sample was large enough, then provided your questions gave answers in a quantitative form, you could choose people in equal proportions, and apply a weight to the results within each subgroup to reflect the population proportion; this can get complicated, though, and you may want to refer to Selltiz *et al.* (1981) for an overview of further particulars.

The main drawback with this method is that, while it splits the sample into subgroups to reflect diversity in the proportion in which it occurs in the population, it doesn't give each person in the population an equal chance of being selected into the sample. You simply bring each person into one or other subgroup until you have the total number of people required by that subgroup, and the people you didn't get round to have no chance of being included. This might distort the conclusions you're seeking to make, due to an uncontrolled or unrealized influence. In our local government example, for instance, suppose you were to bring in respondents on the basis of availability, by working from the more junior managers upwards till your quotas were achieved. But a person's position in a bureaucracy is likely to be related to age, so the people old enough to have had private sector experience would be more likely to be in more senior positions. So you might find yourself introducing a bias due to seniority and age into the 'private-sector-experienced' group without realizing it.

Nonprobability sampling methods have the advantage of flexibility, and are particularly useful in the first, familiarization cycle through the issues you're investigating. They afford a better opportunity for collaboration with your respondents than probability methods, and allow great scope for inference and judgement in interpreting results. You can find a useful presentation of additional forms of nonprobability sampling, and an excellent discussion relating particularly to small samples, in Miles and Huberman (1994).

Probability sampling methods

All of these involve a deliberate and explicit selection of respondents into the sample from the population, made in advance of your data-gathering. The essential thing is to choose sample members at random, so that each population member has an equal chance of being selected, and so that the particular combination of people whom you select into the sample is neither more nor less likely to have been chosen than any other combination. The mechanics of the process are straightforward.

- Decide on your sample size in advance.
- Take your sampling frame (at its simplest, a list of the population) and number each person; note whether the highest number has one digit (a population no larger than nine people!), two digits (maximum 99 people), or three digits (maximum 999).
- Get hold of a set of random number tables (these are published separately, e.g. Murdoch and Barnes (1986), Nelson (1980), White *et al.* (1979) and are reproduced as an appendix in many statistics textbooks); ignore the fact that the numbers are printed in blocks across the page.
- Stick a pin at random into the tables, then move systematically up, down, or across the columns of numbers: focus on every single digit, or every pair of digits, or every triplet of digits, depending on your population size.
- When this is the same as a number you allocated to a person in the sampling frame, choose that person for your sample.
- Continue; if you come across the same number again in the random number table, ignore it and go on to the next
- Stop when you have the sample size that you want.

This procedure lies at the heart of each of the following probability sampling methods.

Simple random sampling. This involves a straightforward sampling frame of all the people in your population (whether this is an organization, department, or section), not classified in any other way. You'll be generalizing the results from your sample on to this population and not beyond it; so, for example, if you decide that you're interested in an issue in which the department is the population, and if you draw your sample within this departmental frame, you can't subsequently generalize any direct conclusions about how people outside the department would have answered your questions. Of course, this isn't a problem: if you know in advance that you want to generalize beyond the department to the organization, make the organization your population and sample within that.

The disadvantage with this arrangement is that you lump everyone in the sample together, without making any further distinctions. If that's what you want, that's fine. Suppose, however, that you're interested in generalizing findings to subgroups of the population as well as to the whole (for example, to see whether males answered consistently differently to females; salaried employees as opposed to wage-earners; managers in production as opposed to managers in marketing, in a study of both functions)?

Stratified random sampling. If so, here's what to do. Divide the population into subgroups on the factor in question, and keep the lists separate in your frame; you then choose subsamples at random, following the above procedure, within each separate list. The sum of each of the subsamples gives you your total sample size. Table 9.1 shows you some examples of stratification.

As you can imagine, it's procedurally important to keep track of the number of people in each subgroup. This is especially so if your design is more ambitious and you're stratifying in more than one way: for example, if you want to contrast the responses of line managers as opposed to managers in specialist functions (a first stratification), and within this, males as opposed to females (second stratification). Table 9.2(a) shows an example of a sampling frame summary (total numbers in the various groupings) for a three-way stratification I once produced for a national study of job satisfaction among Irish police sergeants (Jankowicz and Walsh, 1984).

Stratified random sampling is the most powerful means of generalizing findings based on samples of populations; its disadvantages are ones of sheer practicality. It can be very time-consuming to draw up lists of large numbers of employees, while travelling costs to scattered locations, if it's that sort of project, can be prohibitive. (Remember, you're choosing truly at random from the population: so combinations of locations separated by large distances are as likely to occur as locations next door to each other.)

Cluster sampling. Sometimes called 'multistage sampling', cluster sampling addresses these kinds of issues. Instead of sampling from within each subgroup on a particular stratum, a subset of subgroups is chosen at random and the others are ignored. This subset becomes the sample; additionally, if the numbers of people involved are still too large with respect to the intended sample size, simple random sampling is done within each of the subsets.

This is the most common form of probability sampling. There are technical disadvantages concerned with the efficiency with which your sample data gives you information about the population characteristics when cluster sampling is compared with stratified random sampling, but I would imagine that these factors are likely to be less important to the validity of a management project than the various issues and constraints I reviewed in section 6.2. If you want further particulars on these technical disadvantages, a good review is provided in Selltiz *et al.* (1981).

Table 9.1 Alternative levels of stratification; different cases

A In a study of an entire company, you decide that the company is the population.
Total number of employees (let's say) is 1000; this is your **population**. If you choose 40% of the employees at random to be your **sample**, you end up with 400 people, whose responses you are prepared to generalize directly to all 1000. This is an unstratified random sample.

B If in the same study, you wanted to focus **only** on the salaried staff (of whom there are 300) and ignore the 700 wage-earners.
Total number of salaried employees is 300 people; this is your **population**. If you were to choose 40% of these at random, you'd have a **sample** of 120 people.
Note, you can **only** generalize to the other 280 salaried employees, and not to the 700 wage-earners. It is still an unstratified random sample, but the population is different to Case A above.)

C You're back with the population of Case A, and decide to stratify all 1000 employees on the basis of their salary status, choosing 40% of each group, and drawing at random within each group. The 1000 are your population.

Sampling frame summary	Population	Sample
Salaried employees	300 × 40%	= 120 your first subsample
Wage-earners	700 × 40%	= 280 your second subsample
Total	1000	400 your total sample

The 400 people are now a random sample stratified by salary status.

D You decide to stratify on the basis of a second factor, sex of employee, taking 40% of each subgroup to provide your subsamples. The 1000 are still your population.

Sampling frame summary	Population			Sample		
	Male	Female	total	Male	Female	Total
Salaried employees	270	30	300	108	12	120
Wage-earners	350	350	700	140	140	290
	620	380	1000	248	152	400

You have sampled at random within each subgroup of the sampling frame summary, taking 40% of each subgroup. The 400 people are now a random sample stratified by salary status and by sex. Note how the subgroups add up, as they should, to the appropriate stratum totals shown in Case C. Note also that the 12 female salaried staff subsample is as representative of all the female salaried staff as the 108 male salaried staff subsample is of all the male salaried staff. The fact that there are fewer of them is a property of the population (the regrettable situation in which there are fewer females than males in managerial/professional positions) rather than of the sampling technique.

Table 9.2(a) A sampling frame summary for a stratified random sample with three strata.

The three strata were: type of post (five categories); location (two categories); and length of service (two categories). The two location categories are DMA (Dublin metropolitan area) and Country (Irish Republic beyond Dublin). Titles of some corresponding types of post vary for historical reasons, but 'Station House Officer' in the DMA fulfils the same role as 'Sergeant in Charge' in the Country; 'Section Sergeant' in the DMA fulfils the same role as 'Duty Sergeant' in the Country. Thus all categories of type of post are replicated in both DMA and Country. The numbers in each cell of the table stand for the total number of respondents in the population in each combination of the three strata; the full sampling frame had that many names from which to sample, in each cell. A sample of 20% of each cell was drawn at random. Data correct as of January, 1983. (Reproduced by kind permission of Deputy Commissioner P.J. Moran, An Garda Siochana.)

Type of post	Station House Officer	Sergeant in Charge	Section Sergeant	Duty Sergeant	Detective Sergeant	Detective Sergeant	Clerical Post	Clerical Post	Others	Others	Total
Location	DMA	Country	DMA	Country	DMA	Country	DMA	Country	DMA	Country	
Length of service as a sergeant:											
0 to 11 years	44	211	135	158	145	60	68	14	57	55	947
>11 years	67	306	49	94	23	26	46	21	41	104	777
Total	111	517	184	252	168	86	114	35	98	159	1724

Table 9.2(b) A record of the sample drawn, and of returns received, of the postal questionnaire used in the study

The three figures in each cell stand for: questionnaires despatched – questionnaires returned – returns as a percentage of despatches. Three points should be noted.

(a) Sampling always involves rounding errors: it is impossible to take a fraction of a person into a sample! So 20% of 44 Station House Officers in the DMA with 0–11 years of service is 8.8 people. (b) When 'rounding to the nearest person' to achieve the sample proportion of 20%, it was decided to move up or down to allow for the expectation that some subgroups would, because of pressures of work, be less likely to return questionnaires than others (hence 10 people sampled in this instance, rather than nine): a crude procedure to the purist, better handled in one of the three ways described in the text. (c) It is good practice to have a table like that shown below, to report return rates and provide a summary for the discussion of possible error factors arising from differential returns across subgroups.

Type of post	Station House Officer	Sergeant in Charge	Section Sergeant	Duty Sergeant	Detective Sergeant		Clerical Post		Others		Total
Location	DMA	Country	DMA	Country	DMA	Country	DMA	Country	DMA	Country	Country
Length of service as a sergeant:											
0 to 11 years	10–7–70	44–40–91	27–16–59	32–20–63	29–7–24	12–9–75	13–9–66	3–2–61	11–3–27	11–10–91	192–123–64
>11 years	13–9–69	76–62–82	10–6–60	19–14–74	5–2–40	5–2–40	9–7–78	4–4–100	8–1–13	21–12–57	170–119–70
Total	23–16–70	120–102–85	37–22–59	51–34–65	34–9–26	17–11–65	22–16–73	7–6–86	19–4–21	32–22–69	362–242–67

Both parts of this table are taken from a job analysis study of police sergeants in An Garda Siochana, the Irish Police Force: Jankowicz and Walsh (1984).

A final thought: the census

If you'd like another statement of these sampling methods, with their advantages and disadvantages, you'll find a handy, four-page summary in Miller (1977); a good overview is in Hemry (1990). In conclusion, it's worth remembering that some topics can be handled well by putting your questions to everyone in the organization. Some topics in the small-business sector, and case studies of individual departments taken as the focus for your project, can fall under this heading. In this situation, you're in effect carrying out a census of the entire population, rather than sampling, and again, while validity is a matter of appropriate technique in asking your questions, generalizability beyond the boundaries of your organization or department is a matter for logical inference and reasoning, where the scope of your project involves comparisons with other organizations or departments.

9.3 THE PRACTICALITIES OF DESIGN

As you can see, one of the most important design aspects of your empirical work concerns the decision you make on which is your population, which is your sample of that population, and which other populations are involved in the thesis you wish to establish. These decisions depend very much on your precise topic, argument, and thesis, and you'll want to involve other people in discussing your design with this in mind: certainly your sponsor, and probably your tutor. Moreover, if you've accepted my comments on project work as a collaborative endeavour (the 'New Paradigm' view expressed in sections 6.3 and 6.4), then you'll want to involve the people you'll be surveying – the people in the population concerned – in these design decisions.

Whichever approach you take, you are likely to encounter the following practical questions.

Sample size

How many people should you have in your sample? The answer to this question varies depending on the kind of question which you want to ask, and the form of sampling you adopt. In the case of accidental sampling, the pressures of the situation result in a total 'by default'; if you intend to work with a purposive sample, the sample size will be determined by your feeling that you have approached all the relevant people, a feeling reinforced by the advice you're given by tutor, sponsor, and respondents. If you're using one of the probability sampling methods, then it is possible to determine the sample size statistically, bearing in mind the proportion of the population to sample in order to achieve a given level of accuracy; there is a good review of the issues involved in Sudman (1976), particularly in Chapters 1 and 5.

Reading this, you will discover that the accuracy of your results will depend much more on the variety of different groups and subgroups in your population, and how much time and effort you can afford to spend, rather than on size. So, as a start, look at what, say, 10% of your population would look like. If you've only ten people in the population, the resulting single respondent is unlikely to be representative of the ten, whatever sampling method you adopt; at the other extreme, if the population is 1000, then you're very likely to be in business. However, this does depend on your design. For example, if you're dealing with issues which incline you to stratify your sample in several different ways (by level in the organization and by type of job, say), you may well discover that there are few, or indeed no, people in some of the combinations of level and job type in which you're interested, even in organizations with relatively large numbers of employees!

The simplest way round this problem is to collapse categories in one or more of your strata. (Instead of working with six job levels and ten different types of job, in other words, find a rationale in which it makes sense to classify job levels into three rather than six, and job types into four rather than ten, for example.) Alternatives might be to ignore categories with small numbers of people, combining them into a single 'other' category on the stratum in question; to cluster-sample from only those categories which have large numbers of people; or indeed to eschew probability sampling altogether, and to use quota sampling or purposive sampling approaches instead. You'll find a good discussion of some of these alternatives, with an excellent illustrative case study, in Reeves and Harper (1981b). Notice, though, that the inferences that you can draw from your data – the information you can extract – will be subtly different, depending on the actual alternative you choose.

Non-response

'What do I do if I planned to see 25% of the sales staff and only 10% had time to respond: won't this bias my comparison with the 25% of the technical staff I planned for, all of whom provided me with data?' In a word, 'yes'. But, depending on how you're asking your questions, there are three ways round the problem.

■ In a stratified random sample in which your data consist of numbers and percentages, it might be possible to weight your results in making comparisons between disproportionately responding groups, as mentioned previously.

- As you'll see in Part Three, if you're using postal questionnaires or planned interview schedules, these should always involve a chase-up stage, in which you ask people again for their help. This works, though never completely, and only if you've planned the time to do so!
- Alternatively, if your population is large enough, it is good practice to have a reserve sample, chosen in the same way as your main sample, from which you can randomly substitute people to approach.

It also depends on the kinds of questions you're asking. Other factors, such as acceptability to management, costs of implementation, the existence of powerful influence groups, or sheer practicality, may have a greater bearing on the chances of your conclusions being accepted as sensible, than minor variations in sampling accuracy.

In all cases, however, your procedure is straightforward: try and be as accurate as you can; report the deviation of your actual response rates from the scheme which you planned (a good place to do so is in the table in which you present your sampling scheme: see Table 9.2(b)); and discuss the kinds of bias to which, you feel, the deviation has given rise.

under-graduate

Interpreting your data must **always** be a matter of presenting and discussing the possible sources of error, as well as the more direct inferences and conclusions which the data suggest. If you look ahead to the discussion of project presentation in Chapter 14, you'll notice that so many of the errors of reasoning which merit divine retribution are those in which error sources have been ignored; this seems to be a particular problem at undergraduate level, and especially when considering sampling errors.

MBA

While this sort of mistake is less common, you're liable to make others, arising from the sheer complexity of what you're doing. Consider: you're working with more than one issue; it's conceivable that you'll have to ask different kinds of questions with different kinds of people for each separate issue, so that, in effect, you may find yourself handling several different populations as you apply several different methods and techniques (a survey; a number of case studies; a set of key informant interviews) to address all the issues. Sorting out which are your populations, which are your samples, and which are the outside groups to which you want to generalize will need a clear head in the first place; and keeping track of different sources of error, arising from variations in return rate, will require discipline in reporting in the second.

Combining sampling methods plus an alternative

all

'I know what I need to do; but none of the schemes which you describe seems to fit my situation. Ideally, I need to do a mixture of all of them.' Fine, and why not? If you're clear enough about your situation to be able to recognize that, then only a little further thought will suggest the particular combination of methods to adopt.

Some common combinations are as follows.

- Accidental sampling as you become aware of issues to explore, followed by a systematic slice through the organization to investigate the issues in detail.
- Purposive sampling, especially key informant technique to help you to identify issues, followed by a quota sample of people who may have systematically different views or perspectives on the issues.
- A key informant sample to identify issues, with a horizontal slice of relevant managers, and perhaps a stratified random sample of their subordinates categorized into departmental subgroups.
- Some form of purposive sample, followed by a stratified random sample of employees categorized into managerial versus operative subgroups: this is a common pattern for many undergraduate, questionnaire-based survey projects.

under-graduate

Selltiz *et al.* (1981) also suggest cluster sampling (e.g. to select particular departments) with the advantages of representativeness that this brings, followed by a quota sample (e.g. within each department, stratified by role or position on issues of interest) with the advantages of economy of effort which quota sampling permits.

all

You might like to read their discussion on this theme, of combining probability and non-probability samples. There is also a good discussion of some of the factors to bear in mind when designing empirical work with managers, in Reeves and Harper (1981a).

Finally, you should know that there is one special situation when, in order to be representative, you do not sample within a population at all; instead, you replicate positions along one or more issues or variables. This is when you use the comparative case study method and the details are given in section 10.2.

9.4 IN CONCLUSION: TIMETABLING FOR EMPIRICAL WORK

This chapter started with a reminder of the complexities involved in the management world you're exploring, and a reassurance that this complexity can be simplified, provided you adopt a straightforward approach to the planning of your empirical work. Once you have decided on a design, and chosen the methods and techniques which you'll use (see Chapter 10 and the remainder), all that's left to do is to prepare a data-gathering timetable and stick to it.

If you've followed the guidelines outlined in section 5.2, you'll already have an outline timetable for your project, at the very least as a list of dates and deadlines recorded in your diary. Flesh out this outline in an initial approximation as far as you can, bearing in mind the need to spread your attention evenly over the major issues you've identified during the time that will be available to you. As you begin your data collection, you'll identify further questions to ask and issues to explore; you'll also want to go over familiar territory in more detail, as I suggested in sections 6.3 and 6.4; these will be unpredictable at the outset, so be prepared to amend the timetable from time to time.

How can you plan for the unpredictable? It helps if you can think of the empirical phase of your project work as progressing through four stages: preliminary analysis (often known as the 'pilot stage'), main analysis, synthesis, and implementation, for each main issue which you're addressing. Table 9.3 shows what's involved at each stage, and reveals that the process is periodic: within your work on each major issue, there are stages where your attention expands as you explore all the ramifications in question; and there are times where your attention contracts, as you summarize what you have learnt and pause to take breath before tackling the next stage involved. Martin and Spear (1985) who are the source of this table, point out that you should always plan to 'stop the expansion just before it gets too big to handle', and that you shouldn't expand your attention again until 'you feel you have your information well under control'. The preliminary analysis is the stage at which you think carefully about matters of design; the main analysis, where you put the design into effect.

MBA

It is likely that your project work will involve you in empirical work on several major issues, so that the process described in Table 9.3 is cyclic as well as periodic: that is, you'll be repeating all the stages of Table 9.3 once for each of the major issues you address. It is very likely, as I mentioned at the start of this chapter, that you'll find yourself working on different issues at the same time, being at different stages with each. This usually happens because you're waiting for people relevant to an issue to become available to talk to you, waiting on questionnaire returns, and the like. Keep track of where you've got to in your diary!

under-graduate

In your own case, you're more likely to have taken on a project in which there is only one main issue under investigation, as you'll recall from my comments on research and project methods in sections 6.3 and 6.4. And so you're more likely to go through the cycle just once.

all

Take up your project diary, and, as soon as it's feasible:

■ Make a note of the key issues that your thesis suggests may be relevant (remember, you've already thought about the thesis and written it down somewhere in your diary: see section 5.4).

Table 9.3 Expansion and contraction phases involved in project work

Preliminary analysis (pilot stage)	Opening up the issue Looking at associated issues Identifying stakeholders Testing other questions to ask	Expansion
Main analysis	Following up leads Collecting data Searching for alternative viewpoints	Expansion
	Selecting key aspects Summarizing findings Relating them to what's already known	Contraction
Synthesis	Generating alternative courses of action	Expansion
	Selecting the best next step	Contraction
Implementation	Contacting people involved in the next step Examining alternative time schedules	Expansion
	Selecting a particular plan for the next step Taking the next step	Contraction
Choice	Completion of empirical stage, or addressing next major issue: back to	Contraction
Preliminary analysis	Above	Expansion

After Martin and Spear (1984)

■ If you're an undergraduate, and in a position to do a study based on the exploration of variables rather than issues, state the hypothesis or hypotheses which you'll need to investigate in order to establish your thesis. (See sections 6.3 and 6.4.) | **under-graduate**

■ If you haven't already done so, begin your reading plan, preferably in the shape of a relevance tree (see section 8.2), and continue to make notes on the reading you do. | **all**

- Sketch out a rough design, as suggested by your thesis, if you haven't already done so in preparing your proposal to your tutor, being ready to add to the design and alter it substantially after you've joined your organization and familiarized yourself with the latter through direct experience. At the very least, list the various design conditions suggested by your thesis, and draw up a tentative sampling scheme which seems appropriate to them.

- Preview the remaining chapters, and make a tentative choice of the method you're going to use, giving a little thought to the associated techniques. Then read the appropriate material on techniques in Chapters 11 to 13, and commit the implications to your diary in the form of a precise timetable for your data-collection.

You can expect to come back and expand, or develop, several of these items as time goes on. The issues will become amplified, the reading plan will extend, and the design become more clearly specified or amended in the light of your growing familiarity with the data that begin to emerge.

Methods and techniques $\boxed{10}$

People use methods like pilots fly planes. A largish minority, usually those who haven't done a project before, view their data-gathering as a matter of barnstorming, flying by the seat of their pants. 'We'll take her up for a spin old boy, it's a piece of cake really, nothing to it.' In other words, they may underestimate the technical requirements of the method or methods which they plan to adopt. An interview, for example, is just a conversation with a purpose: and we all conduct conversations every day, don't we? A questionnaire is just a list of questions to which we want answers: what could be simpler than that?

A smaller minority, usually those who've done one or two academic projects before, behave more like the pilot of an aerodynamically unstable, high-performance jet (the kind which drops out of the sky like a brick when its computer system fails). Seduced by technicalities, they worry about details, to the detriment of the relevance and sense of the questions they ask or the information they obtain. Is the reading level of the questions, as measured by their meaningfulness, concreteness, and imagery content, sufficiently matched to the comprehension of the respondents? Is it really permissible to calculate the average of a set of rating scales, since ratings represent ordinal rather than interval levels of numbering? You get the idea.

The remainder come somewhere between the two extremes: they follow a safe but sensible flight procedure. My purpose in this chapter is to provide you with a flight-plan: a set of guidelines by which to approach the methods and techniques which you'll be using. Firstly, we need to clarify terms, particularly those two words, 'method' and 'technique', and explore the distinction between qualitative and quantitative techniques of analysis. Secondly, I'll describe the methods available to you, and outline the circumstances in which you're likely to choose one rather than another. Thirdly, the guidelines themselves. Regardless of the method or technique which you're using, there is a set of activities which you'll have to undertake if you're to be successful, and I'll present these in general terms, going on to use them as a framework for the material on techniques in the chapters that follow.

10.1 METHODS AND TECHNIQUES: DEFINITIONS

In our context, a method is a **systematic and orderly approach taken towards the collection of data so that information can be obtained from those data**. There's a difference between the two, as you'll recall from section 8.3: data are raw, specific, undigested and therefore largely meaningless; information, in contrast, is what you get when data have been arranged in such a way that uncertainty is lessened, queries resolved, and questions answered. Everything you do in your empirical work should be directed to just one end: gathering and presenting data from which the information can be easily and simply derived.

Several different methods are commonly used in business and management project work, and your choice would vary according to the nature and scope of your topic and thesis, the sources of data you're using, the purposes you have in gathering data, the amount of control you're prepared to exert in obtaining these data, and the assumptions you're prepared to make in analysing them. The main methods available to you are as follows.

- **Archival method**, in which you direct your questions at people and at written sources, concerning issues and events in the past in order to understand the present and predict the future, using either historical review or biographical analysis.
- **The case-study**, in which you explore issues both in the present and in the past, as they affect a relatively complete organizational unit (single case study) or group of organizational units (comparative case study), and in which you look to the future by means of the recommendations you make.
- **The survey**, in which you direct your questions at relatively large groups of people, in order to explore issues largely in the present.
- **The field experiment**, in which you identify the relative importance of one or more variables in situations (and these are limited in business project work: see Chapter 6!), where a focus on variables rather than issues makes sense.

Techniques, in contrast, are **particular, step-by-step procedures which you can follow in order to gather data, and analyse them for the information they contain**. As Bennett (1986) suggests, they tell you **how** to do something rather than **what** you're doing, or **why** you're doing it.

There are many techniques relevant in project work. In the remaining chapters, you'll find the most relevant, grouped under the following headings.

- **Semi-structured, open-ended techniques**: the conversation, the individual interview, the key informant interview, and the focus group.
- **Fully structured techniques**: the structured questionnaire, and the structured face-to-face interview, together with material on postal and telephone variants.
- **Additional techniques**: the repertory grid, attitude scaling, and the observational techniques of structured observation and the field experiment.

In looking at these lists of methods and techniques, what is important is that you don't regard the more structured techniques and the methods with which they're associated as 'better' or in some way more 'scientific' simply because they're quantitative, or because many studies go from the qualitative to the quantitative as understanding progresses. As you'll recall from Chapter 6, everything depends on the level of understanding which is possible in the management environment, and structure and quantification are, in themselves, no guarantee of freedom from error. In dealing with unstructured, conversational interview technique, for example, Mishler (1986: 29) makes the same point when he says:

> Alternatives to the standard approach, like unstructured interviewing, tend to be viewed as faulted variants . . . I am arguing, instead, that the standard survey interview is itself essentially faulted and that it therefore cannot serve as the ideal ideological model against which to assess other approaches.

A **qualitative** approach has the following features (Miles and Huberman, 1994: 6).

- It depends on a deep familiarization with a normal or typical real-life situation.
- It involves you in the search for significant themes running through disparate sources.
- It results in a holistic understanding of the situation: of the factors involved and how they interrelate, identifying the less obvious issues as well as those which initially grab your attention.
- It demands that you take your informants seriously in their own language, and from their own point of view, suspending your own personal and project-related preconceptions while you're gathering data, no matter how legitimate those preconceptions might be.
- It seeks to discover how people understand the situation or issue you are investigating, and how that understanding guides their actions.

■ It seeks to develop knowledge by linking the accounts people give to an underlying body of theory.

A **quantitative** approach is complementary. Proceeding from the positivist assumption that if something exists, it exists in some degree, and can therefore be numerically measured, it is characterized by:

■ Involving you in concentrated attention on a limited number of variables and constants which are important to you and which are usually expressed in the language of your own investigation.
■ A search for the significance of relative proportions, in order to identify what is more important or significant and what is less so in the issue which you are exploring.
■ An attempt to understand the ways in which selected factors in a situation are structured or interrelated, in importance or precedence.
■ Abstraction from repeated single observations, in which the meaning or significance of data arises from some aggregation, average, range, or comparison rather than from the individual data points themselves.

Neither approach is best. The 'best' method is the one that is most appropriate to the kinds of questions you wish to ask at the time, in the sort of environment and with the sort of thesis which you're advocating. Often, you'll find that you can combine the qualitative with the quantitative, taking the view that the two approaches are mutually complementary rather than exclusive (see Jones (1988) for the argument in detail, and Siehl and Martin (1988) for an interesting case example taken from the study of organizational culture). Horses for courses.

As we're considering definitions and usages, you might find it helpful to note the following in passing: a **datum is** the result of a single observation, while **data are** what you get when you repeat the observation or make several different observations. 'Data' is the plural of 'datum'; so it's incorrect to say, for example, 'my data has been arranged in tabular form'. In a similar vein, you might note that 'methodology' isn't just a high-powered word for 'methods'. **Methodology** is the analysis of, and rationale for, the particular method or methods used in a given study, and in that type of study in general. So, if your regulations require you to provide a section in your project labelled 'methodology', you're being required to provide a rationale or argument for the approach you adopted to the data, as well as a simple statement of the methods that constituted that approach.

10.2 CHOOSING AND COMBINING METHODS, QUALITATIVE AND QUANTITATIVE

Other than the general comments made in section 9.1 on the matching of designs to methods, and the comments I made in defining the different methods in section 10.1 above, there is no straightforward decision rule which allows you to choose one method for one set of circumstances, and another for another. As you can infer from the discussion, many different factors influence your choice. Moreover, you might find yourself using more than one method or technique, in combination, either because your design calls for it, or because you want to use the results from one method to cross-check the results from another, an approach known as '**triangulation**'. The rationale for triangulation is expressed well by Kane, who represents archival review, questionnaires, interviews, and participant observation as potentially overlapping in scope:

> If you had to stake your life on which of these is likely to represent the most accurate, complete research information, you would choose the centre [of the overlap] in which you got the information through interviews and questionnaire, reinforced it by observation, and checked it through documentary analysis. . . . Here, you are getting not only what people say they do and what you see them doing, but also what they are recorded as doing.
>
> (Kane 1985: 51)

The purpose of this section is to outline some of the advantages and disadvantages of each method, and to describe some common combinations, with a few words on the techniques which apply. Your best approach would be to treat the material as a set of general suggestions, and take advice whenever you're in doubt about which approach is most appropriate. The source should be your tutor or sponsor as usual; however, you should also look at written accounts of method and procedures which appear in the literature you have reviewed. I don't say this lightly. One of the reasons for reviewing other people's work in your field is to discover how they resolved problems of methods, techniques and design in investigating issues similar to your own. If in doubt, then, follow the current practice as written up in the journals and books which describe empirical work done in similar circumstances.

However, always remember that you use more than one method or technique in order to triangulate or develop earlier findings; resist the temptation to take on too many different techniques simply because it sounds impressive in your initial proposal document (see section 3.4) or on the contents page of your project document.

Archival methods

Historical review. The purpose of historical review method is to describe what happened in the past, sometimes for its own sake, but more commonly as used in business and management projects, in order to illuminate the present. It is particularly useful for familiarization purposes, and to trace the development of the issues which you have decided to focus on in presenting your topic. The importance of an issue is due as much to its provenance as to its content, and a longitudinal approach can be very revealing. The historical review is particularly important in projects on financial and accounting subjects, in tracing the current health of an organization, product, or market from the financial and sales records available to you, and, in the sense that it familiarizes you with an issue, can be a useful source of hunches or more formal hypotheses which you subsequently explore with different methods, the case study in particular.

You proceed by 'interrogating the data', putting questions to the text as I've described in the checklist in section 8.3. You may find that some of the very specific techniques and data-sources used in archival work are especially helpful to you: Orbell (1987) is good on this theme, and a must for anyone doing a project with a financial topic in which you need to obtain historical data from organizations other than your own.

You would carry out an analysis of historical financial performance using the same indices that you use for evaluating contemporary business performance in case study analysis, and Table 10.1 will remind you of some of them. But to reduce the analysis of archival material to a set of ratios, even when dealing with financial issues, would be to ignore the rich context of political, social, tactical, strategic and even ethical discourse within which the data were originally produced. Within this context lie issues and themes of importance to the organization as it is today, and these can be uncovered using techniques of **hermeneutic interpretation**. This approach, defined as the identification and interpretation of meanings expressed and embodied in a text by detailed study of the text-in-context requires you to:

■ understand the meanings expressed in individual texts (or indeed object or event);
■ identify subthemes;
■ identify clusters of themes across texts;
■ triangulate with other data, especially documentary;
■ check validity and reliability through collaboration with other people;
■ place the themes into their organizational context;
■ sample key documents systematically, preparing a case report.

Table 10.1 Financial analysis: some commonly used ratios

Liquidity ratios	
Current ratio:	Current assets/current liabilities
Acid test:	(Current assets – stocks)/current liabilities
Profitability ratios	
Gross profit %:	((Sales revenue – cost of sales) × 100)/sales revenue
Net profit %:	((Net profit before tax and depreciation) × 100)/ sales revenue
Return on total assets:	(Net profit × 100)/total assets
Return on capital employed:	(Net profit before tax and interest × 100)/total capital employed
Return on owners' equity:	(Net profit before tax × 100)/equity capital
Share and dividend performance	
Dividend cover:	Profits available for distribution/dividend paid
Price–Earnings ratio:	Market price per share/earnings per share
Funds management	
Debtors' collection period:	(Debtors × 365 days)/sales revenue
Average payment period:	(Creditors × 365 days)/purchases
Stock turnover:	Cost of sales/closing stock
Ability to borrow	
Debt ratio:	(Current liabilities × 100)/total assets
Capital gearing ratio:	(Fixed interest capital × 100)/shareholders' funds, where fixed interest capital = (long-term debt + debentures + overdraft + short-term loans – current cash assets)

After Lancaster and Massingham (1988: 309)

The main problem you will encounter in using historical methods arises because human memory isn't a literal recording medium like an audio or video tape. People are selective in what they notice, have active memorization mechanisms, and are motivated in what they will subsequently recall. Furthermore, they make mistakes! You're advised to use at least two sources of data for information which is crucial to your argument, or which is important in compiling an official record of what has taken place. You can usually cross-check one written source against another, a written source against the results of an interview, and the results of one interview against those of another.

Biographical analysis. On the other hand, there is often great significance in what people remember, and in the shape of the story which they seek to tell, whether these agree or disagree with others' accounts; particularly if you see what you're doing as an exercise in biography, either personal or organizational. Davies (1992) provides an interesting rationale and case study of the value of personal biographies in understanding the historical patterns of behaviour which influence current performance and in providing an account of the way in which personal values underlie, form, and conflict with organizational values; or, as Farrell (1992: 219) puts it in her account of how women managers construe issues of quality, 'in all of these biographical stories the personal and organizational themes are inextricably intertwined'.

Take care in accepting the status of your data-source as a guarantee of his or her accuracy of judgement and recall. The fact that a retired Colonel is the village squire and knows the district intimately, is, for example, no guarantee of the accuracy of his analysis of the reasons why a local stately home and its associated theme park have failed to attract foreign visitors. To be told, as was a student of mine doing a leisure management project, that 'foreigners don't like theme parks so they've never visited ours', flies in the face of common sense: hadn't he heard of Disneyland or the Epcot Centre, for example? It was too late to go back and ask him, but, as often happens when common sense is offended, further, more systematic data collection was stimulated. In this case, data towards a fruitful comparison of the factors involved in developing the grounds of an English stately home into a theme park, with those factors involved in developing a theme park on a greenfield site. While not primarily a biographical study, biographical data were there for the taking, and the Colonel's personal history had a lot to do with the way he interpreted the strategic choices facing him.

As with historical review, biographical analysis can be made to serve two distinct functions. The first would be to provide you with an 'official record': the best account you can devise, despite human frailty, of what 'actually happened', with the results of individual conversations and semi-structured interview techniques cross-checked against archival written records where possible, and **content analysis** would be the technique to use: see section 11.2. The second would be to provide an account of how and why a person or group of people saw events, especially personal experiences, as they did, to provide you with an insight into values, motives and aspirations; in this case, **hermeneutic analysis** would be the appropriate technique. Forster (1994) is a good introduction to hermeneutic techniques as used in historical review method.

You need to be clear about which it is that you're doing at any one time. You will also find that triangulation, a record of the intentions of your data sources, their representativeness, and the internal consistency of the story they tell, are useful safeguards of the validity of the information you receive. See Aspinwall (1992) on validity in biographical analysis, and while you're at it, it would be very useful to read the entire special issue of *Management Education and Development*, from which most of my references in this section are taken.

The usual way of presenting information obtained by techniques associated with the archival method is in the form of a connected account, using tables and diagrams to illustrate the argument which you wish to make. Chapters 5 and 6 of Miles and Huberman (1994) are a very rich source of tables, diagrams and displays well suited to biographical analysis in particular, although they don't provide you with any information on one particularly useful technique, the repertory grid. This is described in Chapter 13 below, and you'll find that Jones (1992) offers an excellent example of a related technique, the change grid, in a study which used biography to understand issues of personal and management development in the health service.

The account must involve a critical appraisal of alternative and competing explanations for the events and issues explored: you're not simply describing what happened. Finally, you need to explain how your review is relevant to the current issues which make up your topic at the start, and present the implications for current practice, throughout and in conclusion.

The case study

Case study method is used when your thesis focuses on a set of issues in a single organization, and you want to identify the factors involved in an in-depth study of the organization or (to choose a smaller unit of analysis), a single department within it. Alternatively, if you have identified a number of variables whose importance to the present organization you wish to explore, it's possible to carry out a comparative case study, in which you ask the same questions in several related organizations as well as your own.

Yin (1994) compares the case study to the experiment, and provides three alternative situations in which you might choose to use the former method:

■ If you're following a theory which specifies a particular set of outcomes in particular circumstances, and use a case study of an organization which finds itself in those circumstances for a critical test of the theory and its applicability to the organization.

■ In order to identify the distinguishing characteristics of an extreme or rare situation in which an organization or organizational unit might find itself. You'd be concerned to compare and contrast, and you'd have to be careful to do more than simply describe.

■ If ever you're given access to an organization, or a process within an organization, which has rarely, if ever, been studied. You need to be careful with this rationale for using a case study, since business organizations operate in a rapidly changing environment and you could argue that every situation is new, and poses unique problems that would repay your study. A useful touchstone would be to ask yourself (and/or your tutor and sponsor) whether the circumstances are sufficiently interesting that something important will be learnt from your study.

In the comparative case study, Yin points out that the design logic is somewhat similar to the logic involved in experimental methods, and different from survey methods in particular. The purpose of your data-gathering in a comparative case is not to **sample** different organizations because you wish to generalize your findings to all other organizations of the same type (as you would do in a survey); it is to **replicate**, that is, to compare the organization you're studying with others in a systematic way, exploring different stances to the issues you are examining, or examining different levels of the variables involved. See Miles and Huberman (1994: 173–6) for more details of this distinction.

My own MBA students have occasionally given me a hard time over this, but a distinction there is! The point is that the organizations in a study using survey method are selected into a sample to be **representative of some population** (see section 9.2); in contrast, organizations are chosen for a comparative case study to be **representative of different possible positions or stances**, regardless of the relative frequency of these stances in the population.

For instance, a manager in a local education authority may have a thesis that information technology will only be utilized extensively by LEAs if administrative as well as educational uses are found for the equipment involved. He or she would choose several authorities, not for the purpose of sampling the range of authorities so that the conclusions can be generalized to all, but in order to examine the thesis systematically: by conducting looking at authorities in which computers are used purely for administration, purely for educational use, and for both purposes together. There may be 200 LEAs which use information technology only for administrative purposes, 400 only for educational purposes, and 600 for both; you are representing the different stances, and obtaining meaningful findings about them, if you carry out a comparative case study of two LEAs of each kind, even though you are not representing the population as you would if you had done a survey with a stratified sample of 20, 40, and 60 respectively. Comparative case studies are not surveys.

The data in a case study are obtained largely through a review of written records, and by means of interview technique, and in this sense, the case study resembles the archival method; where it differs is that direct observation techniques and **stakeholder analysis** (Burgoyne, 1994), would also be available to you. It is unusual to combine the case study with other methods; although, if you have the time and are particularly interested in adopting a comparative approach in order to compare and contrast the same issues in different organizations, you may find yourself using a technique taken from structured interview or questionnaire work.

The method will involve you in at least four stages of work. Bennett (1986) lists them as follows:

1. Determining the present situation.
2. Gathering information about the background to the present situation.
3. Gathering more specific data to test alternative hypotheses about the important factors in the present situation.
4. Presenting recommendations for action; and, where you have the time and the power to have influenced events, evaluating the outcomes of these recommendations after they have been implemented.

Yin (1994) offers a similar list which emphasizes the need to be clear about the unit of analysis (the level at which you're conducting the case study), while Hartley (1994) provides a reminder that your approach in a case study should be based on a theoretical stance, about which you should be explicit: call this the prologue to step 1, in the list given above.

The great advantage of the case study over other methods is that it attempts to be comprehensive, and involves you in describing and analysing the full richness and variety of events and issues in the organization or department in question. Richness and variety, however, will involve you in the full messiness and complications which arise in the real situation which you're describing, as I outlined in section 6.2: which is why a sampling approach which seeks to generalize conclusions as if conditions were identical in other organizations isn't possible.

A difficulty with this method, then, is that you lay your design open to the influence and interruptions arising from day-to-day events to a somewhat greater extent than with the other methods, and you might care to review section 6.3 for ways of handling this situation. The need to use multiple sources of evidence to check out and confirm initial conclusions; the need to manage and maintain a growing database; and the need to construct an inferential chain from thesis, via database, to evidence and final conclusions, are all emphasized by Yin (1994), whose brief but comprehensive guide to case study research is highly recommended to anyone choosing this method.

It also helps if you have a clear idea of the way in which you intend to present your information. The outcomes of case studies used as a **project or research method** are usually presented in narrative and tabular form, according to a structured plan which recapitulates, in greater detail, the stages you went through in doing the work. A good way of getting a feel for this structure is to consider the way in which you normally work up and present a case study used **for teaching purposes** as part of your taught course, since, in effect, this is the kind of structure which your examiner will be seeking to apply in reading your work. Table 10.2 presents one set of headings which are commonly used by students to present their analysis of a classroom case study; at this stage in your programme, you should be familiar with these headings or something equivalent to them. Chapter 7 of Miles and Huberman (1994) suggests a variety of graphical displays which you might find useful in reporting case study results.

If you're following an undergraduate programme, your exposure to the case method in teaching may be somewhat limited, particularly if you haven't yet done much in the field of strategic management or business policy. You might look at any of the following collections of case studies to familiarize yourself with the kind of information which cases present to their readers; on reflection though, students at any level might want to glance at them as examples of analytic approach and reporting style. Doswell and Nailon (1976) address problems in hotel management, arranged functionally; O'Cinneide (1986) covers the range of organiz- ations from small-business start-ups to existing, mature businesses, and takes enterprise, growth and change as his focus. Tyson and Kakabadse (1987) confine themselves to human resource issues at strategic and operational level in a variety of organizations, while Gowler *et al.* (1993) focus on organizational behaviour in general. Boisot (1994) contains four fascinating case studies describing the problem of governance in the post-command economies of eastern Europe and China, written in several different styles. There is a good discussion of case study as a research method in Hartley (1994). Finally, you'll find an account of analysis techniques in the marketing context in Baker (1976), and a procedural guide to case study presentations in Lancaster and Massingham (1988).

The survey method

In contrast to historical review, the survey method draws most of its data from the present. You carry out a survey in order to establish people's views of what they think, believe, value or feel, in order to discover these views for their own sake, or to support an argument that you're presenting, sampling a population of potential respondents in order to generalize conclusions more widely. It's perfectly feasible to carry out a

Table 10.2 One set of standard headings used in the presentation of case study analyses in classroom situations

Where do they come from?	Outline the history and background of the organization or department involved in the case
How did they get here?	What goals, policies, strategies and actions led up to the present situation?
What led them astray?	What constraints and difficulties got in their way, and how did they handle them?
Where are they now?	What is the current situation, and what major issues present themselves?
Where could they go to?	What alternative courses of action are available?
Where do they want to go to?	What course of action is currently being contemplated by the organization?
Where ought they to go to?	What course of action is optimal, bearing in mind the trade-offs involved? How does this compare with the course of action being contemplated?
Where will they go to?	Given the trade-offs and constraints, what course of action do you recommend?
How will they get there?	What needs to be implemented, with what existing and new resources?
How can they get lost?	Since constraints exist and trade-offs must be made, what major problem sources or pitfalls exist?
How will they know they've arrived?	What are the criteria for success, how will they be recognized, and how can they be applied?

business and management project, at any level, by using survey method alone, without combining it with other methods; however, in some projects, the historical survey, a biographical analysis, or perhaps a brief case study, form a precursor which generates hypotheses or identifies issues which you investigate with a larger group of respondents by means of the survey method itself.

Surveys are particularly useful when you want to contact relatively large numbers of people to obtain data on the same issue or issues, often by posing the same questions to all. You'd use one of the many techniques associated with the survey method in situations in which either the relative frequency with which certain views are held is informative (as in the structured interview or questionnaire), or in which particular perspectives arising from different expertise bases contribute to a picture of comparisons and contrasts (as in the less structured, key informant interviews).

The word 'survey' always indicates human respondents: your basic data are obtained by talking to people, either face-to-face, by means of the telephone, or by written questionnaire. And this gives rise to the main problem associated with survey method: you're dealing with verbal reports, either oral or written, and before you can begin interpreting them, you're limited to the data which people are able and willing to report in the first place. Different interview and questionnaire techniques involve different ways of controlling or allowing for this source of error, but, to a degree, you have to take people at their word, even when you're holding one interview to cross-check what another interviewee said! Ultimately, you have to ask yourself if what you have heard sounds genuine and 'rings true', and look for non-survey methods (archival review, structured observation) to verify your conclusions.

You present your information in a narrative report, supported numerically and graphically, with the main points of each table or figure being stated in words immediately after it. A connected account is then used to summarize the information from a group of tables or diagrams which you have presented on a particular issue or theme.

The field experiment

You would carry out a field experiment if you were sufficiently familiar with the situation you were studying, and the events involved, to be able to identify variables whose impact on each other you would observe. You would do so in order to arrive at an explanation of the events, and possibly in order to contribute to a more general theory of such events.

As you will have gathered from Chapter 6, I'm not convinced that there are many situations in which you are likely to use this method. However, I've included this section for two reasons. First, there is no doubt that some undergraduate projects (particularly those in the human resource field) which confine attention to a single issue, usually professional, taken independently from the usual flow of organizational events, can base themselves almost entirely on this method. Secondly, the method provides a rationale for a number of techniques of data presentation designed to test hypotheses in survey work.

In an experiment, the data are gathered by observation of a tightly predefined range of behaviour under controlled conditions. In the simplest case, you confine your attention to two variables and look for a pattern of association between the two. For example, you might want to demonstrate that attendance on a training course makes a difference to managers' job performance. 'Attendance on the course' is the first variable, and, let us say, 'supervisor's ratings of the manager's performance' is the second. You would gather ratings for a sample of managers, tabulating the ratings under two headings, 'Did attend' and 'Didn't attend', and look for higher ratings in the former case.

Suppose that is exactly what happened; then what you could conclude is that the two variables are related. However, you couldn't say anything about the direction of the relationship, that is, the cause. (For all you know, supervisors only sent their best people on the course, as a reward for past performance, and the course made no difference. If so, it was the high supervisor ratings that 'caused' the presence on the course, rather than the presence on the course 'causing' the supervisor ratings!) If all you want is to demonstrate that the two variables are related, this isn't a problem. For example, there are many situations (especially in survey work) in which you want to identify patterns in your observations: that males answer questions systematically differently from females, managers in one function from managers from another, and so on, and the idea of stratifying your sample to identify such patterns by looking for associations in your data makes explicit use of this rationale.

However, if you want to say something about the cause of the relationship, you need to do two more things. First, you must arrange events so that you can be reasonably sure about the sequence of the association (which variable makes a difference if it happens first, and which doesn't). The easiest way is by design: in any study of change, it is wise to obtain two sets of observations, using a 'before–after' design. So, in our example, you could obtain supervisor ratings of the managers' performance before and after the time of the course, for the managers who went on it, and for those who didn't. You'd conclude that the course had a causal impact on performance if the difference between 'before' and 'after' ratings was greater for those who went on the course than for those who didn't. This may not always be possible, however. If it weren't possible in the example given above, you would somehow have to ensure that supervisors sent their staff on this particular course regardless of their opinions of their job performance, so that performance could have no prior influence on course participation.

Secondly, you must eliminate the possible influence of other, alternative variables. In the example given above, you would need to convince yourself that only attendance on the course influenced performance, by controlling the impact of other factors that could possibly account for the performance. It is plausible, for example, that managers with a heavy and stressful workload didn't have the time to attend the course, while the ones who went were the unstressed managers with a light workload. It could just be, then, that the final ratings of job performance were due to the stresses of a heavy workload, rather than to course attendance. (High workload = stress = can't cope with the job = poorer ratings and no time to go on the course; low workload = no stress = copes with the job = higher ratings and has time to go on courses.) Just because your results are consistent with your expectations, doesn't make them valid.

Generally speaking, the way to eliminate the effects of external factors is by some form of control, and drawing a sample of managers who are matched in some way – equal in status on the whole range of possible factors that could form an alternative explanation for your observations – is sometimes practicable. But this does require you to know enough about your population to be able to anticipate the factors which need to be controlled; and it also assumes that you have sufficient power to arrange control (in our example, that you have the freedom to influence who goes on the course, and who doesn't).

This may not be the case, and you have two alternatives. First, you could draw a purposive sample by deliberately deciding to observe only those people whom you knew to be equal on the factors requiring control. Secondly, you could simply sample at random from your two different groups (in our example, from among those attending the course, and those not attending the course), and assume that the effects of the various factors involved would cancel each other out. In both cases, you would need to start with a fairly large population, and to know quite a lot about the people involved.

On very rare occasions, you may have sufficient control to be able to dictate, in effect, how people arrange themselves into groups for your research purposes. You'd be operating in the realm of the controlled, laboratory experiment (for all that it occurred in the field of the workplace) rather than the field experiment as such, and you would be able to carry out some very powerful work, albeit on a restricted number of variables. However, this situation is beyond the scope of my account, and if you were faced with such an opportunity, you'd need to look elsewhere for guidance. Bennett (1986: 38) will give you a flavour of the issues involved in control, and there are many textbooks of experimental design to which you can turn for further particulars. Anderson (1966), though dated, is a very useful reference in your circumstances, since it presents a very clear and readable account of experimental design arrangements, and some appropriate analytic statistics, in a convenient 140 pages.

Field experiments are reported in a fairly standardized format, in which you specify the sample size and provide details of procedure and design in terms of three kinds of variable:

- the independent variable: the one which you regard as possibly the cause of the effect you're observing, and which you take control over by, for example, assigning people to different groups with respect to that variable;
- the dependent variable: the one which you hope will express the effects of your activities, (which you hope depends on the independent one) and which forms the focus of your observations;
- the controlled variables: the ones which would get in the way of your causal explanation and whose effects you have therefore tried to eliminate.

10.3 A FRAMEWORK OF GENERAL GUIDELINES FOR EMPIRICAL WORK

Before you started this chapter, I would imagine that you saw the preparation of your empirical work as a matter of organizing some questions to put to your respondents. And so it is, but remember: your job is to gather and present data in order for your reader to arrive at information. And before you can ask useful questions of your **respondents**, or interrogate your written sources, there are some important questions which you must ask of **yourself**. These are shown in Table 10.3. (The questions that you'll be devising to pose to your respondents are such a small part of the whole process that I've had to outline the item in bold so that you can find it in the table.) Ignore the other parts of the table, and you'll end up with lots of data and very little information: if you're to be successful, then, regardless of the method you will be using, you should think through every question you're planning to ask your respondents, in the light of all the other issues raised in Table 10.3.

These questions are also shown in the remainder of this section, in the form of a set of headings, with some general material on each. I use these headings in Chapters 11 to 13 to structure material on the various techniques I present there, so the material which follows is a general introduction to the more specific material covered in those chapters.

Design

The sampling method and the design format are the main issues which you will need to address, the latter referring to the actual design used, whether examining contrasting modes of operation, time-sampling, a before–after design, and so on. These have been described in section 9.1.

There is only one further point to be made at this stage and, though it

Table 10.3 A checklist to be used in preparing the questions to ask

---

1. **Design**

   For each major issue to be investigated, what kind of sampling method is appropriate?

   What size of sample should I choose?

   Should I combine several sampling methods?

   Should I stratify the samples?

   What kind of design format is appropriate?

2. **Elicitation**

   What kinds of steering instructions should I provide, and how are these best provided, given the questions I wish to ask?

   Are there any expectations which my informants are likely to have of me and my role, which might influence or bias their response? How should I address this issue and, particularly, how can I involve the respondent in this procedure?

   What answer format is appropriate to each question?

   What is the question which I wish to ask?

   How should I record the answers which I receive?

3. **Analysis**

   What methods are appropriate in analysing the answers I receive, given the questions themselves, the format in which answers are to be given, and the way in which responses will be recorded?

   What kind of summarizing method is most likely to be relevant to these kinds of answers?

4. **Write-up**

   What sort of approach and style are likely to be appropriate in writing up the kinds of information I am likely to obtain?

   While I can't provide a firm answer as yet, are there any kinds of information which is more likely to appear as an appendix; what other kinds will be essential to my argument and should appear in the body of the text?

A pilot study will answer many of these questions

---

may seem banal, it's often neglected. When it comes to the use of particular techniques, design is a matter of small details as well as of the grand plans for arriving at accurate descriptions and causal explanations which we've been considering hitherto. For example, if several questionnaires are sent to a central location in each of a number of companies, is the addressee informed about how he or she is to distribute them to the respondents? How are the completed questionnaires to be returned – centrally or individually? Simply addressing a large envelope containing questionnaires and a generalized covering letter may not be sufficient.

The procedures by which the various techniques are administered are an appreciable design consideration.

Elicitation

Elicitation, the actual asking of questions, involves you in four kinds of activity.

Steering. This is the first. You have to tell your respondents how they are meant to tackle your questions: in which order, which ones to answer and which ones to miss out, and so on. I'm sure you can anticipate section 12.1 in expecting that in a questionnaire, for example, steering instructions of this kind are printed in front of each question, or group of questions. You know the sort of thing: 'If you answered "Yes" to Q2, please skip Q3 and go straight on to Q4.'

It may come as a surprise, however, to hear that **all** of the techniques involve some sort of steering instructions. Nevertheless, it's true: if you're using interviews for your survey, you still have to prepare a set of steering instructions aimed at yourself as the interviewer, and this activity is as important as the preparation of the questions which you will be asking. In an observation study, your very presence as an observer, and the way in which your role has been presented to the people you're observing, will act as a form of steering: legitimizing some kinds of answers, priming respondents to expect you to be interested in some kinds of events and not in others, whether you intend this or not. All of the material in section 7.2 applies.

The form of answers. This calls for another kind of activity, well in advance. Whatever method you use, your respondents will expect to be informed of how they are to make their answers to your questions, either literally in the form of instructions to 'Please choose the alternative that best expresses your views on this question', or metaphorically in the case of experiments, by being told that only one form of behaviour, that which gives data on the dependent variable, will be attended to by the experimenter. You will have to provide an explicit form of words which specify the form of answers, for each question or group of similar questions which you will be asking. Even in an informal, relatively unstructured conversation, the form of answer is implied by the process, as opposed to the content, of the conversation and the questions involved, and you'll need to give some preparatory thought in advance.

Eliciting answers. At last: this is what it's all about! Well, yes, provided all the other activities have been attended to. There are more detailed guidelines on how to ask questions in order to elicit answers, in the relevant sections on particular techniques; at this point, it's worth noting that very often, the precise wording of your questions will be influenced by the other three elicitation activities, as well as being determined by the nature of the data you were attempting to obtain.

For example, in an interview exploring the development of a strategic plan, you might say 'Please tell me how many meetings with other division heads you attended on this issue', if you choose to make an inference about the importance managers ascribed to the plan, and you'd record each answer in the form of a number. In contrast, your question would be worded 'Please tell me in your own words how you felt about the plan at that time' if you felt that inferring importance from frequency of attendance was too risky, and you were looking for a verbatim response. You would then record it as a literal quotation.

Furthermore, the way in which you would analyse answers to these questions would depend on the wording: the first example would call for a tabulation of the answers given to you by all the interviewees to whom you posed this question, while the second would demand some form of content analysis of their varying verbatim answers.

Recording. Recording answers, then – the particular form in which you do so – is also something which you have to decide in advance, for each question or group of similar questions which you plan to ask your respondents. A verbatim record, or some form of quantitative tally (defined as some mark you make on behalf of each respondent to record his or her answer: a tick in the simplest case, or a ranking, rating, or number in more complex instances) cover the possibilities.

Analysis

This is an activity in which you do two things. Firstly, you familiarize yourself with your recorded data until you perceive patterns emerging, either those which you had in mind when you sought to build your argument or explore the thesis by posing the question you did; or fresh patterns, which are new and unexpected. Secondly, you have to tabulate the data in such a way that these insights or perceptions are informative: obvious rather than hidden, lost in a maze of primary data.

Perceiving. This involves a great many different techniques, from content analysis to the calculation of frequencies and proportions all expressed in the form of tabular and graphical displays, together with a variety of analytic statistics, the latter being particularly common in the case of experimental method. In all cases, what you are doing is bringing together the responses of all your respondents (keeping subgroups separate in the case of samples which you have clustered or stratified), to see what general findings and trends emerge.

As I suggested in discussing the elicitation of answers above, you will need to have thought through the analysis methods in advance, in order to design the questions you wish to pose. However, once your data have been collected, the information they contain won't be obvious to you and, within the limitations posed by the form which your data take, you might wish to explore. A very good way of doing so if you're working with figures is to use a spreadsheet-based statistical package (e.g. STATVIEW) running on a microcomputer; for qualitative analyses, you will find a great range of different packages listed in the appendix to Miles and Huberman (1994).

Analysis is often a matter of exploration: casting data in one form, then another; analysing it one way, then another, to see what emerges. That's not to say that you don't have a number of hunches which you wish to test or issues you want to verify, in which some particular way of inspecting your data hasn't been decided in advance. Rather, I wish to emphasize the richness of your data, given the kinds of management issues which you're investigating, and the value of familiarizing yourself with these data thoroughly in order that the unexpected can be recognized and novel information identified. Information doesn't reach out from the data and grab you by the throat!

Summarizing. This is the essential next step. Having identified findings, trends, and meaningful patterns in the data – having obtained information, in other words – you need to cast the data into a final form which expresses the information involved, as clearly and obviously as possible; some form of numeric table, graphical display, or list of verbal points, is usually the final step in an analysis. As you will see if you glance at Miles and Huberman (1994), perceiving and summarizing are closely interdependent.

Write-up

You may feel that thinking ahead to the time when you write up your information is an unnecessary activity at this stage. However, a little time spent in considering the kinds of write-up which your design, your questions, and their analysis make possible, is very advisable at this stage, while further particulars can be left until you begin writing, having cast your eye over the material in Chapter 14.

Presenting. Presenting findings is frequently a matter of style. You may as well know in advance that some types of design and questioning lend themselves to one presentation style, and others to another, especially if you have personal preferences for one of them. For example, a project in which the empirical stage is largely dependent on a series of interviews with key informants may call for a content analysis, followed by a narrative account of the main findings of the analysis. In contrast, a highly structured questionnaire may require you to tabulate rankings and ratings, presenting much of your information in numeric form. Are you more comfortable with one form rather than another?

MBA

A more likely occurrence in your case is the need to combine several different forms of questioning, analysis and reporting. It would be wise to think them through, to the presentation stage, well in advance, so that you know which issues you will deal with, and present, in which way.

all

Presenting findings really involves two distinct activities:

■ presenting their content: the substantive information which you have prepared from your data, in the context of the argument you are developing;
■ presenting evidence about their accuracy and credibility.

You would do the latter by showing that the substantive information is consistent with other information which you have obtained, either primary (empirical data you gathered yourself) or secondary (consistency with the findings and ideas of other authors), as part of the argument your project document presents. You may add to the weight and credibility of your presentation by citing any measures of reliability of the particular techniques which you used in your data analysis, at this point in your text. There is more on this in section 11.2, in the discussion of content analysis.

Locating. Locating your results in the right place is probably the most important influence on the way in which your reader obtains information from the data which you will be presenting. As you carry out your analysis (and especially during the summarizing stage of analysis), you will need to bear in mind the position in your project document where different kinds of results will be presented. What sort of material should you present in your text, and in what order; how should findings be related to objectives; which should be confined to an appendix, and which displayed in the main body of your account?

To put it into a nutshell, you should aim to present information in just the right quantity at just those places where they will support your argument best, at just the point at which you imagine your reader will require them if he or she is following the argument as you intend it. As well as writing your project document, you should be tracking how your reader is following it, at every point in the text you are creating!

One of my students once submitted a very interesting and workmanlike IPD professional project on the topic of infectious diseases at work. A major key to success lay in her decision (prompted, it must be said, by myself as tutor) to reorganize her material, so that technical descriptions of various bacterially propagated infectious diseases were confined to an appendix. As originally placed, in the main body of her text, they were long enough, and detailed enough, to have obscured her findings on health and safety practices among employees potentially exposed to infection hazards in a local authority cleansing department, to the point at which the reader had great difficulty in discerning the information from the wealth of data which she had supplied.

In principle, this issue is straightforward enough: present just the material which is required to establish your findings in the body of your text, and additional, illustrative, or highly technical material in an appendix. In practice, it depends very much on the kind of finding which you're trying to establish, and the particular way in which your data support the argument you're presenting in arriving at your information. As a rough guide, that means that direct findings (classification headings and frequency counts thereunder, totals, averages, trends, other descriptive and analytic statistics) should go in the body of the text, together with sufficient of the data which gave rise to them for the reader to understand that your argument and conclusion aren't arbitrary. The remainder would then go to an appendix. More specific guidance is given, where necessary, in the account of the various techniques.

10.4 IN CONCLUSION: THE IMPORTANCE OF PILOT WORK

At this point you might argue that the answers to some of the procedural questions posed in Table 10.3 are arbitrary, since you might see several ways of answering them and have no way of recognizing which is more likely to lead to success. The purpose of the proposal document is to make a first stab at this issue, and of the pilot stage of your project to finally resolve any doubts. If you look back to section 5.2 and Table 5.2, you'll remember the importance of timetabling for the piloting of your questions with an appropriate subsample; you may, at this point, find Table 5.3 with its standard times for project activities useful too. You'll recall that section 9.1 discusses the idea of preliminary analysis in the context of design, and you might find that a glance back at Table 9.1 is also helpful.

Generally speaking, you pilot your empirical work by asking the questions that you intend to ask, in the form you intend to ask them, of a small number of people taken from the same population as your sample.

You then analyse the answers in the way you have planned, to see if the results are indeed likely to give you the kind of information which you are seeking. This is your last opportunity, before committing yourself to the time and effort involved in your main data collection, of making sure that the issues mentioned in this chapter have been adequately resolved. Namely:

■ That the method on which you've decided is appropriate. Would the results be more illuminating if you were to use a different method, or combine several?

■ Are the techniques appropriate? And, specifically, how can you use them to overcome the particular problems associated with each method: the partiality of memory; people's ability and willingness to respond; the sheer volume of data with which you'll be faced, some more and some less informative; and the problem of accurate inference-making from the data before you?

■ On reflection, are the sampling method and sample size appropriate, and is the form of design which you've chosen best suited to the kinds of conclusions you'd like to draw?

■ Have you given the right guidance to your respondents on how to answer your questions, what the questions are, how they're to make their answers, and how answers are to be recorded? And, in intimate association with these issues:

■ Will you be able to analyse the answers you receive; is there a better way than you'd anticipated, of making the data informative to yourself? Have you chosen the most relevant form of tabular or graphical display, and does this provide you with the most appropriate form of analysis?

■ Finally, will the findings be informative to your readers, given the way in which you anticipate you'll be reporting them?

Naturally, some of these issues can only be addressed in the light of the specific techniques which you'll be using. The following chapters cover them in detail.

Semi-structured, open-ended techniques

11

The techniques presented in this chapter are all **semi-structured**. In other words, they involve asking questions whose **content and sequence aren't fully specified in advance**. You'd use them in situations in which you have a clear idea of your purpose (you should always have that!), a general idea of the kinds of content which you wish to explore, and a rough notion of the sequence in which you'll do so. You'll allow both the content and the sequence to vary with different respondents, in order to be sensitive to the way in which your interaction with particular individuals is progressing. The techniques are also **open-ended**. That is, they use a form of questioning in which your **respondents are encouraged to answer in their own words**: while you might have some hunches about the kind of answers to expect, you wouldn't be prepared to specify them in advance.

Four techniques are involved: the **conversation**; the **individual interview**; the **key informant interview** and the **focus group**. Because they're relatively unstructured and open-ended, they provide you with large amounts of rich, fertile, but disorganized data. Your task in analysing the results will be to organize, to till this soil for the information it contains; and the main technique you'll be using is called **content analysis**. This involves you in creating categories which classify the meanings expressed in the data, and then in coding, tabulating and illustrating the data themselves. The good husbandry involved will mean pruning, selecting and discarding some (often lots) of the data you've obtained.

The purpose of these techniques is to provide you with the bulk of the data which you require when you're using historical review, biographical analysis, or case study methods. However, they have an additional purpose when used with the survey method. In survey work, they're the means by which you conduct an initial, relatively unstructured pilot study in order to identify the questions to ask, the answer categories to provide, and the sequence to be followed in the more structured main study.

11.1 CONVERSATIONS AND STORYTELLING

During your project period, you'll spend a lot of your time talking inform-ally to other people. Some of it will be gossip, some will be storytelling and some will involve conversations: all of it is valuable, often in a rather vague and unspecified way, in providing you with background about the personalities, procedures, culture and values of your organization. Given that you'll be doing it anyway, why not do it explicitly?

Design

A straightforward way of providing an explicit focus is to turn a spontane-ously occurring chat towards some purpose related to your project, controlling and maintaining the dialogue to this end. Sometimes, how-ever, as Burgess (1982c) indicates, you can initiate a conversation with a clear, project-related intention in mind, and this raises the possibility of holding a series of preplanned conversations in which you follow a rationale by which you group your respondents according to their job title, role, or status within the organization. Are the data you're likely to get from Marketing different from those obtainable from Production, for example? Is the culture, and hence the 'flavour' of your conversations, likely to differ systematically according to the division or region in which you do your informal, conversational wandering around?

Elicitation

'Without allowing people to speak freely we will never know what their real intentions are, and what the true meaning of their words might be' (Cottle, 1977); 'If you want to know what a person thinks, why not ask? He might just tell you' (Kelly, 1955). And there, in a nutshell, you have the complete set of skills involved in elicitation.

The first quotation suggests that you must know how to listen properly. This means knowing how to:

■ keep quiet without interjecting your own stories into the narrative, using your own comments to clarify the other person's meaning or elicit fresh meanings from him or her, rather than to initiate fresh topics of your own;
■ be sensitive to the nonverbal signals as well as the verbal, so that you can hear the emotions and feelings expressed by your informant, as well as the words.

The second suggests that this isn't a passive process! Putting the two together, you won't find out unless you ask, but the asking must be relatively non-directive.

Steering. In a structured interview, steering is always done directively: you tell your respondents how you want them to address your questions, often as a result of their answers to previous questions. For example, 'I'm asking this question because you said you had shopfloor experience before becoming a manager; now, bearing that experience in mind, could you tell me. . . .' In a conversation, steering is a matter of conveying your purpose to your respondent, possibly in so many words, but more frequently by implication through the direction your comments and follow-up questions may take. If your respondent has already given you his or her thoughts, then exposing your own can stimulate additional material; sharing your own feelings (assuming they're relevant and it's done in response rather than in initiation) can deepen the affective content of the answers you hear.

Directiveness is a matter of degree, and you might find Table 11.1 useful in illustrating the range involved. You could consider extending the range of your conversations to include storytelling. The stories your respondents have to tell are obviously important with the historical method, but can form a useful part of case study and survey methods if you consider that, as well as offering content, they're good indicators of your respondent's quality of experience, assumptions about self, and the organization's values as perceived by your respondent. Mair (1989, 1990) provides a rationale for the value of storytelling as a form of psychological and sociological investigation, and Boje (1994) a thought-provoking account of why it matters to examine the assumptions underlying the stories we tell in and about organizations. Tommerup (1988) provides an interesting example, which focuses on the stories employees of Hughes Aircraft told about a succession of their chief executives, as a way of understanding the culture of the organization involved. (If you need a review of the basic material on organizational culture to provide a conceptual underpinning to the narratives you gather, you'll find Pheysey (1993) a convenient handbook of basic ideas.)

To return to technique: 'self-characterization' is a very effective non-directive procedure for eliciting personal stories (Kelly, 1955). You ask your respondent to describe him or herself, in the job being done, from a separate but sympathetic viewpoint. The wording you use is important: if the respondent's name is Mary Welsh, for example, you'd ask her to 'Tell me a little about Mary Welsh, as if you were someone who liked her, and knew her well.' You'd make sure that Mary replied in the third person singular about herself; in other words, you would steer her away from the word 'I' and towards the words 'she' or 'Mary'.

Format. When you're holding a conversation, you tell your respondent about the format in which you'd like your questions answered by the way

Table 11.1 The range of non-directive elicitation and steering

---

Range of techniques available to you in semi-structured work

Parallel monologues	Pinteresque dialogue: 'questioner's' concerns with his/her own issues, 'respondent' with his/her own; no steering occurs.
Gossiping	Steering occurs mutually: respondent's direction steered, somewhat loosely, by the questioner's issue, and vice-versa; several topics or themes involved.
Storytelling	Other than an indication by 'questioner' that he or she's willing to listen, steering left to the discretion of the respondent: respondent tells his/her story and determines the issues.
Informal conversation	Steering occurs mutually, though often on one issue as determined by one of the participants.
Research conversation	Steering by questioner within the bounds of the respondent's story and questioner's purpose; respondent takes the dialogue where he or she wishes.
Semi-structured interview	Steering by questioner to cover certain previously identified issues within a topic predetermined by questioner; broad direction preset by questioner.
As above	With firmer steering given by means of: (a) 'devil's advocate' question: respondent presented with an opposing point of view to clarify his/her position (b) hypothetical questions to discover respondent's reactions in certain circumstances (c) questioner asserts an 'ideal' position, to discover how respondent sees the ideal (d) questioner offers interpretations to seek agreement and/or stimulate counter-arguments.
Structured interview	Steering by questioner following predefined topic, issues and sequence; other material offered by respondent treated as marginal or ignored.

in which you use spoken English, by the way in which you respond to non-verbal signals, and by your mutual use of a variety of social skills. In other words, there aren't any particular techniques other than the ones you dispose of as a language user, and you'll rarely make a deliberate statement of the form 'Please indicate your preferences by ranking the alternatives'.

Now, it isn't my place to teach you English (with one tiny exception: see section 14.2). However, it's worth remembering that the tone of a conversation is something that's set mutually, and that, to a degree, you can shape and model the form of your respondent's answers deliberately by the form of language you're using yourself, if you choose to do so. (Interest shown in the other person creates interest in yourself; the extent to which you use metaphors in your utterances will influence their use by your respondent; agreeing, nodding the head, and appropriate eye-contact induce your respondent to expand on his or her material; and so forth.) Your role as an interviewer, whether in a highly structured survey interview or a non-directive conversation, is never neutral, and the meaning of your respondent's answers is something created by both of you. If this issue intrigues you, have a look at Mishler (1986). A project that uses historical review or case study method will demonstrate an awareness of this issue in its discussion of methodology, and will avoid oversimplifications of the 'only objective methods were used' variety.

Eliciting answers. That's up to you, and the content of the questions you wish to interject into the conversation. You may find it helpful to examine the material on structured interviewing in section 12.2 , however: some of the material, especially on the sequencing of topics to be discussed, is relevant.

Recording answers. By definition, you're unlikely to be doing much recording in an unstructured conversation. The place for the tape-recorder or the notepad and pencil is in one of the other forms of semistructured technique, and you'll find yourself largely dependent on your memory as a recording medium. It's good practice to make a few notes in private as soon as possible after the conversation, however. Obviously, you'll record the gist of what you remember, but you should also highlight any points which you might want to explore in more detail in subsequent conversations with your respondent, or by using a more structured technique. Your project diary is probably the best place for this, even if you intend to use a separate record book for your data.

Analysis

Perceiving. The analysis of data you've obtained conversationally is, likewise, fairly unstructured. There are few structured techniques to apply, since you've relatively few data recorded systematically, and there is a danger that your analysis would be invalid if you used a technique which demands more robust data than those at your disposal. Analysis is still possible, however, and an informal content analysis of the various conversations you've had is very useful: see the description in section 11.2. However, analysis of conversational data is as much to do with yourself as with the material your respondent has provided. Useful questions to ask yourself are as follows.

- How do the data I've obtained today compare with the other data I've already obtained? Are there any apparent trends? How frequent are various kinds of answers in comparisons to others? What picture seems to be emerging?
- What concepts and research from my background reading seem relevant to the data I've obtained?
- How did I personally feel about the conversations at the time I had them?
- Did the answers ring true?
- How can I confirm any initial impressions I formed?
- How much of myself went into it, does this matter, and to what extent do I need to discount it?

A useful way of perceiving patterns in your answers to these questions as you mull over the narrative is to record the answers in the form of a memo to yourself. Miles and Huberman (1994: 72–6) have some useful ideas on how you can be systematic about this technique, and prompt the thought that a simple classification and content analysis of a set of such memos is a useful way of developing a set of propositions for more formal investigation later on in your data-gathering activities.

Summarizing. This then becomes a matter of presenting the main themes mentioned and issues raised, in the form of a set of summary points. It is unlikely that these will be quantified in any way; some statement of the limits of their usefulness, bearing in mind the extent to which you put yourself into the data, is wise.

Write-up

Presenting. Since your recording was fairly informal, you won't be able to include large amounts of data in your project document: you'll be limited to impressions, judgements, summary statements and so forth.

There are, nevertheless, two situations in which you have to present such impressions. First, if your regulations require you to describe the organization in which you carried out the project (particularly common in professional and diploma programmes), then your impressions of the organizational culture, climate, and values will form a useful supplement to the more factual material concerning your organization's ownership, structure, market and customers.

Secondly, whether recorded using the memo technique or not, initial impressions are often a very good source of ideas for subsequent datagathering using more structured techniques, and in outlining your choice of topic, issues explored, and choice of design and techniques, it is useful to include a statement of these impressions in your project document as part of your rationale for doing so.

Locating. And so, if you do report them formally, the results of conversational technique are presented in the body of the text of your project, rather than as an appendix. They're often an integral part of your argument.

In conclusion

All of this may seem that I'm making a mountain out of a molehill. If you'd do all of this anyway, that's fine. However, if some of this is new to you, or helps to legitimize your feelings that informal methods are 'allowed' in project work, that's even better. But remember the message I expressed in Chapter 6: while the techniques you're using may be relatively unstructured and open-ended, the responsibility for ensuring their validity is still there. That means that there's a need to check your impressions; a need to have repeated conversations with the same respondent and with others; and, almost always, a need to check your conclusions by using other semi-structured techniques, or to progress to a more formal stage of your data-gathering by using a structured technique, in a pilot–main study format.

11.2 THE INDIVIDUAL INTERVIEW

As indicated in Table 11.1, a semistructured interview differs from a conversation because the topic and issues to be covered have been determined in advance, because you have previously determined the sample of people whom you intend to contact, and usually because your attempt to prevent biases from affecting your data occurs **before** data collection, rather than after.

Design

The design of a series of semistructured individual interviews starts with an explicit statement (use your diary!) of the purpose in holding the interviews. You'll find that it helps if you think of the purpose as some central issue which you need to resolve: a major question which arises from a particular facet of your thesis; or a critical part of your argument which you need to substantiate empirically. Thinking about this major question suggests a number of aspects, each of which merits one or more questions to be put to your respondents. Usually, the aspects are listed in no particular order (with the exception that the more straightforward, easy-to-answer, descriptive and less personal aspects should be dealt with at the start of your interview). Under each aspect, then, you list a number of questions which you intend to cover with your respondents. You're prepared to be flexible about the order in which you'll pose them, depending on how each interview progresses; what's important is that you obtain answers to all of them by the time any one interview is complete. As a secondary issue, you'll remain open and sensitive to new aspects, issues, and answers offered to you by the interviewee.

By this stage, you will have identified the population you're dealing with, drawn a sample using an appropriate technique (see section 9.2) and specified the strata or groupings, if any, of respondents within the sample. The plan is to cover the ground with all your respondents and analyse the results according to the subgroupings (whether managers in one department answer systematically differently to managers in another, for example).

As you can see, an important difference between the conversation and the semistructured interview lies in the way in which you plan to minimize bias. In the conversation, bias is handled indirectly, by repeating conversations on a particular issue with the same or different respondents, or by triangulation (using some different technique and looking for compatibility). In the semistructured interview, while these other techniques are open to you, you primarily handle bias by a careful design of the interview itself: biases arising from the sequence in which you address subject-matter, from any inadvertent omission of questions, from unrepresentative sampling, and from an uncontrolled over- or under-representation of subgroups among your respondents.

Elicitation

In the conversation, effective elicitation is a matter of linguistic and personal intuition and flair; in semistructured interviewing, elicitation is often regarded as a matter of skill, and I would imagine that you will be familiar with the idea of 'interviewing skills' from some part of your taught course, or from your earlier reading. In a sense, the semi-structured interview demands greater skill than the fully structured interview. For a start, there's more face-to-face, 'on the hoof' flexibility and adaptability involved, precisely because the social encounter hasn't been fully structured in advance. Moreover, the purpose of a semistructured interview is often to obtain information about personal, attitudinal, and value-laden material, and you're likely to be dealing with matters which call for social sensitivity in their own right.

This subject is a large one, and the best I can do is to refer you to one or more of the following: King (1994), Smith (1972), Torrington (1972), and the latter part of Kornhauser and Sheatsley (1976), to be read with 'unstructured interviewing' in mind. Most deal with matters of interviewing skill as well as offering an in-depth treatment of interviewing in general.

If you haven't yet had the opportunity to look at the 'interview skills' approach during your taught programme, try Roberts (1985). It's directed at employment interviewing rather than research or project interviewing, but is very useful because it deals with situations from the point of view of both interviewer and interviewee, and focuses on the skills element in particular, all in a convenient format. Chapters 3, and 5 to 8 of the second part directed at trainers, summarize the skills involved, and provide a good review of issues for your write-up of methodology.

under-graduate

Steering. This is a matter of two contending forces: a directive force on the part of your respondent, in the sense that he or she has a role in determining the sequence of questions and the way in which these are to be interpreted; and a deliberate, explicit but not rigid effort on your part, in bringing the respondent back to the main flow of the interview when the occasion is right. (Rather like sailing, in fact: the wind provides both energy and direction, while your hand is at the tiller to harness this energy and channel the direction onto the bearing you want.) Whyte (1982) is particularly good on this topic, and offers you a scale of 'restrictiveness' which you can use to increase or decrease the directiveness of the dialogue at any one point. It's shown in Table 11.2.

all

Format. In the semi-structured interview, you don't provide your respondent with pre-set answer categories; however, you can of course influence the options available to him or her, and this is a matter of degree. The least directive approach is the 'projective' form of questioning, in which you ask a fairly vague or apparently unrelated question, and take the answer, not at face value, but as indicative of a perception, belief, personal value or motive which, you infer, predisposes your respondent to answer in that way.

Table 11.2 Varying the directiveness in steering a semistructured interview

Non-committal utterance ('uh-huh'); nod of the head	Encourages respondent to continue on same topic with minimal influence on direction of answer or introduction of new question; though a pattern in the utterances, e.g. only nodding when the same point is made, can reinforce development or repetition of the same point
Repeating interviewee's last utterance verbatim but with a questioning inflection	Increases the encouragement to expand on the same point
Probing the last utterance	Raising a question on the same point or remarking on it: interviewee encouraged to develop the point
Probing the idea just before the last utterance	More directive because it doesn't follow the interviewee's lead to the same extent that probing the last utterance would
Probing an idea expressed earlier in the interview	A deliberate choice by the interviewer to go back to something the interviewee said earlier
Introduction of a new question on the same general theme	More directive exercise of interviewer control
Introduction of a new theme	More directive still

After Whyte (1982)

For example, instead of asking the respondent to state what he or she thinks of his or her own effectiveness as a manager, you might ask a general question about managers as leaders, in the form 'how would you define leadership?', or, more directively, 'what are the constraints that managers in the company must handle?' You'll interpret the answer as an indication of your respondent's own effectiveness. As you can see, projective questioning is very context-dependent; nevertheless, the following general guidelines apply.

■ Projective questions in which you are looking for answers about perceptions are easiest and safest to handle; questions designed to elicit personal values and, particularly, motives, require the greatest amount of sensitivity on your part.

- Projective questions calling for answers about the respondent's immediate boss, and about his or her colleagues, are likely to be more tricky than ones which refer to the respondent him- or herself.
- Using projective questions requires a high level of pre-existing rapport: your respondents would be unhappy if they construed your questions as 'loaded' (which they are), and put this down to malevolent intentions on your part (which they're not).
- Before using a projective question, always consider the alternative of coming clean about your difficulty. A form of words such as 'Look, I feel shy about asking this question, but I'd appreciate your help as I think this issue's very important', followed by a direct, **non-projective** question, is often safer and just as effective.
- The more projective questions you use, the more you have to interpret the result, and the more your own judgement will influence the validity of the answers received.

If you haven't encountered this form of questioning before, have a look at Schlackman (1989); written by a very experienced market researcher, this short article is a very convenient compilation of eight different verbal and graphical projective techniques.

The most directive format for answers in a semi-structured interview is one in which you follow an open-ended question with an indication of the context or scope of the answer you expect. For example, a sentence beginning 'What did you do when the marketing proposal was rejected . . . ?' (an open-ended question) might be completed with the words '. . . how did you handle the staff who'd prepared it?' if you want to limit the answers to issues of delegation rather than issues of personal reactions, alternative proposal development, or anything else. And clearly, completing the sentence with the words '. . . did you recognize a training need in the staff who prepared it . . . [pause] or did you put it down to the opposition from other departments?' would turn an open-ended question into a closed question, more appropriate to a fully structured interview technique.

Eliciting answers. Again, the content of the questions is up to you. You might note, though, that the semistructured interview is a good technique for questions dealing with feelings and attitudes, and any situation in which you're uncertain about the range of possible answers you'll obtain. It's commonly used with the case study method, and fairly frequently in the first stages of survey work.

Recording answers. You should do this as systematically, thoroughly, and completely as you can. If your design requires you to carry out a large number of relatively brief interviews (20 minutes or so), you'll probably cover the ground adequately by making handwritten notes during the interview (having asked your respondent's permission at the outset). Read over and revise them immediately afterwards, and make an appointment for a very brief subsequent meeting (five minutes or so on the same day as your interview) to resolve any issue which looks important and wasn't properly recorded in your notes. An elegant alternative is to telephone your interviewee to express your thanks for the interview, using the phonecall to clarify anything you missed in your notes.

Ideally, your notes should be in the form of a précis rather than a paraphrase or synopsis (see section 5.3 for the definition of each); it is very useful to record key points, or particularly interesting or apt expressions, as direct, word-for-word quotations, for subsequent use in your write-up.

You'll need to consider the use of a tape-recorder if your interviews are any longer than half an hour. The most important factor, and one which first-timers often forget, is the time it takes to make a written transcription: at least seven hours of work for every hour of interviewing, if you're to do it properly (see Table 5.3, and believe!). A written, literal, word-for-word transcript which records all the 'ums' and 'ers' is an essential prerequisite to any form of analysis: you can't make an analysis directly during playback.

Analysis

The main technique associated with semi-structured interviews is called **content analysis**. As the name suggests, its purpose is to describe systematically the content of your respondents' utterances, and classify the various meanings expressed in the material you've recorded. It isn't the only way in which you would analyse the data you have obtained, and you might find yourself presenting information in the form of a connected narrative (in a study following the case study method, for example), or by means of a series of verbatim quotations taken from the interviews. But all reporting of semi-structured interviews assumes that you present findings which are representative of what was said, and content analysis is a powerful means for familiarizing yourself with what's there, quite apart from your readers. Content analysis is also important in the analysis of more structured interview and questionnaire materials: see Chapters 12 and 13.

Perceiving. Literally that: an active and judgemental process that classifies the answers you obtained. It involves five stages:

- preparation, in which you identify your unit of analysis (what counts as an utterance to be classified: a word? sentence? whole conversation?);
- categorizing, in which you either use a set of categories taken from the literature, or devise a set of categories of your own by reading over your written transcript: a set of categories under which you will classify each utterance;
- coding, in which you assign each utterance to one and only one category;
- tabulating, in which you count the number of utterances under each category;
- illustrating, in which you present the categories and list the assertions under them: all, or a representative set.

Table 11.3 provides you with a procedural guide, and a worked example showing the result of a simple content analysis of the answers to one open-ended interview question.

It is important that the categories which you construct are reliable. If you are using categories drawn from a pre-existing theory or rationale, then it's important that, before you use them to classify your data, you make a brief, explicit list of the defining characteristics of each category: that is, of the signs that you will be looking for in order to put each assertion into one category rather than another. Reliability is a bigger problem in those situations in which you have no pre-existing categories in mind, and have to draw them up in the first place as a result of reading, and perceiving, the dominant themes in your interview transcripts. That's because there is no pre-existing list of defining characteristics, and because you have to invent these, as well as the categories themselves.

In either case, the issue of reliability boils down to a simple question. Would someone else perceive the same categories as you did? The way to answer this question is to hand a photocopy of the uncoded transcripts to a colleague whom you ask to recognize categories for him- or herself. You would then compare the two category sets, your own and theirs, and argue over them until something more useful emerged and agreement on the defining characteristics was obtained. This would then be tested by seeing if you were both agreed on the coding: the assigning of utterances to categories. You should consider involving one or more of your respondents in this role. (See the rationale presented in section 6.3: if you're working collaboratively, they're often very well qualified for this particular task.)

Summarizing. Tabulation is the most common way of presenting the information available in content-analysed data. If you want to make inferences from the numbers of utterances under each category, then a

Table 11.3 Procedural guide: tabulating and presenting content-analysed data

The steps to follow	Example
Specify the sample:	All 33 members of New Product Development department
Indicate if stratified and how:	17 in the Industrial Products division, 16 in the Consumer Products division
Indictate how many responded in each stratum (to provide the columns of the table):	32 (17 and 15 + 1 unavailable on day of interview)
Prepare the unit of analysis:	The whole of the respondent's reply is treated as a single entry under one category, regardless of number of sentences
Prepare the data:	A transcript of the 32 conversations with the relevant part of the interview highlighted; each coded with a number, 1 to 6, according to the categories below
Specify the categories, how derived, and what defines each category; (to provide rows of the table)	Derived from consideration of all the data; defining characteristics in italic 1. *Plan inappropriate* in view of what *competitors* are doing 2. *Plan unviable* since the proposed *divestments* the inappropriate* 3. *Plan unviable* since planned *acquisitions don't match company policy* 4. *Plan viable* but needs *further development* 5. *No view either way* 6. Miscellaneous

(Code the data)		Industrial Products		Consumer Products	
		n	%	n	%
Tabulate the data, calculating percentages, using the total of each column as the base for each column	Plan inappropriate in view of what competitors are doing	8	47	7	44
	Plan unviable since the proposed divestments inappropriate	4	24	3	19
	Plan unviable since planned acquisitions don't match company policy	3	18	3	19
	Plan viable but needs further development	1	6	1	6
	Miscellaneous	0	0	1	6
	No view either way	1	6	0	0
	No answer	0	0	1	6
	TOTAL	17	101	16	100

Check that total percentages sum to 100, allowing for rounding errors	Presenting in whole numbers here, so after dividing by the column total round back to the nearest whole number.
Illustration: prepare a verbal description of the table, to be used when presenting the table in the project document	'The majority of respondents (82%) expressed unfavourable views about the plan, the most common being that competitors' activities were insufficently taken into account. This is true in each of the divisions in which the respondents are located. Only a small minority (one person in each division) felt the plan was viable, and that with reservations; one further person refused to commit him/herself. The miscellaneous comment concerned some of the personalities involved and does not add to the information expressed.'

table to this effect, perhaps stratified according to your sampling design, will reveal relationships to you, and permit a variety of descriptive and analytic statistics to be carried out on the numbers. If you're less concerned with the numbers, then a list of the various utterances, or representative examples, can be reported in a table in which the columns are the category headings that you've used; Miles and Huberman (1994: chapter 5) provides other alternatives to the table of numbers, as does Morris *et al.* (1987).

As presented, such information is formally identical to what could have been obtained by a structured interview or questionnaire question (often due to the unit of analysis being set to be equal to the respondent's entire utterance in response to the question, regardless of how many sentences were involved), and many of the reporting conventions of the more structured techniques apply: see Chapter 12.

This isn't surprising. The answer categories for fully structured interviews and questionnaires were obtained through content analysis in the first place, whether the categories derive from some theory, or are developed from a pilot study, or are developed informally 'in one's head' on material obtained by conversational techniques. Structured techniques may look more 'objective' because the answer categories are specified before the questions have been asked, but where do you think they came from? Someone, somewhere, has carried out some form of content analysis in order to arrive at them in the first place, and has had to grapple with the resulting problems of reliability in categorization. For further particulars of content analysis procedures, try the latter half of Holsti (1968).

Write-up

The results of semi-structured interviews can be presented in a variety of ways, from the continuous narrative which blends empirically obtained information with your own interpretative comments, to a formal, tabular summary accompanied by the results of statistical tests.

Presenting. There's no more to be said about the narrative account, other than to remind you to be careful in the inferences you draw from your information. Tables 8.7 and 14.2 will remind you of the pitfalls involved. Tabular presentation is exemplified in Table 11.3, and described in more detail in section 12.1. There is a third way of presenting semi-structured interview material, and that involves the use of illustrative quotations.

You can give a highly informative presentation of your findings by stating the main issues you were exploring in the interviews, and, for each issue, presenting the relevant categories from a content analysis, with one or more verbatim quotations taken from the interview transcripts in order to illustrate the points being made. It's surprising what a dramatic impact a list of verbatim statements can have on your readers: statements which all say the same thing (they're grouped under their category headings, remember), but in slightly different ways, with all the weight of experience, the awareness of practical detail, and the practitioner wisdom (you hope) of the people whom you interviewed in gathering the data.

You will recall from my account of the general framework in section 10.3 that your write-up should always include some information on the reliability of your findings, and the argument was first stated in section 10.2 in the discussion of triangulation: by now, I hope you'll be taking this need for granted. This is the place to include any evidence you have obtained on the reliability of your content analysis category system, for example; two indices are provided in the Figure 11.1 procedural guide.

Locating. By definition, a narrative account blends empirically derived information with reasoned argument, and would therefore appear in the body of the text; either spread out in crucial locations over most of your project document (as in the case of many MBA projects: see Table 4.2), or confined neatly within the boundaries of an 'empirical section' (a little like Table 4.1). A tabular presentation which focuses on numbers and proportions would more likely be presented in an empirical section, each table followed by a verbal statement of the information presented as in Table 11.3. As you will see in Chapter 14, the place for long lists is normally the appendix; however, if you're careful in your selection, and can present your argument in an interesting and, possibly, entertaining

Purpose: To demonstrate the absence of idiosyncrasies in the allocation of responses to categories when coding those responses? Also, to demonstrate the extent to which a careful discussion of your category definitions has increased the reliability of coding.

Procedure

1. Record the category into which you have coded each item.
2. Record the category into which a colleague has independently coded each item.
3. List the categories down one side of a sheet of paper.
4. Repeat them along the bottom of the sheet of paper.
5. Into the cells of the matrix thus formed, enter the number of items you and your colleague have placed in each cell.

Your content analysis is reliable to the extent that you both agree: so all of the items should lie on the diagonal of this matrix, and there should be no outliers.

A simple percentage agreement score

1. Sum the items which lie along the diagonal, and express this sum as a percentage of the total number of items $\frac{15+10+12+14+16}{96} \times 100 + 69.8\%$

Intuitive enough, but biased by the sheer number of coding categories: the fewer the categories, the easier it is to get a large percentage by chance alone: impossible to compare percentage agreement scores across separate content analyses which have different numbers of categories. So you need to find a way which **removes** the effect due to chance.

Cohen's Kappa (Cohen, 1960)

The number of codings on which you both agree, minus the number of codings for which agreement would be expected by chance given the marginal totals; as a proportion of the total number of codings minus the number of codings for which agreement would be expected by chance.

To find the level of chance agreement

1. Find the proportion of the total codings which each person has allocated to each category.
2. Multiply together the corresponding proportions (your own and your colleague's); sum the result.
3. Multiply this sum by 100.
4. And now work out the value of Kappa.

A value of 1.0 would reflect perfect agreement, while 0 represents the level of pure chance.

Example: the result of following steps 1 to 5

Your list

	Commun- ications problems	Prod- uction difficulties	Defining the market	Willingness to cooperate	Client's product knowledge	Total
Communication problems	15	1	2	4	2	24
Production difficulties	–	10	–	2	–	12
Defining the market	3	–	12	1	–	16
Willingness to cooperate	5	2	–	14	1	22
Client's product knowledge	2	4	–	–	16	22
Total	25	17	14	21	19	96

Colleague's list

You: $24/96 = .25$; $12/96 = .125$; $16/96 = .167$; $22/96 = .23$; $22/96 = .23$

Colleague: $25/96 = .26$; $17/96 = .17$; $14/96 = .15$; $21/96 = .22$; $19/96 = .20$

$(.25 \times .26)+(.125 \times .17)+(.167 \times .15)+(.23 \times 22) +(.23 \times .20)=.2079$

$.2079 \times 100 = 20.79$ gives the number of codings to be expected by chance.

Number of codings on which you agree: $15 +10 +12 +14 +16 = 67$; total codings 96;

$$\text{Kappa} = \frac{67 - 20.79}{96 - 20.79} = .614$$

Cohen's Kappa is a very common measure of agreement, and it is worth using as a supplement to the simple percentage agreement score. In both cases, your objective is to discuss the result with your colleague, exchange views of what exactly you mean by each category, and repeat the whole content analysis and coding with the objective of improving on the two measures of agreement. (Repeat both analyses after you have done the second coding and trust that the values of both measures are higher!) Actually, there is a more accurate agreement measure than Kappa. Kappa ignores the fact that, in most instances, you and your colleague will have more agreements than disagreements, and assumes that you have a fair idea of the kinds of errors you are both likely to make – an assumption which may not be warranted in the first of your two codings. If you're in a situation in which the absolute degree of agreement is important to your argument, rather than the fact that you can improve on your first coding, use the measure described in Perreault and Leigh (1989).

Figure 11.1 A procedural guide to reliability calculations in content analysis.

way, here's one situation in which a longish list of verbatim quotations from your respondents can be placed in the main body of the text, as a supplement to the tabular account. It isn't there to add interest, however, but to move your argument onwards at key stages in your presentation.

11.3 THE KEY INFORMANT INTERVIEW

Key informant interviews differ from other forms of interview largely because respondents are chosen on the basis of their idiosyncratic, specialized knowledge, rather than being randomly chosen to sample the range of issues you are investigating, and this has important consequences for design. According to Tremblay (1982), the technique is especially useful in:

- defining the essential characteristics of some issue by drawing on the personal experience and understanding of the people involved – the way in which such concepts as 'management of change', or 'customer orientation', are understood and interpreted in practice in your particular organization, for example;
- identifying the boundaries, constraints and extremes within which these definitions are seen to apply;
- increasing your knowledge of the issue itself.

Design

This technique uses purposive, 'snowball' sampling (see section 9.2): you take the guidance of your early respondents into account in choosing subsequent interviewees. Moreover, you also involve early respondents in determining the kinds of questions you will ask of your subsequent interviewees. As a result, your advance planning must include arrangements to prevent your respondents from running away with the design, and you do this in two ways. Firstly, by determining the criteria for respondent choice in advance, bearing in mind:

- their role, job title, and position in the organization;
- their likely knowledge of the issue involved;
- their willingness to help, and potential articulateness in doing so;
- their likely perspective on the issue, so that idiosyncratic views can be controlled.

Secondly, by recording subsequent deviations from the list of people you initially chose as interviewees, presenting both the initial and final list as a table in your write-up, and commenting on the likely differences this might have caused to the information which you obtain.

Elicitation

Since this is a form of semistructured interview, all the general comments made in sections 11.1 and 11.2 apply, with the following specific pointers.

Steering. For any one respondent, you would proceed from the general to the particular, asking questions which define terms and determine broad boundaries before proceeding to particular details. As the sequence of interviews progresses, you incorporate questions which check the information you have obtained from your early respondents, and look for particular viewpoints and comments on these early impressions from the current respondent's perspective, always remembering to cover the general ground with the current respondent first.

Format. The comments made under this heading in sections 11.1 and 11.2 apply.

Eliciting answers. Again, the content of the answers you're looking for depends on your purpose. Remember, the individual expertise of your respondents is what's being drawn on with this technique, and so you might wish to include some questions which help to establish this: how long the person has been in his or her job, any particular professional background which might have helped to formulate their views, and so forth.

Recording answers. The comments made under this heading in section 11.2 apply: you will need some form of recording medium, and in the case of longer interviews, this might well involve a tape recorder. Bear in mind that different expert interviewees might offer you data expressed in the language of their particular expertise. Thus, an accountant might give you a table of financial ratios, or a senior manager, a page showing the results of a SWOT analysis, and so on. Take these when you leave, in addition to any personal record you make, even if you don't currently plan to present them during your write-up.

Analysis

Data obtained from key informant interviews are well suited to a content analysis in which the categories reflect the major perspectives arising in the interviews.

Perceiving. As before, you're identifying what people have said, and the emphasis which they have given it. Do people with different roles or expertise bases converge on an agreement about the issues involved, or do their individual perspectives vary in significant ways? How frequently do different people express these similar or dissimilar views? How does their position and role affect the nature of the data which they provide? Moreover, which data are as you'd expect, and which are informative because they're surprising?

Summarizing. As before, you'd do this by means of a narrative account and/or by counting the number of people who have given different kinds of answers. Bearing in mind that it's the individual's specialist views which are particularly important, and that there may only be one of each kind of interviewee (one chief executive, one group chief accountant, and so on), you may want to present information initially under job title headings, before going on to summarize the views on which there is agreement and the views on which there is disagreement, concluding with a statement of the significance involved.

Write-up

There's not much more to say under this heading that I haven't already implied under the headings immediately above, and in section 11.2.

Presenting. What makes your data informative to the reader is its provenance: who said it and why, as much as what was said!

Locating. Locating your findings in the main body of the text, preceding and illuminating the findings of a larger probability sample drawn from employees in general, is a common, and very informative, way of proceeding. If you have lots of findings from individual job holders, one respondent for each job, you might consider making these an appendix, and just presenting a summary in the main body of the text. If so, you'd need to make sure that the list of job titles was presented as a table in the main body, when you describe the sample of respondents.

11.4 THE FOCUS GROUP

This is a form of group interview in which the data arise from **dialogue and general discussion among participants**, rather than from a dialogue between yourself as investigator exploring his or her story with a single person as respondent. It is particularly useful for discovering the range of views and attitudes present within an organization or part of it, and offers you the opportunity to observe the processes by which people interact, and hence to infer something of the culture and climate of the organization as well as providing you with data about the content of people's views on the issues which you are exploring. However, because several people are interacting, your control over the sequence of questions dealt with is less than in the one-to-one interviews described above, and the data are somewhat more difficult to analyse; moreover, they're restricted to publicly expressible material. If you use focus groups in your project work, then, you might consider triangulating by using one of the individual forms of interviewing as well.

Design

If your purpose is simply to familiarize yourself with the variety of views on a topic, a pair of focus groups will do; however, if you're examining different perspectives, or exploring a variety of issues on which people's views are likely to vary depending on their role or company position, you'll need to organize a larger number. (One group alone is never sufficient, since the data may simply reflect individual personalities, raising problems for the generalization of your findings to your organization as a whole.)

Each group should consist of similar kinds of people who have enough in common that they can enter into a discussion about the topic in question, but who preferably are unfamiliar with each other on a regular, day-to-day basis. The latter may seem surprising, but consider: if they know each other and communicate regularly, they'll take a lot of things for granted. Yet these are just the things (values, norms, assumptions and beliefs based on a common organizational rather than personal history) that you want to uncover, by the skilful and careful way in which you conduct the discussion. Ideally, you create a situation in which the focus group is led to **discover** them for you. While it's appropriate to mix people doing different kinds of job at the same organizational level, Krueger (1988) is probably correct in suggesting that you shouldn't mix people across organizational levels, for the above reason, and the additional one that people in supervisor–subordinate relationships to each other may be inhibited in what they are willing to say to each other.

Table 11.4 lists the main factors involved in designing focus group activities, most of them self-evident. Notice the distinction that's made between the focus group members, and other people in the organization whom it may be possible to involve in the design of the group. You'll recall the rationale for, and value of, doing so from section 6.2. In the case of focus groups, there are two good ways of involving people in a cooperative venture:

■ by discussing your purpose, and the sort of information sought, with the kinds of people in your organization who would be most interested

Table 11.4 Designing focus groups

Determining purpose
- What kind of information is being sought?
- Why is it being sought: what project issues will it illuminate?
- Consider involving members of the organization (but not future focus group participants) in identifying issues, questions, and type of focus group participant to recruit
- Who else will have access (including feedback to the focus group participants themselves)?
- A written statement of the above, for discussion with people who will use the results: stakeholders and other interested parties in the organization, tutor, sponsor

Determining number and size of groups
- one to four groups for fairly structured, exploratory work
- six to eight groups for relatively unstructured work requiring full content analysis of data
- four to twelve people in each group: small groups may be biased by existing relationships between participants, individual expertise, uncooperative respondents; larger groups raise difficulties in controlling and recording subgroup conversations
- add 20% extra to each group to allow for 'no-shows'

Determining focus group participants
- which different categories of people will be involved?
  - Members of different departments?
  - Holders of different types of post?
  - Members of different professional groups?
  - Advisory/service groups?
  - Customers/clients, potential or actual?
  - Big customers/small customers?
- Different focus groups for different categories

Determining timetable
- A day or so to determine questions, especially if these are developed cooperatively
- A half-day for preparation, briefing of other people involved in observation/ recording
- A half-day per focus group activity
- A further day for preparation and administration of recordings, per focus group
- A week or so for typing transcripts
- Another week for analysis
- A week for write-up and report

After Krueger (1988) and Morgan (1988)

in, or affected by, the conclusions and recommendations of this part of your project. Involve them in planning, and consider the possibility of using one or two of them in acting alongside you as group facilitators (always assuming that this doesn't bias your results); take feedback from them after they've seen the results;
■ by feeding back the results to your focus group members.

Elicitation

You elicit data in a focus group by facilitating ('leading', 'moderating' are synonyms) a group discussion focused on a particular topic. You do so by posing a sequence of questions which stimulate, maintain, and direct the flow of discussion; this discussion must:

■ be broad-ranging but relevant;
■ provide data that are as specific, concrete and detailed as possible;
■ explore feelings with sensitivity, while bearing in mind the personal context.

To do this well requires some experience of group discussion and a fair degree of interpersonal skill; if you're a beginner, and intend to base the bulk of your empirical work round the focus group technique, then a careful reading of Krueger (1988) will give you an excellent start – Chapters 4 and 5 and his procedural appendices in particular.

Steering. A relatively small number of questions (five to eight, no more) are posed, ordered from the more general to the more particular, and preceded by a statement of the purpose in holding the group and a number of statements in which you set the context for the discussion.

It's useful to think of the set of questions as a route within which discussion will be channelled, and, in contrast to the semistructured interview, you shouldn't diverge from the predetermined order in which you ask the questions. Indeed, the skill in focus group facilitation lies less in the posing of the questions, and much more in:

■ making appropriate interjections and probes to maintain discussion on a particular question;
■ tolerating silences at points where these might encourage fruitful *sotto voce* comment;
■ anticipating the flow of discussion and steering it away from dead-ends;
■ legitimizing varying viewpoints;
■ preventing some individuals from dominating the discussion at the expense of others.

Format. As with all the other types of semi-structured interview, your questions are open-ended; as with the individual interview, you can delimit the form of answer by adding a qualifying statement to the question. In contrast to these, however, you're advised to avoid direct 'why' questions, since these can inhibit the flow of discussion; use a 'what prompted/influenced you' or a 'what sort of features attract you to/lead you away from' form of question instead. Other than these format guidelines, focus group technique explicitly avoids any attempt to indicate the form in which answers are to be provided, because the 'answers' to questions are often an emergent property of the discussion, to be identified during the analysis, rather than a specific response to a direct question.

Eliciting answers. What you will ask depends on your purpose. Since the intention during the group is to stimulate a natural and free discussion, and all of your attention will be devoted to matters of interaction and process, it is good practice to memorize in advance the questions you'll ask, and the possible probes for each.

Recording answers. For similar reasons, you won't be able to make extensive notes during the focus group. If you want to capture complete verbatim utterances, use a colleague in an assistant facilitator role, whose entire job it is to act as a scribe. You'll depend on the tape recorder for the bulk of your recording needs, however.

Analysis

An adequate analysis of material obtained from a set of focus groups takes plenty of time. This is partly because written transcripts have to be prepared from the original tape-recordings, partly because the analysis procedure itself is fairly unstructured, and partly because of the additional safeguards you have to provide in order to preserve the validity and reliability of the information you obtain.

As soon as possible after each focus group is completed, you should sit down, with your co-facilitator if you used one, listen to the tape recording, and discuss the main themes which you see as emerging. These should be summarized in a brief written report, which reflects your discussion of themes, subthemes, relevant participant characteristics, key utterances or phrases used by the participants, notes on significant non-verbal incidents, and an impression of the mood and feelings expressed in the group. The value of a co-facilitator (someone who was also there!) is immense: can you agree on the contents of this report? If you don't have another person in this role, then each point in the notes should be written with the following questions in mind.

- How can I prove it?
- What evidence can I cite?

Perceiving. The next step is to analyse the content of all of the focus groups you have conducted, with your topic and project issues in mind. You've a mass of raw data in front of you, and you're setting out to simplify it by perceiving, summarizing, and providing evidence, so as to identify the themes and subthemes which emerged in the discussion. Inevitably, as with all semistructured work, something of yourself will go into this analysis. You will have had a number of hunches, expectations, and propositions related to the thesis of your project before you come to the data, and these will form a background against which you look for the themes themselves. How best to prevent them from prejudicing your findings while using them to guide and inform all your efforts?

You have several possibilities: to stick closely to the **raw data** themselves, carrying out and presenting a content analysis along the lines discussed in section 11.2, or to stand back from the data a little and write an **interpretation**, based on your prior hunches and on the material in front of you, with supporting evidence in the form of verbatim quotes that reflect consensus and key disagreements. Memos written to yourself (see section 11.1) could be content-analysed as evidence. Somewhere between these two extremes lies the possibility of providing a descriptive account: a summary, with relatively little interpretation, of the data before you, again supported by evidence in the form of direct quotations. Krueger (1988: 128), who has identified these possibilities, provides you with some useful examples of each approach.

Whichever approach you adopt, you're setting out to discover themes. You do so by:

- reading through all your summaries to identify potential themes and trends;
- reading through all the transcripts, identifying the material which followed in response to each of your questions, to refine your perceptions of themes and trends;
- listening again to all the tape recordings, looking for evidence to confirm the results of the previous step;
- bearing in mind the membership of the different focus groups that you conducted, and the way in which this may influence the themes which people expressed.

You need to listen to the meanings expressed in the words people use, the context in which things were said, and the consistency with which these were said; in all of this, as Krueger (1988) puts it, you're trying to 'find the big ideas'.

Summarizing. The results of all this activity are summarized in the form of a series of statements. Each statement expresses a main theme, and is followed by evidence in the form of a narrative account of the gist of what was said, with some information about the degree of consensus with which it was said, and some illustrative quotations.

Opinions are divided about the way in which consensus is expressed. Krueger (1988) feels that there is no place for numeric data (along the lines of a content analysis which states how many utterances were coded under each category or theme). Other writers, Morgan (1988), for example, feel that, so long as the numbers are only used to give an impression of the impact or main thrust of the feeling (percentages and the like), numeric data can be useful, particularly in contrasting the strength of feeling on an issue between focus groups consisting of different kinds of people.

I would advise you to follow Morgan, but avoid the temptation of carrying out any statistical tests of significance on these numbers. In other words, you can use them in a descriptive way, to identify the main thrust of consensus; to do any more would be to make statistical assumptions that aren't warranted. Many of your focus group members will make repeated statements on one theme, which on feedback to the group turn out to be relatively lightweight, while others make just one, quiet, but deadly effective utterance, which sums up the mood of all. Your data categories aren't statistically independent (a property required for any form of statistical test), and the frequency of utterances doesn't reflect the impact of the ideas being expressed.

Write-up

You would write up your findings as a single account, and not group by group.

Presenting. Krueger (1988) provides a number of examples suited to one-off reports. As your own presentation will be just a part of a more complete document, I'd suggest that you present the context, followed by a set of headings each of which represents one of the themes you identified, with a descriptive summary, and a list of relevant quotations. One or two tables which summarize the main thrust of the trends on a particularly important issue (especially if these express some difference of emphasis between different categories of participant) would also make sense; but generally, the presentation of the information in focus group technique, in contrast to questionnaire technique, is not structured around tables.

Locating. This account would be placed in the main body of the text, preceded by an account of the issues and themes which you selected for investigation by the focus group technique. A summary and conclusions might follow immediately, or form part of a broader statement which summarizes the results of accompanying individual interviews or any other technique which you have used. The place for a full report, or summaries of the findings of each separate group if they are particularly pertinent, would be in an appendix.

11.5 A NOTE ON THE VALIDITY OF WHAT YOU'RE DOING

Chapter 6 presented an argument to the effect that project work done in the style of a study, rather than according to the rules of hypothetico-deductive method, is more likely to cope with the realities of in-company existence. If this is true, then some of the techniques I've described in this chapter are quite sufficient to provide you with realistic and valid information, on a stand-alone basis, and quite good enough to build an argument round a conceptual model, or support some thesis you wish to establish (or to reveal lack of support, if the realities as you're forced to perceive them are such!). Others, like the conversational technique, may require supporting evidence obtained by using one of the other techniques.

You should always remain aware of the sources of error that face you, and the first step in doing so is to re-read the description of the technique you wish to use, paying particular attention to the methods for coping with error. Having said that, it's also true that any of the techniques described in this chapter can be used as a means of piloting and developing categories and hypotheses for the more structured techniques which are described in the following chapter, the validity of which will be all the stronger because of the rigorous work you've already put in. When used for pilot work in this way, any of these techniques could be used on its own.

Fully structured techniques | 12

This chapter presents two commonly used techniques: the questionnaire, and the form of interview in which a questionnaire-like interview guide is followed by the interviewer. It also describes two procedural variants, the postal questionnaire and the telephone interview. All of these techniques are **structured**. In contrast to the semi-structured techniques presented in Chapter 11, that means that the content and sequence of the questions have been determined in advance, and that little that happens as people provide you with answers will make any difference to this. Likewise, the **form** of answers which you will accept from your respondents is determined in advance. However, this isn't as inflexible as it might seem. There is scope for the inclusion of some open-ended questions within a fully structured questionnaire, for example, and it is good practice always to provide an 'other, please specify' answer category, either explicitly in a questionnaire, or by careful questioning in a structured interview.

The value of this approach is that it allows you to standardize your questioning to such an extent that a more numerate, statistically-based analysis is possible, and permits you to test out hypotheses more explicitly, always assuming that the situation permits. Moreover, as Selltiz *et al.* (1981) point out, a properly devised, standardized method is likely to be cheaper to administer, may permit you to cover more respondents, can provide greater feelings of anonymity, may require less skill and sensitivity to administer, and allows your respondent more time to think about his or her responses than any of the semistructured techniques. This is especially true in the case of postal questionnaires. Table 12.1 summarizes these and other characteristics of postal questionnaire work, face-to-face interviewing, and telephone interviewing. As you can see, there isn't a single 'best buy' for all situations.

All these characteristics involve decisions which must be addressed during the course of your design. Not one of them is an inherent property

Table 12.1 A comparison of the main structured techniques

H stands for high, M for medium, and L for low levels of the characteristic shown at left.

Characteristic	Postal questionnaire	Face-to-Face interview	Telephone interview
Design and sampling issues			
Control over inclusion of all population in sample	M	H	M
Control over selection of respondents into sample	M	H	H
Chances of answers being given by someone else	H	L	L
Sensitivity to distortion by respondent substitution	H	M	H
Chance of controlling bias due to selective non-response	L	H	H
Refusal rate	H	M	L
Response rate with varied populations (public at large)	M	H	H
Response rate with homogeneous, highly selected populations	H	H	H
Questionnaire construction issues			
Likely acceptability of longer list of questions	M	H	M
Likely success of complex questions	M	H	L
Likely success of open-ended questions	M	H	H
Likely success of steering questions	M	H	H
Likely success of boring-but-necessary questions	L	H	H
Likely success with personal and sensitive questions	H	M	L
Likely success in avoiding missed questions	M	H	H
Issues of bias			
Likely success in establishing anonymity/ confidentiality	H	M	M
Chances of avoiding bias due to social desirability of answers	H	L	M
Chances of avoiding 'interviewer' bias	H	L	M
Chances of avoiding contamination by others	M	M	H
Feasibility of assistance being available to investigator	M	M	L

Table 12.1 continued

Administrative issues			
Amount of time required to set up and implement	H	H	L
Potential costs	M	H	L
Control over costs	H	L	M
Sensitivity of costs to geographical distance from respondents	L	H	M

After Dillman (1978) and Frey (1983)

of the technique in question, and desirable results won't happen spontaneously. Indeed, you might be surprised by the amount of advanced preparation that will be required before you can use a structured technique.

12.1 THE STRUCTURED QUESTIONNAIRE

You begin the development of a structured questionnaire in more or less the same way as you do the semi-structured interview. In other words, as I described in section 11.2, an explicit statement of your purpose will suggest a major question which you wish to explore, and you spend some time in mapping out a number of questions, each of which will provide you with data about various aspects of the major question. Beyond that, the procedure is substantially different, since you must also provide the steering information, the format of answers, and a system for recording answers to each of the questions, in such a way that your respondent can express his or her intentions straightforwardly without further prompting by yourself. (After all, in the case of a postal questionnaire, you won't be physically present!) Furthermore, you will have decided on the format in the light of your plans for the analysis of your data.

Before proceeding, let me establish a convention of terminology. As you will gather from the following sections, it's possible to elicit data in a variety of ways, and only one of these takes the form of posing a question (a sentence which ends with a question mark!), to which a number of answers are provided. Occasionally, for example, you'll be asking your respondent to look at a set of phrases and tick just one of them as most representative of his or her views: no question as such, no answer sentence either. To avoid confusion, let's call the string of words by which you elicit data an **item**, any string of words which expresses a potential answer an **alternative**, and the action a respondent makes to indicate his or her views, a **response**.

Design

By now, you will be clear on the form of design to use, will have decided on the size and nature of the sample which you wish to draw, and will know enough about the issues you wish to explore to have decided on a particular sampling method. If this is still unclear, you'd be advised to do either or both of the following.

- Re-read section 9.2 on sampling, section 9.3 on design and on sample size.
- Discuss the results of any semi-structured technique which you have already used with your tutor or sponsor in order to work out the design and sampling implications of the present phase.

If you have divided your sample into subgroups of respondents (by quota, stratified, or cluster sample methods), or if you are interested in the responses of different kinds of people irrespective of sample subgrouping, then the major design issue which remains is for you to prepare items to be used to identify, record, or confirm your respondents' membership of the various subgroups.

For example, if you have a sample stratified by number of years of service in the organization, you'll want to develop an item which gets your respondents to tell you how many years they've served. With some forms of sampling, you would have found this out in advance, needing to know this in order to draw up the sample subgroups in your sampling frame; but though you may know this for each subgroup in total, you may not know it for each named individual. And in any case, it is essential standard practice to confirm information of this kind. Similarly, if you intend to break down people's responses on any other basis, quite apart from their membership of a sample subgroup (for example, because you're exploring an issue and have subgrouped respondents according to their views on that issue: see the material entitled 'handling non-technical problems' in section 6.3), you must make sure you provide an item which will allow you to group in this way.

There is more on this in the analysis section below; for the moment, let me stress that good design involves you in identifying, in advance, two entirely distinct kinds of item: those which provide you with straightforward descriptive data, and those which will help you to turn these data into information by analysing responses according to the categories of people in whose differing patterns of response you're especially interested.

Elicitation

Designing the items themselves is an iterative process; you'll find yourself cycling through the activities outlined below several times, for each item you're preparing, as you refine it for eventual use. Table 12.2 is intended as an aid in this activity. You should use it as a checklist to be applied to each item as you develop it.

You may find it helpful to write each item on a filecard, to allow for subsequent amendment and reordering as necessary. Other important details will also be written on this filecard, so make sure you buy a pack of the larger-sized index cards.

Steering. Your first concern will be for the sequence in which to present your items to respondents. Next, you will need to decide if a given item is to be answered by all respondents, or is to be skipped by some respondents because of the way they answered items earlier in the sequence. You might like to number each card in the order in which that item is going to be presented to respondents, writing the substantive item itself on the card in capital letters. Generally speaking, items which elicit personally sensitive data, those dealing with feelings or which require some thought, and those concerning issues on which the respondent may not have made up his or her mind, should come later in the sequence. Factual and more straightforward information should come first.

Clearly, some personal data are factual and straightforward. No one will mind giving you their name, department name, or, assuming it's relevant, their sex. It's important to have them, particularly if your sample is divided into subgroups and these data are to be used in cross-tabulating other, less personal data. Your inclination will be to put them at the start of your questionnaire, but consider: some people are very sensitive about certain factual details about themselves (e.g. age, salary, union membership). A common practice in cases where personal details include sensitive, as well as factual data, is to put all the personal details questions together at the end of the questionnaire, the rationale being that by then, rapport will have been established with the respondent.

As your set of items develops, and you realize that the sequence will depend on the individual's responses to previous questions, you'll need to add a form of words which tells the respondent which question to address next: 'If you chose alternative (a) to this question, please skip question 16 and go on to question 17'; or, 'If your answer to the previous question was "Yes", please give a reason in your own words in the space provided below' are some possible examples of explicit steering instructions. You might like to write these on to the filecard in lower case lettering, below or above the words which express the substantive content of the item itself.

Table 12.2 A checklist for item-by-item questionnaire design

Design and sampling
1. How is the respondent's membership of sample subgroups ascertained or confirmed?
2. Does this particular item do the above, as distinct from providing substantive data?

Elicitation: steering
1. What form of words is most appropriate for the steering instructions?
2. Is the item in the right place in the sequence?
3. Is it led up to in a natural way? Does it come too late or too early in terms of arousing interest?
4. Is the response likely to be biased by responses to previous items?

Elicitation: format
1. What response format is most appropriate for this item?
2. Where free-choice and multiple-choice formats are used, does each set:
   - cover all the possible alternatives?
   - provide categories that are mutually exclusive?
   - provide an appropriately worded 'don't know' category?
3. Where rating-scale format is used, is the scale:
   - anchored at each end and at various points by a suitable operational description?
   - centred with a middle point so that genuine indifference can be indicated? (Unless you suspect that people will 'sit on the fence': in which case, use an even number of alternatives.)
   - of no more than nine points (people can't apply a consistent framework over more than nine)?
4. Where a set of rating scales is used:
   - are position preferences controlled for?
   - is "yea-saying" controlled for?
   - is social desirability controlled for?
   (The first two involve using wording such that agreement with the meaning expressed in the item means ticking the right-hand end of the scale for some items, left-hand end for others; the second is a matter of appropriate wording or the use of paired comparison techniques)
5. Where ranking format is used is the respondent:
   - told whether tied ranks are acceptable?
   - asked to rank fewer than twelve or so alternatives? (Again, problems in being consistent when ranking large numbers of alternatives: use paired comparison format if necessary.)

Eliciting answers
1. With respect to item **content**:
   - is this item really necessary to the issue being explored?
   - are several items required to cover the issue? (e.g. asking how strongly a person feels, as well as what the person thinks)

Table 12.2 continued

- will the respondent have the information required for a valid response? (consider using information cards or 'flashcards' to remind about possibilities)
- is the item sufficiently concrete and specific? But also
- is the item general enough and free of spurious concreteness?
- will the response really indicate an informed judgement, or just elicit a stereotype?
- is it too specific, personal, too early or too late in the sequence to be answered honestly?

2. With regard to item **wording**:
   - does it avoid obscurity? (e.g. does 'PC' stand for an IBM-compatible micro, any personal computer, political correctness, or a police constable?)
   - does it avoid undefined qualitative words (e.g. words like 'quite', 'usually', 'frequently')
   - is the basis for answering specified? (e.g. are you looking for a neutral, informed, personal, behavioural, ethical, or moral basis underlying the response)
   - does it mislead through hidden implications or words evoking stereotypes? (e.g. 'International Manager'; 'Good European')
   - is it too personal ? (e.g. 'How much do you earn?': better provide broad bands and ask respondent to tick one); but also, can it be expressed more directly?

Recording answers

1. Is the respondent told explicitly how he or she is to indicate the response? (Ticking one alternative, ticking more than one alternative, ranking, rating, filling out a table, answering in his or her own words.)
2. Is the respondent asked to check the consistency of responses? (e.g. ensuring that percentages sum to 100; knowing what to do to indicate an equal preference)
3. Will the item require illustrative material, or a flashcard to summarize the alternatives?
4. Is the respondent asked to check that essential details have been provided? (e.g. name, location)

Analysis

1. Is the planned method of analysis consistent with the wording of the item and its content?

   See Figure 12.1 on methods of analysis to be used after the questionnaire has been returned – but make sure that this issue is considered when the item is first being written!

After Kornhauser and Sheatsley (1976); Dillman (1978)

Occasionally, whole sections of the questionnaire must be skipped, depending on the responses to previous items, and you'll need to keep track of whole wodges of filecards. If your questionnaire involves several such contingent sequences of questions, you'll find that a simple flowchart is helpful for recording the order of the cards, and for keeping track of the alternative sequences through them. This may seem a little pedantic but, believe me, it's very useful for the time (and it will come!) when you, or the member of a pilot group of respondents on whom you're testing out your questionnaire, wonder if a better questionnaire sequence is required.

Whether you need to keep track of the items in this way depends partly on how long your questionnaire is going to be. Common sense suggests a dilemma: people like attractive, well-laid out questionnaires with plenty of space on the page (especially if you include some open-ended items); on the other hand, they lose interest if the questionnaire has too many pages. There's more on this issue in the eliciting answers section below; for the meantime, you should plan on using filecards and a flowchart if your questionnaire is longer than ten items or three pages of final typescript.

Format. A variety of response formats is available to you, the most common being the fixed-alternative forms (multiple choice, free choice, ranking, and rating), and open-ended forms.

Multiple-choice format is the most common and straightforward: you ask your respondent to choose a single alternative from a list of several which you provide. You always include an 'Other, please specify' alternative; with some kinds of question an appropriately worded 'Don't know' alternative will also be informative without causing offence. **Free choice format** allows the respondent to choose one or more alternatives and, again, should offer an 'Other, please specify' alternative. **Ranked format** asks the respondent to put all the alternatives into rank order on some quality specified in the item; using an 'Other, please specify' alternative is not advisable since analysing the item will be very difficult, and so you need to have thoroughly pre-researched ranked format items, to be sure that your set of alternatives is completely exhaustive without the 'Other' alternative. **Rating format** involves the respondent in assigning 'points' to each alternative, and usually provides a scale by which he or she can do so. Finally, **open-ended format** simply states the item and requests the respondent to answer in his or her own words.

These formats are exemplified in Figures 12.1 and 12.2 (with the exception of rating scales, which are described in section 13.2). As you ponder over the content of each of your items, you should decide which answer format is most:

■ likely to provide you with the most useful data about your respondent's views;

Components	Text as it appears in the questionnaire (italics excepted: see notes below)
Item	Q.8 *IN YOUR VIEW,* WHAT IS THE MOST IMPORTANT PRIORITY FOR THE *CHAIRMAN* OF A *FINANCIAL INSTITUTION*?
Recording instructions	Please put a tick in the box beside the *ONE alternative* which best describes your view.
Alternatives	(a) To understand the basic concepts which underlie the various forms of financing which the institution offers to its clients ☐
	(b) To foster an entrepreneurial spirit in which appropriate levels of risk can be contemplated and evaluated ☐
	(c) To encourage the development of a clear, and commonly shared, vision of the institution and its future ☐
	(d) To ensure that the corporate strategy and mission statement permeate decisions taken by staff at all levels ☐
	(e) To develop an appropriate organizational structure, and avoid alterations to it ☐
	(f) To remember the paramount importance of the shareholders in setting objectives and evaluating priorities ☐
	(g) OTHER: Please specify, in your own words, in the space below:
Steering instructions	*Public (government) funding organization*: please skip Q.9 and go on to Q.10; Q.9 is aimed at *privately owned* financial institutions.

In this study of the chairmen of boards of financial institutions (banks, discount houses, insurance companies, merchant banks, venture capitalists, and government funding organizations...

Notes on italic text:	
1. *IN YOUR VIEW*:	A personal viewpoint (as distinct from, say, a corporate or board view)
2. *CHAIRMAN*:	It is tempting to use 'Chairperson' but, following evidence that the practice among this population is to use 'Chairman', the latter is used in order to match the expectations of the sample members. A difficult choice: do you stick to your principles or maximize return rate?
3. *ONE alternative*:	The item is written in multiple-choice format, i.e. choose one item from several.
4. ☐:	Analysis will involve tallying ticks in each box across the whole sample.
5. Public/private:	The sample has been stratified on this basis, so the tallies will be done separately for each subgroup.

Figure 12.1 Deciding on response format.

■ easily analysed for the information contained in the data it will provide.

In other words, the format isn't something you can decide without thinking ahead to the time your questionnaires have been returned and your data are available for analysis. On the one hand, if the format doesn't match the wording of the item to the appropriate analysis method, the item will confuse the respondents and the results will lack validity; on the other hand, a format that is inadequate in this regard will also confuse you, when you have to get down to the mechanics of the analysis and realize that you haven't thought things through. Indeed, one of the most common reasons for missing a project submission deadline arises when a student leaves the detailed planning of his or her analysis until all the data are in!

Eliciting answers. Now you come to the specification of the item content. This consists of two parts: the item itself, and the set of alternatives. As Table 12.2 suggests, there are issues of both content and wording which you should bear in mind as you write. A good item is strictly necessary, covers appropriate material, is suited to the comprehension and knowledge level of the sample, is appropriately specific, avoids stereotyped answers, and comes in the right place in the questionnaire sequence. Moreover, it's worded precisely, doesn't take a knowledge of in-house or professional acronyms for granted, is non-threatening, avoids vague words, and indicates the basis on which the response is to be made.

It's possible that you will construct the alternatives from the knowledge of the issues which you gained by your earlier use of less structured techniques: conversational, key informant interview, focus group, or whatever. The alternatives may be ones which you informally judged to be appropriate as a result of that earlier experience, or they may be categories which you explicitly derived from a full content analysis of the earlier data. Their content will depend on this prior thinking, while their wording will depend on the answer format which you have chosen, as well as on the guidelines outlined in Table 12.2. Add the item and the alternatives on to your filecard.

The wording of your item and alternatives has a great bearing on the final length of the questionnaire, and, clearly, if the questionnaire is perceived as being too long, the responses are likely to be careless, or, indeed, non-existent. Some items may require a brief sentence of background and rationale; some demand a longish list of alternatives, while others, the open-ended ones, require you to provide at least 8 cm inches of space into which your respondent will write their response

IN YOUR VIEW, WHAT IS THE MOST IMPORTANT PRIORITY FOR THE CHAIRMAN OF A FINANCIAL INSTITUTION? Please put a tick in the box beside the ONE alternative which best describes your view	Public n	Private n	Public %	Private %
To understand the basic concepts which underlie the various forms of financing which the institution offers to its clients	4	8	10	13
To foster an entrepreneurial spirit in which appropriate levels of risk can be contemplated and evaluated	2	12	5	20
To encourage the development of a clear, and commonly shared, vision of the institution and its future	10	15	25	25
To ensure that the corporate strategy and mission statement permeate decisions taken by staff at all levels	5	11	13	18
To develop an appropriate organizational structure, and avoid alterations to it	8	7	20	12
To remember the paramount importance of the shareholders in setting objectives and evaluating priorities	5	4	13	7
Fulfilling responsibilities to government	5	0	13	0
No answer (no. of respondents)	1	3	3	5
Total (no. of respondents)	40	60	102	100

A straightforward analysis. In the two leftmost columns, tally all the responses in each category across the sample, keeping the two sample subgroups separate; report the tallies, together with information about the number of people not answering the question. Total of tallies downwards plus 'no answers' (plus 'don't knows', if any) must equal sample size and must aways be reported. Where subgroups exist and are of unequal size, calculate % values and report these next to the basic frequency data, in the two rightmost columns. (The '102%' total was bad luck: an awkward divisor!).

Figure 12.2(a) Procedural guide: the analysis of multiple choice responses.

verbatim. If you begin to get the impression as you prepare your filecards that the questionnaire is simply going to be too long, you might decide to use an entirely different technique, the face-to-face structured interview being the obvious alternative to choose. How long is 'too long'? Well, that depends on many factors, especially those which help to retain your respondent's interest in the topic you're covering (see Table 12.3); but Howard and Sharp (1983) offer a useful rule of thumb for postal questionnaires when they suggest that anything longer than 10 pages, or taking longer than 15 minutes to complete, is likely to be too long.

HERE IS A LIST OF PRIORITIES TO WHICH A CHAIRMAN MIGHT SUBSCRIBE. Please tick any one or more which you feel are important.	Public n	Private n	Public %	Private %
To understand the basic concepts which underlie the various forms of financing which the institution offers to its clients	16	30	10	13
To foster an entrepreneurial spirit in which appropriate levels of risk can be contemplated and evaluated	5	49	3	22
To encourage the development of a clear, and commonly shared, vision of the institution and its future	43	58	26	26
To ensure that the corporate strategy and mission statement permeate decisions taken by staff at all levels	25	48	15	21
To develop an appropriate organizational structure, and avoid alterations to it	32	21	20	9
To remember the paramount importance of the shareholders in setting objectives and evaluating priorities	19	18	12	8
Fulfilling responsibilities to government	23	0	14	0
No answer (no. of respondents)	1	3		
Total (no. of responses)	163	224	100	99

Not quite so straightforward since, in free choice format, each respondent ticks as many boxes as he or she wishes. In the two leftmost columns, tally all the responses in each category across the sample, keeping the two sample subgroups separate; report the tallies, together with information about the number of people not answering the question. Notice that the total at the bottom of the columns represents the sum of ticks, **not** the total of respondents. Use the latter when working out % values, and report these in the two rightmost columns.

Figure 12.2(b) Procedural guide: the analysis of free-choice responses.

Recording answers. When you've specified the alternatives, you must then decide on the wording you will use to instruct the respondent on how he or she is to make a response. You might imagine that most sensible people would be able to work it out for themselves just by looking at the item. However, as you'll realize from your ruminations on answer format, different formats call for different recording methods. If you don't tell the respondent which of these answer formats to use, you'll end up assessing the respondent's intelligence rather than his or her responses to the item in question, thus increasing the unreliability of the data you collect. Add the wording of the recording instructions on to your file card.

HERE IS A LIST OF PRIORITIES TO WHICH A CHAIRMAN MIGHT SUBSCRIBE. Please rank them from 1 to 7 to express your own view of their relative importance. '1' means 'highest' and '7' means 'lowest'. They are priorities, so no two can have the same rank.	RESPONDENTS (Public-sector only) There would be as many columns here as there are respondents, plus a column for the sum of ranks. (Only the first and second respondents' columns are shown in this example.)			PUBLIC SECTOR
	1st,	2nd...	....Sum of 39 respondents	Sums, ranked
To understand the basic concepts which underlie the various forms of financing which the institution offers to its clients	5	7	480	6
To foster an entrepreneurial spirit in which appropriate levels of risk can be contemplated and evaluated	7	6	504	7
To encourage the development of a clear, and commonly shared, vision of the institution and its future	2	1	120	1
To ensure that the corporate strategy and mission statement permeate decisions taken by staff at all levels	3	2	190	3
To develop an appropriate organizational structure, and avoid alterations to it	1	4	170	2
To remember the paramount importance of the shareholders in setting objectives and evaluating priorities	6	5	458	5
Fulfilling responsibilities to government	4	3	265	4
No answer (no. of respondents)				1
Total (no. of respondents)				40

Analysis of ranked data involves:
- Summing the rank given to each alternative, **across** the sample or subsample left to right across the respondent columns: (as in the first two columns above, which show the first and second respondents' ranks), into a column of rank sums for the whole subgroup (the third column above).
- Ranking these rank sums, the lowest getting rank 1, and putting the resulting values into another column (the fourth column above).
- Repeating the above steps for each of the remaining subgroups of the whole sample.
- The resulting sets of rankings are directly comparable between subgroups, and would be collated into a final table for presentation and discussion. You wouldn't report the individual respondents' rankings (columns 1 and 2 above).
Notice that:
- The respondents must be told the direction of ranking ('1' means 'highest'); and how to handle tied ranks (in this instance, they aren't allowed).
- Totals of respondents are reported, as always. (There are only 39 respondent columns in our example since one respondent didn't provide us with data!)

Figure 12.2(c) Procedural guide: the analysis of ranked responses.

Table 12.3 The factors which maximize response rates in survey work.

Factors maximizing response	Examples
1. Rewarding the respondent by:	
• Showing that you value them and their help	Sharing information on why and how they were chosen
	Personalizing communications
• Expressing this verbally	Saying 'thank you' in writing or orally, in advance as well as after data return
• Viewing them as experts whom you wish to consult	Telling them why their knowledge is relevant
	Appealing to their personal expertise
• Showing how the study supports (or at least is not in conflict with) their values	Showing how the research is relevant to issues which currently concern them
• Offering tangible rewards	Where available, a token payment to establish 'ability to deliver'
• Making the questions and method used to pose them interesting to the respondent	Good technique in using the particular data-gathering method involved
2. Reducing costs to the respondent by	
• Making the task appear brief	Evidence of clear structure (layout and clarity of questionnaires; brief summary of points to be covered in interview)
• Reducing the mental and physical effort involved	Clarity of expression of questions asked
	Simplifying data return
	Making appointments to suit respondent
• Eliminating the possibility of embarassment	Making more personal questions easy to answer by (a) avoiding them! (b) appropriate wording (c) appropriate sequencing
	Informing about anonymity and security arrangements
• Avoiding any impression of subordination	'Asking a favour'; but also, involvement in design/evaluation of the questions being asked
• Eliminating any direct monetary cost	Supply of pre-stamped, pre-addressed return envelope
	Paying your way in interview situations where a meal is involved
	Meeting direct expenses
3. Establishing trust by	
• Providing some token in advance	A confirmatory thank you card or phonecall before the questionnaire is returned/ interview conducted
• Establishing status and legitimacy	Reference to your university
	Reference to in-company sponsor/support
• Building on pre-existing reward–cost outcomes	Reference to previous relationships between you/supporters and the respondent

After Dillman (1978)

The words in which you tell your respondents how they are to tackle the item (the format instructions and recording instructions) have a great influence on the perceived style and 'flavour' of your questionnaire, and these in turn play an important part in the respondent's decision to cooperate with you. The word 'please' is at your disposal, and the only issue is whether including it with the recording instructions of every item isn't a bit repetitive. Make a judgement when you've seen how the whole set of file cards reads.

By this time, each card is beginning to look crowded. It contains:

- a number indicating its place in the questionnaire sequence;
- the wording of the steering instructions;
- the wording of the item;
- the wording of the alternatives;
- the wording of the recording instructions.

Shuffle the cards into sequence, and compile them into a typed, A4 format to provide a master of your questionnaire ready for photocopying.

Analysis

There is a great variety of techniques available, from the simple description of sample responses by means of frequency counts over item alternatives, to a more complex use of analytic statistical tests, single or multivariate, for a single sample or for various subgroupings of your sample: the latter made possible by the fact that your questionnaire is highly structured. This isn't the place for a review of all of them, but you'll find a brief account of the main descriptive methods helpful, followed by an indication of the existence of analytic statistical measures, and a reference to further information about them. My concern at this stage is to provide you with an overview just sufficient for you to be able to complete the writing of your questionnaire items, with particular reference to the different formats outlined above: remember, you can't complete your decision on format without an awareness of the analysis method you're going to use.

Set a cut-off date for the return of the questionnaires by which you will begin your analysis, incorporating a period for any chase-up or re-posting you have planned in the case of tardy respondents (see section 5.2). On this date, compile all your returns and look through them all, rejecting any respondents who have omitted or botched responses to so many items that their questionnaire is unusable. (If a respondent has omitted a response to just one or two questions, you can treat him or her as a 'no answer' when analysing that question; too many non-responses, or too many improperly answered items. mean that the questionnaire must be rejected. 'Too many' is a matter for your own judgement!)

From this moment on, treat the analysis of the resulting set of questionnaires as an accounting exercise; in other words, you have to account for the total number of respondents in this resulting set in your analysis of each question. Responses to tables have to add up to this total, the subtotals of subgroups must sum to this same total; the sums of response alternatives plus 'don't know' plus 'no answer' responses must sum to this total; in short, your reader must get a clear picture of the answers of the sample as a whole, across all items.

Perceiving. As Figures 12.1 and 12.2 indicate, your first step is to do a brief content analysis (see section 11.2) of the 'Other, please specify' responses to find a few (one to three, usually) categories to add to your list of alternatives for each of the items. Your analysis will then be carried out on the full set of alternatives. (Look at the alternatives in Figure 12.2 in contrast to Figure 12.1: the alternative 'Fulfilling responsibilities to government' has been added to the former, reflecting the views of five public-sector respondents.)

Next, you have to aggregate the data across all respondents; and, finally, you look for patterns in the data, in order to discover the information contained. You might do this for the data as a whole, or you might aggregate within subgroups of respondents, and there are two ways of doing the latter.

Firstly, if your sample is clustered or stratified, you'll want to examine the responses of people within the different clusters or strata, in order to draw comparisons or make contrasts. So, for example, if the sample is clustered on the basis of salary status (salaried versus wage-earning), you'll keep the data separate for each of these groups (see Table 9.2). Secondly, it is possible to obtain unexpected and interesting information by crosstabulating: breaking down the answers to one question, by the answers to another. So, for example, if you asked respondents to specify their length of service with the organization, you could see if long-serving respondents answered systematically differently from short-serving respondents, even though you didn't originally stratify the sample by length of service.

Indeed, when you're exploring an issue, it's possible to break down the answers to each item by the answers to every other single item, provided your sample is large enough and that you haven't got too many alternative answers to the items involved. The availability of user-friendly micro-computer packages makes this sort of exploration very straight-forward and tempting, but you should consider the costs:

■ you end up with masses of data and you need time to identify the usable information;

■ you increase the risks of Type 1 errors if your package allows the automatic calculation of analytic statistics (if you're familiar with statistical analysis, note the danger; if you're not, ignore the point: you shouldn't be using the statistics the package offers, so seductively, in the first place!);

■ you may become confused about the generalizability of your findings.

The last point needs some explanation. If you've subgrouped your sample (by cluster or stratified sampling), you've kept control over the sample and can validly generalize your findings to the population. So, if you've stratified by length of service, a significant difference in answers to a particular item between long-serving and short-serving members of the sample would indicate a real difference among long- and short-serving employees in your population. In contrast, if you hadn't stratified by length of service, but did a breakdown of answers to a particular question by length of service anyway, any difference between the long- and short-serving respondents would be true of the sample but not necessarily of the population.

Explore the data by all means, but focus your primary attention on the issues, hunches and hypotheses which you developed originally as relevant to your topic and thesis. And keep it simple: you're looking for patterns in the data, which usually boils down to three issues.

■ Is there a trend?
■ In the case of comparisons (e.g. between subgroups) are the answers the same?
■ If not, is there a trend to the contrasting answers: have the respondents answered systematically differently?

At the simplest, descriptive level, you report plain frequencies: tally and report the number of people who chose each alternative answer: see the procedural guide in Figure 12.3. If you're comparing the responses of different subgroups of different size, you should turn the frequencies into percentages within each subgroup, and report both. Multiple-choice, free-choice and ranked formats involve different variations on this theme, as illustrated in the procedural guide in Figure 12.2.

At a more complex, analytic level, you compute an appropriate analytic statistic which informs you if the difference or trend in the data is statistically significant, that is, large enough to represent an actual difference or trend in the population, rather than occurring only 'by chance' in your sample, i.e., as a result of factors which you haven't anticipated, didn't control, or aren't even aware of. This is a matter for a more specialist textbook, and Groebner and Shannon (1981) together with Siegel and Castellan (1988) are particularly helpful for people who feel confident with analytic statistics and have designed their questionnaire appropriately.

(being the salary figures of 70 male managers shown in Figure 12.4)

Continuously distributed data

Information can be extracted from this confusing mass of data by drawing up a frequency table and expressing the figures as a frequency graph, histogram, or pie chart.

1. If you don't already have one in the form of questionnaire item alternatives, create a set of 5–15 mutually exclusive intervals into which you can code each data item.
2. Count the number of items in each interval across the sample and list the resulting totals in a column of frequencies.
3. Check that the total of the frequency column equals the sample or group size; if not, repeat step 2.

Frequency graph: a graph of intervals (along the horizontal axis) and frequencies up the vertical axis. The points on the graph can be joined together.

Histogram: the same, but with the points on the graph represented by horizontal lines, joined to their neighbours by verticals.

Frequency graph

Histogram

Salary intervals	Frequ.
>=28,000	1
26,000–27,999	10
24,000–25,999	5
22,000–23,999	5
20,000–21,999	1
18,000–19,999	8
16,000–17,999	7
14,000–15,999	8
12,000–13,999	9
10,000–11,999	12
8,000– 9,999	4
6,000– 7,999	0
Total	70

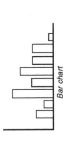

(being the 163 ticks placed into one or other of the 8 multiple-choice alternatives of Figure 12.2(a)

Data in discrete categories

Information can be extracted from this confusing mass of data by tallying in groups and expressing the figures as a bar chart or pie chart. While the bar chart looks at first glance like a histogram and while pie charts are used for both sorts of data, you can't use a histogram, or worse, frequency graph for these: the figures express the number of tallies allocated to distinct, non-continuous categories.

1. If you haven't already done a content analysis of new verbatim data, create a set of mutually exclusive questionnaire item alternatives. Usually, though, if you're working with a structured questionnaire, you already have item alternatives: the boxes people tick.
2. Count the number of responses in each box ('tallying') across the sample and then list the resulting values in a column, each next to its item alternative.
3. Check that the totals of these values equals the sample or group size; if not, repeat step 2.

Bar chart: a diagram of item alternatives along the horizontal axis and frequencies up the vertical axis. Vertical bars are drawn with heights proportionate to tallies. If the bars are drawn touching each other, that is only for visual purposes: remember, they represent non-continuous categories!

Item alternatives	Tallies
To understand the basic concepts…	4
To foster entrepreneurial spirit…	2
To encourage the development…	10
To ensure that the corporate…	5
To develop an appropriate…	8
To remember the paramount…	5
Fulfilling responsibilities to…	5
No answer	1
Total	40

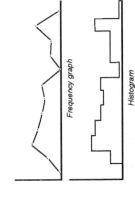

Bar chart

You wouldn't include any 'no answer' frequencies in your frequency graph or histogram. I suggest you do so in a bar chart, or pie chart when the latter is with discrete data. In all cases, don't forget to label the axes, provide a title, and prepare a verbal summary of the main finding(s) demonstrated.

Figure 12.3 Procedural guide: simple data descriptions.

However, there is one statistic, chi-square, which is so useful for picking up relationships in tabular data that I've included it here as a procedural guide, Figure 12.4. (There is a different computational procedure which you could use if you're working with a 2 × 2 table, which gives a slightly more statistically accurate answer, but the difference isn't worth worrying about: the formula I've used is a general one, suitable for a table with as many columns and rows as you please, and it was convenient to use a 2 × 2 table as an example. Refer to Siegel and Castellan (1988) for further details, and in all cases in which you have a lot of 'expected values' less than 5.) Remember, too, that whenever you establish the **statistical significance** of your data, while you have provided the best possible proof that your information expresses what is happening in the population, you have not necessarily said anything about the meaning – the **psychological significance** – of your information. The two are distinct, and the latter depends on the rationale that lies behind the relationship you're examining, which in turn depends on your design, as I've presented in section 9.1.

Before leaving the subject of analysis, perhaps a final few words about using a computer are indicated. With a sample of less than 100 people and a questionnaire of 15 items or so, you'll probably finish the job faster if you do most of the analysis by hand, with a calculator for any percentages calculations or analytic statistics that an individual question may require. That's assuming you don't have an appreciable number of cross-tabulations. The reason is simple: it takes time to learn how to use a package, cross-check the results with some sample data which you've hand-computed, and then key in all of your main data. And in any case, you shouldn't ever use a microcomputer-based statistics package to compute analytic statistics unless you know enough about the statistic to be able to do it by hand. Worst of all is the student who runs every computer-based statistical test in sight, and then goes to look for a tutor to interpret the results!

With samples of 200 and over, the time lost in learning the system and inputting the data is amply repaid by the speed and convenience of a computerized analysis, while between 100 and 200 sample size, it's difficult to say, and depends very much on the number of cross-tabulations and analytic statistics you need to compute.

If you're using a computer for analytic statistics, the manual that comes with the package will provide a good guide to the versions of the formulae used and a statement of the assumptions entailed in each. Whether you use SPSS or not, you might care to refer to the original SPSS manual (Klecka *et al.*, 1975), since it's so clearly written that it's worth referring to for its account of statistical approaches to survey analysis.

Comments

You would work out the value of chi-square if you have a table of distinct categories arranged vertically and horizontally, and you felt there might be a trend or relationship in the data. It is particularly useful where you are comparing two columns of figures which are tallies, for two separate subgroups of a sample, of responses which have been categorized using the same set of answer categories for both subgroups.

Rationale

Take the simplest case: a 2 × 2 table, such as the one at the bottom right of Figure 12.5.

Salary	Males	Females
>= 14,000	45	39
< 14,000	25	66
Total	70	105

Is there a trend? In the population from which this sample is drawn, do the males earn more than the females? Or is this just an accidental characteristic of this particular sample?

How big would the top left and bottom right values have to be, how small would the bottom left and top right values have to be, before you felt that the relationship in this sample was so large that you couldn't put it down to accident, and concluded it

Salary	Males	Females
>= 14,000	35	52
< 14,000	35	53
Total	70	105

You'd conclude there was no trend.

40	47	45	42
30	58	25	63
70	105	70	105

Salary	Males	Females
>= 14,000	69	1
< 14,000	1	104
Total	70	105

You'd feel pretty sure there was!

Males	Females
55	32
15	73
70	105

And in these examples, your certainty that there is a real trend in the population increases from left to right.

was true of the population? (Remember, we're assuming that you've done all you can to draw a representative sample!)

Computing chi-square

You follow the same rationale. You work out the chances that the figures you actually obtained are so different from the 'no-trend' pattern that you can no longer continue to believe there's no trend; so there must be a trend!

1. If you haven't already done so, work out all four marginal totals and the grand total for your actual figures.

Observed: the figures you actually obtained

Salary	Males	Females	Total
>= 14,000	45	39	84
< 14,000	25	66	91
Total	70	105	175

Now, what would the figures look like if there wasn't any trend? Well, that's set by the marginal totals (we assume that your sample still had the same number of males and females, and the same total of people earning above and below £14,000). so, to find out what the 'no-trend' figures would be . . .

. . . 2. For each observed figure, work out its expected value if there was no trend by multiplying its two marginal totals together and dividing by the grand total

That's 84 × 70/175 = 33.6; 84 × 105/175 = 50.4; 91 × 70/175 = 36.4; and 91 × 105/175 = 55.2

Next, notice that your certainty that there is a trend depends on the difference between the observed figures, and the no-trend, 'expected'.

Expected: the figures you'd get if there were no relationship

Salary	Males	Females
>= 14,000	33.6	50.4
< 14,000	36.4	55.2

3. So, summarize your degree of certainty by summing differences between observed and expected, as a proportion of what you'd expect if there weren't any relationship, first squaring the differences to get rid of awkward minus signs.

(45 − 33.6) squared/33.6+
(39 − 50.4) squared/50.4+
(25 − 36.4) squared/36.4+
(66 − 55.2) squared/55.2
equals chi-square, 12.13

Statisticians have worked out all possible combinations of differences for you and published the results in a table, called the 'Table of critical values for chi-square'. Using this, you can find out how certain you can be that there is a real trend in your data: that the sample reflects a real trend in the population, rather than just an accidental sampling error.

4. For a 2 × 2 table, look in the top line in the body of the table. Going from left to right, find the value nearest to and smaller than the value you calculated. At the top of that column you'll find the probability that the value you got was indeed accidental rather than reflecting a real trend.

5. By convention, you regard your value as statistically significant if this probability is equal to or less than 0.05, that is, 5%. You could be wrong – but there are only 5 chances in 100 of being wrong: a safe bet!

6. Finally, if you're working with a table bigger than 2 × 2, (C − 1) x (R − 1) where C=no. of columns and R=no. of rows, tells you which row of the table of criticall values of chi-square to refer to in step 4 above. Use row 30 if this figure is 30 or more than 30.

Figure 12.4 Procedural guide to the computation of chi-square.

Summarizing. In the case of questionnaire data, this involves casting the data into a form which best displays the trend or relationship to your reader, a knack which you'll develop with practice. It boils down to two things: highlighting the information you wish to convey; and choosing a graphical form in which to display it.

Figure 12.5 provides two examples of the first. In the first example, casting the frequencies into percentages **across** subgroups (an unusual way of computing percentages, since it's usually done downwards, **within** subgroups) makes the relationship between salary and sex of employee dramatically obvious; in the second example, the idea of relationships as patterns (in this case, a trend across the diagonal) emerges. You can analyse a trend within a table by means of the chi-square statistic: see the Figure 12.4 procedural guide.

As for the second, the most common alternatives to a tabular form are the frequency distribution, bar-chart, and pie-chart, labelled with the item alternatives as appropriate, and with the results of any analytic statistics superimposed: refer back to the Figure 12.3 procedural guide.

Write-up

Presenting. Questionnaire results are presented according to a common pattern as follows.

■ The purpose of the particular section of the questionnaire is stated; then, for each item in the section.

■ The wording of the item itself is presented, without steering instructions or recording instructions.

■ The format is stated, if it isn't obvious from the data.

■ The data are presented, in tabular or graphic form, with the alternatives shown in the appropriate position in the table or graph, and making sure that every member of the sample is accounted for. Each table or figure must have a number and a title; the axes of a graph must be labelled.

■ A verbal statement is made of the information contained. Table 11.3 provides an example.

■ General comments or statements are made to link the item just presented to the item to be presented next. What I have in mind here is that there should be a logical, step-by-step progression of ideas and discovery across the set of items as your argument is built.

■ A summary of the findings of the section is provided, in the form of bulleted statements. (This point is part of a bulleted statement: a clause, sentence, or short paragraph beginning with a small black square and being part of a list, the whole set being inset from the left

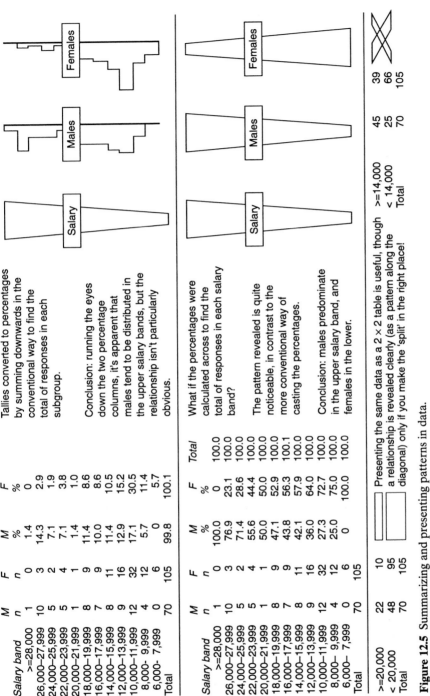

Salary band	M n	M %	F n	F %
>=28,000	1	1.4	0	0
26,000–27,999	10	14.3	3	2.9
24,000–25,999	5	7.1	2	1.9
22,000–23,999	5	7.1	4	3.8
20,000–21,999	1	1.4	1	1.0
18,000–19,999	8	11.4	9	8.6
16,000–17,999	7	10.0	9	8.6
14,000–15,999	8	11.4	11	10.5
12,000–13,999	9	12.9	16	15.2
10,000–11,999	12	17.1	32	30.5
8,000– 9,999	4	5.7	12	11.4
6,000– 7,999	0	0	6	5.7
Total	70	99.8	105	100.1

Tallies converted to percentages by summing downwards in the conventional way to find the total of responses in each subgroup.

Conclusion: running the eyes down the two percentage columns, it's apparent that males tend to be distributed in the upper salary bands, but the relationship isn't particularly obvious.

Salary band	M n	M %	F n	F %	Total %
>=28,000	1	100.0	0	0	100.0
26,000–27,999	10	76.9	3	23.1	100.0
24,000–25,999	5	71.4	2	28.6	100.0
22,000–23,999	5	55.6	4	44.4	100.0
20,000–21,999	1	50.0	1	50.0	100.0
18,000–19,999	8	47.1	9	52.9	100.0
16,000–17,999	7	43.8	9	56.3	100.1
14,000–15,999	8	42.1	11	57.9	100.0
12,000–13,999	9	36.0	16	64.0	100.0
10,000–11,999	12	27.3	32	72.7	100.0
8,000– 9,999	4	25.0	12	75.0	100.0
6,000– 7,999	0	0	6	100.0	100.0
Total	70		105	100.0	100.0

What if the percentages were calculated across to find the total of responses in each salary band?

The pattern revealed is quite noticeable, in contrast to the more conventional way of casting the percentages.

Conclusion: males predominate in the upper salary band, and females in the lower.

	M	F			M	F
>=20,000	22	10		>=14,000	45	39
< 20,000	48	95		< 14,000	25	66
Total	70	105		Total	70	105

Presenting the same data as a 2 × 2 table is useful, though a relationship is revealed clearly (as a pattern along the diagonal) only if you make the 'split' in the right place!

Figure 12.5 Summarizing and presenting patterns in data.

margin!) By the time your reader has got to the end of the section, he or she is likely to be forgetting the earlier findings you presented, and needs a summary of all that has been presented so far.

Locating. All of the above is placed in the main body of the text, either in one single major section (Figure 4.1), or in several different sections in which different issues and aspects of your thesis are explored and relevant ideas taken from reading are presented (Figure 4.2). It should be followed by a general summary of the findings, in the form of a connected narrative, and should precede a discussion of the implications of these findings.

Supporting data, data to amplify your findings, and less relevant information are presented in an appendix. People often wonder how much to provide in their appendices. That depends on the nature of the work they're doing, but you might find the following guidelines useful. First, the questionnaire itself must be appended; secondly, supporting data which can be sensibly organized in some way should be appended (for example, the table which you analysed to recognize a particular finding, before you recast it into the form presented in the main body of the text; or a list of 'Other, please specify' responses grouped into the categories which you added to your list of alternatives); unorganized raw data that are simple lists of responses must not be appended.

Postal questionnaires, return rates, and confidentiality

You'll be getting your questionnaire to the respondents by post. Have a look at Table 5.3 and remind yourself how much time this involves. (You might also take note of the amount of time required for pre-testing the questionnaire.) Once it's out of your hands, it's out of your control, and you've no means of helping the respondents to give you clear and accurate answers. So you should try it out on yourself, one or two colleagues, and possibly on a small pilot group of respondents taken from the same population as your sample.

You should also prepare and pre-test the covering letter which will go with the questionnaire. At the very least, this should contain:

- a statement of who you are and who is supporting you;
- a statement of the purpose of the questionnaire;
- a request for help, in which you should primarily try and show how completion of the questionnaire may be of ultimate benefit to the respondent. (Most requests for help state how the questionnaire will be helping the student. While this is a legitimate thing to do, it's best seen as a secondary issue: the reality is that many recipients are more interested in satisfying their own needs rather than yours.);

■ a statement that the respondents' material will be treated responsibly;
■ an expression of thanks in anticipation.

Return rates. This is also a good time to review all of your procedures, to check that you've done all you can to maximize cooperation by your respondents. In a sense, you already know a lot about this: it was the underlying theme of the material in Chapters 6 and 7. Generally, you obtain cooperation by adopting a cooperative stance to the whole research endeavour; that is by trying as far as possible to explore issues about which your respondents have a sense of ownership, and adopting a negotiating stance in bringing together their interests with your own legitimate needs to satisfy your formal project requirements. However, your scope for doing so if your questionnaire is posted to total strangers is somewhat limited. What to do?

This is a field which has been well researched, much of the work having been summarized by Dillman (1978), who addressed himself specifically to the issue of how best to maximize the response rate of participants in questionnaire and telephone interview surveys. He draws on a theory in social psychology, exchange theory (Blau, 1964; Thibaut and Kelley, 1959) to provide the following rationale. People will cooperate with you and provide data if you show that it is worth their while, in the sense that:

■ cooperation is in some sense rewarding to them;
■ the rewards outweigh the costs to them, in terms of money, time and effort;
■ they are convinced that they can trust you to keep your side of the transaction.

Table 12.3 summarizes the major factors which Dillman's extensive survey and programme of research have established under each main heading; examples are given at the right of the table. I'm sure you will be able to think of further examples, especially if you work with the idea of maximizing reward–cost differences to the respondent's advantage. I would imagine, for example, that some of the incentives (particularly the financial ones) may be beyond your means.

This issue is worth spending some time and effort over. It would be a pity if your otherwise excellent project work were marred by a low rate of return on the questions you've asked. What sort of return can you expect, as a baseline, as it were? Well, that depends very much on the method you use and the topic of the research, quite apart from your use of any of the procedures listed in Table 12.3. But think of it in this way. Assume that 5% of any group will reply simply because they like being asked questions; with a little luck, another 5% will be free or have the time easily available to do so. That's 10%. Not of your population, remember, but of your sample! If you think of a 10% baseline, you'll have a useful rule of thumb for reminding you that you must do all you can to find the other 90%. Here are some further suggestions.

■ If you're surveying people within your own organization, use the organization's own headed letterpaper or memo paper for your covering note, and convey the university's involvement by mentioning it in the note itself.

■ It is standard practice to chase people up, once, some two weeks after despatch.

■ Provided you have their prior permission, using previous respondents' names and perhaps active efforts to encourage later respondents, assuming both know each other and time permits a staggered response.

■ Familiarity with you and with what you're doing. A respondent may not be part of your group of active supporters, but is still more likely to help if you know each other, have attended the same meetings, drunk in the same bar and eaten in the same canteen together.

■ Promises of copies of the final report on the data, or an abbreviated version, can be useful; demonstration that action will follow, to the extent that this is within your power to provide, is even better.

Appropriate use of techniques like these, and a systematic approach to the factors listed in the table, have led Dillman and his co-workers to report average postal questionnaire return rates of 74% of sample size (returns averaged over 48 questionnaire surveys; individual figures for return rates vary between 50% and 92%). Telephone interview figures using the same approach (which Dillman has called the 'Total Design Method') are: average rate of 91% of sample size (returns averaged over 30 telephone surveys, range 73% to 99%): see Dillman (1978: 21–33).

These figures are extremely high, and perhaps beyond the means of any individual, unsupported by the resources of a survey centre, to achieve. My own return rate in the study of Irish Police Sergeants (see Table 9.2(b)), working in a situation nearer to your own, was 67%. In retrospect, while all the applicable factors of Table 12.3 were used, the most important ones were:

■ informing respondents in the covering letter that sponsorship and funding came from the Association of Garda Sergeants and Inspectors, the respondents' own professional body; coupled with

■ despatch of questionnaires through official police channels, accompanied by a covering note from the relevant Assistant Commissioner as well as my own letter; followed by

■ a chase-up letter two weeks after despatch of the initial mailing.

Confidentiality and security. A final way in which you can encourage cooperation is by making, and communicating, adequate arrangements to encourage a feeling of safety among your respondents. There is a good general rule to apply: unless you have explicitly obtained your respondents' agreement to mention them as providers of particular items of data, you should use the information they give you anonymously. There are various levels of security involved.

Once given, a promise on your part not to reveal names must be kept. Your data could then be labelled, in your own records only, with the name of the respondent only so that you don't confuse the respondent's data with someone else's.

The use of a simple letter or number code by which to identify the set of data given you by a particular respondent is a very common procedure. You keep a list of names and corresponding code numbers in a safe place, the paper or electronic medium on which you have recorded the data being identified only by the code. The use of codes is essential if this degree of anonymity has been requested, and you are following a before–after or similar design which involves you in going back to your respondents: don't just remove their names from their dataset, or you'll never be able to put the two sets of data together for analysis! If you have used number codes in drawing up the sample (see section 9.2), the number you used then can be used as your anonymity code.

Security is also provided by the use of data which have been partially or completely processed, (tables, percentages, distributions, or general narrative summaries), so that individual responses, whether previously identity-coded or not, aren't reported in your project report. This is also a very common form of arrangement, and is used in combination with the previous one. You store raw data identified by an identity code, and you report processed data in which the individual provenance or ownership isn't identified. Of course, with some kinds of information, your in-company readers, being lively and curious people, will try to work out who said what; in fact, with small samples or stratified subgroups, you'll often hear respondents say things like 'Oh yes, that particular comment sounds just like old Fred in Marketing: I wonder if I can recognize his answers to the other questions?'

This should be discouraged, and there are two ways of doing so. Collapse subgroups in your dataset to remove the stratification when you present the findings to your readers (whether the data are figures or verbatim comments); or convey the findings in your own words, possibly under a 'Miscellaneous' heading. The verbal comments at the bottom of the 'Table as presented' section of Table 11.3 provide an example of the latter.

Finally, there may be situations in postal questionnaire work in which your respondents don't even wish you to know who said what. These are rare, but the procedure is to number-code the questionnaires and put them into envelopes yourself, asking someone else unconnected with the organization to assist you by addressing the envelopes in which the questionnaires are despatched once you have sealed them. Your assistant would then open and destroy the envelopes when the questionnaires were returned, handing you the questionnaires without looking at them.

It gets a little more complicated when you have to approach the respondent again, e.g. in the case of a before–after design. You could adopt double-blind procedures, with the assistance of a colleague as before, but these may be rather too elaborate for your needs. Something that works well in these circumstances is to ask respondents to provide their own code number, based on, say, the year, month, and day of birth of a close relative, and to remember to use the same code on the two separate occasions (Selltiz *et al.*, 1981).

Of course, no security system is perfect. Even with double-blind procedures, if your intentions were malign you could get together with the other person and decipher the coding arrangements. It is your job to assure your respondents that your intentions are benign.

You have another responsibility, and that is to keep your data in a secure place. At the simplest level, they should be kept under lock and key, away from the organization itself. More sensitive data can be kept in a safe: you might ask your tutor if he or she has access to one in the department. If you keep data in a microcomputer, ask your computer technician if he or she has one of the many commercially available security programmes, and install it in your micro with your own unique password. Finally, if the data are kept on a mainframe machine, your computer technician should be asked to make appropriate user number arrangements so that only you can access the relevant files.

Under the terms of the Data Protection Act, any respondent has the right to a print-out of his or her data entries. You should check the implications with the member of staff in your department or teaching institution who has responsibility, and be prepared to supply a print-out of the respondent's own file to the respondent if he or she requests it.

Before leaving this subject: don't forget the general issue of the confidentiality of your completed project document: you might like to look at section 7.4 again.

12.2 THE STRUCTURED, FACE-TO-FACE INTERVIEW

A glance at Table 12.1 will remind you of the advantages of the interview in comparison with the questionnaire. As far as business and management project work is concerned, probably the most important of these relate to the ease with which you can express complex ideas and cover the ground thoroughly. As Chapter 6 suggested, matters of business strategy, policy, and practitioner concern are often difficult to break down into a small number of unambiguous, single questions. The advantage of the interview over the questionnaire is that you are present yourself, and can, within the structure you have previously designed, amplify the meaning of the items, and explain the intentions behind your questions, in a way which isn't possible with the structured, postal questionnaire.

Every structured interview follows a written interview guide: a document which looks very much like a questionnaire, and provides item sequence details, steering instructions, items, alternatives, and recording instructions. In fact, all of the information which you would have recorded on file-cards in order to create a questionnaire (as described in the previous section) is also, with occasional changes to wording, required in preparing a structured interview guide. Use file-cards in the same way.

The purpose of the guide is to ensure that you handle the interview in essentially the same way with each of your interviewees. Memory can fail you, you might be tired, the need to explain your intentions to the respondent may cause you to forget the thrust and direction of your question sequence, something which your respondent says may be so interesting that you go off on a complete tangent – if you're not careful, a structured interview can turn into a semi-structured one or even a conversation, which is fine if that's what you want, but if you're reading this chapter rather than Chapter 11, I assume that your intention is otherwise!

Because of the close similarity between interview guide and questionnaire, I'll assume you're familiar with section 12.1, and confine my material to issues that are unique to the structured interview. I'll also assume that you've read the material on individual interviews in section 11.2: some of the material is related, and the rest forms a useful contrast of which it's useful to be aware.

Design

Apart from the need to be explicit about the items which will be used for breaking down answers to other items (see the relevant material in section 12.1), and the general issues of design, there are no particular points to be made here.

Elicitation

When you elicit data in a structured interview, you follow your previously designed guide, but react appropriately to the verbal and non-verbal signals by which your respondent indicates his or her understanding of the items and their alternatives, to the level of interest which your respondent expresses, and to the digressions and comments he or she initiates.

Steering. And so, just as with the questionnaire, you prepare steering instructions in advance: only in this case, they consist of notes to yourself. In reacting appropriately to your interviewee, you'll need to use techniques from the more directive end of the range shown in Table 11.2. In other words, you take the initiative in introducing new themes as you move from one section of your guide to the next, you determine the items and their sequence within each section, and you're active in redirecting the respondent's attention when the conversation momentarily diverges from the course you have set.

You can set the direction from the start of each main section, by providing a fuller rationale for what you're doing than you'd be able to in a questionnaire. Decide on the wording in advance and write it into your guide at appropriate places. As the interview progresses, you'll find yourself responding in one of five ways, depending on what the respondent says and does:

■ recording responses and proceeding to the next item in the sequence as you receive a direct response;

■ amplifying the wording or meaning of an item if the respondent misunderstands the item as first expressed. if you feel in advance that some items will require an amplifying phrase, you should write an appropriate form of words, in brackets after the main item, in your interview guide;

■ maintaining the flow of the interview after a digression by the respondent, bringing him or her back to your sequence as skilfully as you can without further action;

■ remembering and perhaps noting a comment which, while it's a digression, has a bearing on a subsequent item; when you get to that item, you'll be able to refer back to the comment the respondent made;

■ noting and responding appropriately to any other comment which you hadn't expected, and therefore hadn't planned for in preparing the guide, but which is nevertheless relevant to the theme of your work, before proceeding with the main sequence as before. When you're designing the interview guide, you might like to leave a wide margin at the side of each page in which you can record such comments. You might also use this 'personal margin' to record any significant non-verbal activities which you feel might be useful during analysis.

Format. As with questionnaires, most interview guides tend to present similarly formatted items together: it would be unusual to jump from a multiple-choice item to a rating item to a ranking item and back throughout the whole sequence of items. So you're likely to find that you need to give the format instructions just once before the set of items in question, and that all you need to do is to occasionally remind the respondent of the format, in advance of the item itself. 'Now, for the next four questions I'm going to give you a number of alternatives, and ask you to rank them . . . [several items later] . . . and again, how would you rank the following?' Decide on the wording of the format instructions in advance, and write them onto a file-card at an appropriate point in the sequence.

Eliciting answers. Your cards, and the resulting interview guide, will show the item itself, and the set of alternatives you regard as responses to the item. When you prepare the interview guide leave sufficient space in which you can write down verbatim responses to any open-ended items being used. Record these literally, rather than attempting a précis or synopsis.

You'll elicit answers in one of three ways.

- By reading out the item and the alternatives. Because you will keep the interview guide in front of you as you conduct the interview, the respondent won't have any record of the item and the alternatives, and is likely to forget the alternatives soon after you've stated them. To prevent this, you'll need to prepare a set of flashcards: stiff cards bearing the alternatives, typed in block capitals and preferably in a large typeface, which you hand to the respondent as you read out the item.
- By reading out the item, listening to the response and doing an instant content analysis before classifying the response under one of the alternatives written in the interview guide. When you're preparing the guide, you may need to include a brief statement of the defining characteristics beside each alternative, to help you in classifying the responses appropriately: see section 11.2 under the 'perceiving' heading for further particulars of content analysis.
- By reading out an open-ended item and recording the verbatim response, for subsequent content analysis.

I say 'reading out', and if you're to maintain reliability you will need to stick to the same form of words, and as far as possible, similar procedures, with all of your interviewees. However, a series of readings from a script makes for no eye contact and a very dull social encounter; the ideal to aim for is a thoroughly practised procedure: not necessarily a completely memorized script, but sufficient familiarity so that an occasional glance at your interview guide is sufficient to remind you of where you are, what you need to say, and where you'll be heading next.

Recording answers. You'll be doing that yourself, as I've implied already. In contrast to the semi-structured interview, this is a straight-forward procedure, since you know what format of answer to expect, and you have all the relevant alternatives in front of you. You record the responses in the interview guide itself. The guide has been prepared and laid out appropriately, and at this point you're acting as scribe for the respondent. As you'll have gathered from the foregoing, you'll have little use for a tape recorder if the structured interview is your main data-gathering method.

Analysis

Perceiving and summarizing. These are almost exactly the same as in the questionnaire: see the appropriate headings in section 12.1. The only difference (and this isn't universal practice, but is nevertheless a good one) is that you should scan all the interview guides before you start the analysis, to see if you've written any comments in the 'personal margin' which might be relevant to your handling of individual items.

Write-up

Presenting and locating. Again, the procedures used in the questionnaire will apply.

12.3 TELEPHONE INTERVIEWS: CONVINCING RESPONDENTS OF YOUR BONA FIDES

The telephone interview can be a very convenient way of contacting your respondents, especially if they work for your own organization but at distant locations. You might argue that it's is just a face-to-face structured interview with the non-verbal behaviour removed, as it were, and that the same general guidelines as for the interview apply. However, there's a little more to it than that, precisely because the face-to-face element is missing, and good telephone interview technique provides lessons in interviewer–respondent relationships which are relevant to any form of structured survey in which people unknown to you are surveyed.

Imagine that you're sitting at your desk, or at home, and the telephone rings. A strange voice asks you if you wouldn't mind answering a few questions for a survey they're doing. How would you react, especially if you're in the middle of an important job and the questions appear to be a little personal? Much the same, you might imagine, as if you'd received an unsolicited questionnaire, or phone call asking you to take part in a face-to-face interview. How can one best establish one's personal bona fides and minimize intrusiveness when dealing with strangers?

The approach is taken from Dillman (1978) and Frey (1983), both well worth reading if the telephone survey is to be your main data-gathering technique. They provide you with excellent guidelines on design and procedure, though their comments on sampling (directory based or random dialling) are more appropriate to marketing surveys of the general public than to in-company business project work.

Firstly, just as in the postal variant, where a letter accompanies the written questionnaire, you should send your respondents a brief letter or memo which says enough to provide assurance, but not sufficient to dispel curiosity, which gives an approximate time and date in the near future, and which additionally provides a return telephone number for the respondent to use if the proposed time is inconvenient. Provide the name of an appropriate senior person (your sponsor or tutor) and their phone number in case your respondent wishes to check you out. Use headed paper, your university's or your organization's as appropriate. Finally, do all you can to assure the respondent that you're not selling anything.

It's wise to give some thought to the best time to call your particular respondents; this will involve a decision on whether the best place to contact them is at home or at work. Once you start the phone calls, keep a careful record to prevent you calling people twice over, just as you keep a record of despatches in the case of the postal questionnaire; keep a note particularly of other people answering your intended respondent's phone, and information on when your respondent will be available for interview. It's easy to forget such details when you're engaged in making a series of phone calls to a variety of people.

The remaining guidelines apply particularly to the telephone interview itself. Make the call as planned, and check that the time is convenient, calling back if it isn't; give your respondent a fair opportunity to refuse, by stressing that participation is voluntary.

You need to have prepared your opening comments very carefully (it's here that most refusals occur), to include your name, where you're calling from and why, information on how the respondent's number was obtained, a reminder of the letter you sent, and a statement of how long the interview will take.

If the respondent has any questions, answer them fully, and then start on your interview guide. The items should flow sensibly and obviously, from one to the next: unlike the face-to-face interview, you don't have quite the same freedom to explain apparent inconsistencies. The first items should capture attention and relate directly to the purpose of the interview, with the personal background items kept until the end. Because you're not able to show your respondents a flashcard which summarizes a large set of alternatives, you'll need to split up longer items into two or more stages: the first which asks for a general expression of their views, and the second which examines the issue in more detail depending on the initial response, asking for a statement of how strongly they feel, for example. Both Dillman (1978) and Frey (1983) provide detailed examples.

When you've finished, say thank you and describe what will happen next, in the form of feedback on some of the results if you've planned to provide this.

Further techniques $\boxed{13}$

In the previous two chapters, the more commonly used techniques associated with business and management projects were presented. The purpose of this chapter is to outline three further techniques which are relatively little-used in the business and management field, and which may have a useful part to play in project work.

The first of these, the repertory grid, is valuable for open-ended work at any level, from undergraduate through Diploma and professional to Masters. A curious hybrid, being highly structured but with contents completely determined by the respondent, it lends itself particularly to exploratory work in undefined situations, and for pilot work prior to the use of other techniques. The second, attitude scaling, may be used at any level in its rough-and ready form as part of a structured questionnaire or interview guide and can, if properly developed, form the entire empirical core of a project, especially at undergraduate level. Finally, the third 'technique' is really an approach to the observation of people at work, and is given in two contrasted variants, structured observation and field experiment. I include the former because I believe the skills to be highly relevant to in-company work, and the latter because, if one is to use experimental method at all (see Chapters 6 and 10), the relevant techniques should be well understood.

All of these techniques are sufficiently different from those presented in Chapters 11 and 12, and from each other, that the standard scheme of headings (Design, Elicitation, Analysis, Write-up) isn't very helpful in outlining them. What follows is a more connected account, but the relevant matters arising under each of these headings are dealt with.

13.1 THE REPERTORY GRID

Most of the techniques I've previously outlined require you to make assumptions about the way in which your respondents are likely to view the issues you're investigating. For example, all of the fully structured techniques require you to specify the alternative answers from which respondents must choose. What happens if the respondents don't find these alternatives helpful, though? What if they view the issue in a completely different way? With a semi-structured technique, you can back off to a degree and change the basis of your dialogue to one which matches the respondent's assumptions while you're talking together but, with a structured technique, the best you can do is to provide 'Other, please specify' alternatives at appropriate points.

The repertory grid allows you to address the respondent's assumptions and personal understanding of the issues directly, without the slightest need to anticipate the alternatives which he or she has in mind. It's ideal whenever you want to identify the individual's perspective and view things from his or her own point of view, whether as part of a pilot study in order to determine what your subsequent questions and alternatives should be, or as a detailed form of key informant interview. It's less a case of 'Other, please specify', and more a case of 'No other: you specify'.

The technique involves three phases of activity: conducting a form of structured interview with the respondent; analysing the individual results; and aggregating the results of several interviews into an overall set of findings.

The grid interview

The purpose of a grid interview is to elicit your respondent's constructs. A **construct** is a way in which the respondent thinks about the issue you're exploring; a particular way he or she has got of giving meaning to, i.e. construing, the issue in question. In sum, it's an active perception of how things are. Now, the ways in which meaning is expressed vary enormously depending on the subject-matter, from single adjectives and noun phrases like these:

pleasant – unpleasant
solvent – insolvent
strategic – operational
niche product – commodity product

to more complex sentence structures like these:

likely to slow the growth of the company – likely to foster expansion
insufficient managerial experience – substantial managerial experience

But what all constructs have in common is that they're always expressed as a **contrast**, like the examples I've listed above. You can't understand what a person means by 'good' without knowing what he or she has in mind as a contrast: to say 'good' as opposed to 'poor' is to express a very different meaning to 'good' as opposed to 'evil'. Go on: try it out explicitly, by saying to yourself (as in 'this is a good piece of work'), 'good–poor'; and then, 'good–evil'. Don't you feel the weight of the connotations and implications of the latter 'good' as they unfold into your awareness?

The grid interview consists of four components:

- the **topic**, in which you agree the subject-matter under discussion;
- the elicitation of **elements**, in which you arrive at examples or components of the topic for further discussion;
- the elicitation of the **constructs** themselves;
- the **rating** of elements on constructs, to identify the particular meanings being expressed.

The interview itself is conducted in eight steps, which are listed in Table 13.1. Each step must be followed faithfully, and it's in that sense that the interview is highly structured; however, the content of what you discover is completely in the hands of your respondent, and in that sense, the grid interview is entirely open-ended. Figure 13.1 shows an example of the results of this procedure: it's a completed grid sheet which records the results of an interview with a senior manager, in which his constructs about doing business in eastern Europe are recorded.

The best way to learn the technique is to conduct a grid interview with yourself, following the steps outlined in Table 13.1. Choose some topic which sounds interesting, and about which you'd like to record your own constructs. May I suggest 'My friends and colleagues' as a topic, and a list of five different friends/colleagues at work as the elements? And, just to make things interesting, add two further elements: 'Myself as I am now', and 'Myself as I'd like to be'. Use a photocopy of Figure 13.2 on which to work. Write the elements into the diagonal lines at the top of the figure, and use the spaces at the left and the right to write in the ends of each construct. As soon as you've elicited each construct, rate all the elements on the construct using a five-point scale, following the convention that the left end of the construct defines the '1' end of the scale, and the right end of the construct defines the '5' end of the scale. Put the rating of each element into the appropriate box in the row of boxes devoted to the construct with which you're working.

As you go through this grid, you may learn several things about your views of your friends that are new to you. A grid is a very good way of getting to the root of an issue, by expressing perceptions explicitly. Carried out with someone else as a respondent, it creates an opportunity for the person to make up his or her mind on an issue which mightn't previously have been thought about carefully, or thought through in any

Table 13.1 Eliciting a repertory grid

The basic procedure is in eight steps:

1. Agree a **topic** with your respondent.
2. Agree a set of **elements**, and write these in at the top of the grid sheet.
3. Explain that you wish to find out how he or she thinks about the elements, and that you'll do this by asking him or her to compare them systematically.
4. Taking three elements (A, B, C), ask your respondent 'Which two of these are the same in some way, and different from the third?'
   Provide assurance that you're not looking for a 'correct' answer, just how he or she sees the elements.
5. Ask your respondent why: 'What do the two have in common, as opposed to the third?'
   Write down the thing the two have in common, on the left side of the grid sheet; and the opposite of this (the reason the third element is different) on the right of the grid sheet, making sure that you've obtained a truly bipolar expression – a pair of words or phrases which express a **contrast**. This is the person's **construct**.
6. Present the construct as a rating scale, with the phrase on the left standing for the '1' end of the scale, and the phrase on the right standing for the '5' end of the scale.
7. Ask your respondent to rate each element on this five-point scale, writing the ratings into the grid as he or she states them. Occasionally, check that the directionality of the scaling is preserved, i.e. that your respondent shouldn't be using a '1' when he or she is offering a '5' and vice versa.
8. Your task is to elicit as many different constructs as the person might hold about the topic. So, repeat steps 4 to 7, asking for a fresh construct each time, until your respondent can't offer any new ones; use a different triad of three elements each time: B, D, E; A, D, F, and so on

A few additional pointers: once familiar with the above procedure

- You don't always have to actively offer three elements; you might ask your respondent to look at all the elements together, and for him or her to choose any three which express a particularly strong contrast that hasn't yet been offered as a construct.
- If you get the feeling that a construct is too vague (e.g. 'good leader–bad leader' where the elements are people) you can always ask 'In what way?' and press for a more behaviourally specific definition of each end of the construct, writing these into the grid sheet.
- Alternatively, if you're trying to discover constructs which are more basic/fundamental to your respondent, don't record the construct offered, but ask him/her: 'Which end of the construct do you prefer – and why?' Express the reason given as one end of a new construct, which you then record in the grid sheet together with its opposite.

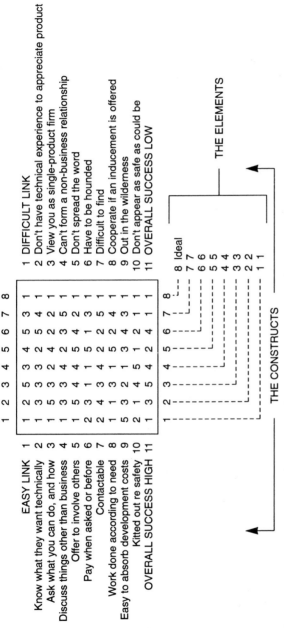

		1	2	3	4	5	6	7	8		
EASY LINK	1	1	2	5	3	4	5	3	1	1	DIFFICULT LINK
Know what they want technically	2	1	3	3	3	2	5	4	1	2	Don't have technical experience to appreciate product
Ask what you can do, and how	3	1	5	3	2	4	2	2	1	3	View you as single-product firm
Discuss things other than business	4	1	3	3	4	2	3	5	1	4	Can't form a non-business relationship
Offer to involve others	5	1	5	4	4	5	4	2	1	5	Don't spread the word
Pay when asked or before	6	2	3	1	1	5	1	3	1	6	Have to be hounded
Contactable	7	2	4	3	4	2	2	5	1	7	Difficult to find
Work done according to need	8	1	3	3	1	5	4	4	1	8	Cooperate if an inducement is offered
Easy to absorb development costs	9	5	3	2	1	3	4	3	1	9	Out in the wilderness
Kitted out re safety	10	2	1	4	5	1	2	1	1	10	Don't appear as safe as could be
OVERALL SUCCESS HIGH	11	1	3	5	4	2	4	1	1	11	OVERALL SUCCESS LOW

THE CONSTRUCTS

THE ELEMENTS

8 Ideal
7 7
6 6
5 5
4 4
3 3
2 2
1 1

Notes

1. Elements were six UK companies with which the manager trades; element 7 was a particular Polish company with which he had recently developed trading links; and element 8 was 'My ideal trading partner'.

2. The constructs were elicited as described in the text, with the exception of those shown in capitals, which were supplied by the researcher to assist in subsequent data analysis.

3. The ratings are given in the body of the table.

4. The usual convention was followed: the left pole of each construct defines the '1' end of the scale, and the right pole of each construct defines the '5' end of the scale.

The meaning captured by the grid can therefore be easily read back. For example, this manager rates company no. 1 as 'A firm in which they know what they want technically – they don't lack the technical experience to appreciate our product. It's difficult for us to absorb the development costs of trading with them, however, since they're located out in the wilderness.' And so on.

Figure 13.1 An example of a completed repertory grid.

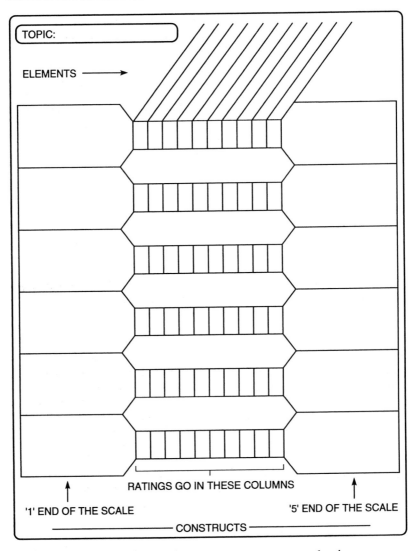

TOPIC:

ELEMENTS ⟶

RATINGS GO IN THESE COLUMNS

'1' END OF THE SCALE   '5' END OF THE SCALE

CONSTRUCTS

Figure 13.2 Grid sheet for recording elements, constructs and ratings.

detail. Perhaps you can see the potential value of the technique as part of a key informant interview?

In practising with your own grid as I've suggested, you may, likewise, learn something new about yourself. This could arise from the content of the constructs you've got about your friends and colleagues, or from the way, now that you come to think of it systematically, that you rate particular individuals on particular constructs. Or it might come from a

Table 13.2 Issues and procedures in repertory grid interviewing

What makes a good element?
- A feeling of ownership on the part of the respondent; so, usually you ask the respondent to nominate the elements. But not exclusively; you might want to supply an element that's relevant to the topic, as I did in when suggesting you add the 'myself' elements to your own list of friends and colleagues (see text).
- Anything can be an element: people, places, institutions, job responsibilities, different business strategies – the list is endless, provided it's not a construct. Avoid words with easy opposites, and words that are qualities rather than actions or things.
- Nouns make good elements; the less abstract, the easier they'll be to handle.
- Verbs and clauses are useful, but more tricky. Use the '-ing' form, i.e. not 'To make a decision', but 'Deciding'; not 'The delegation of responsibility' but 'Delegating'.
- A usable set of elements (i.e. one that your respondent will find easy to work with during the grid interview) covers the topic evenly and is 'all of a kind'. Try not to mix abstract nouns with concrete nouns and complicated verbal forms. (How would you construe 'the Olympic Ideal', 'bicycles', and 'Saturday afternoons spent in acting as a sports coach'? It's possible, but messy.)

What makes a good construct?
- Whatever expresses your respondent's meaning fully and precisely.
- A pair of words or phrases which are opposites, and as specific as possible. Don't accept as an opposite, the same words with the word 'not' stuck in front of them. 'Good–Not good' doesn't convey much meaning, whereas 'Good standard–Poor standard' tells you it's not a case of 'Good' as opposed to 'Evil'.
- Encourage your respondent to be as specific as the topic demands. Avoid 'motherhoods' by asking 'in what way exactly?'. Thus 'Performance adequate–Performance inadequate' conveys much less meaning than '>10% return on capital employed–<10% return on capital employed' if the topic deals with financial performance, and less meaning than 'Experienced enough to carry out the more difficult tasks–Requires constant monitoring and checking' if the topic involves an employee performance appraisal.

What makes a good set of ratings?
- Whatever helps your respondent to express the position of the elements on the construct involved.
- Five- or seven-point scales are useful; more points on the scale is spurious precision.
- Encourage the respondent to use the full width of the scale: if it is a five-point scale, there should be at least one rating of '1' and one rating of '5' along each construct.
- Use ratings, and not ranks; identical values for some of the elements are quite appropriate.

consideration of the kinds of constructs you discover you're using. Are they all evaluative, or are some purely descriptive? (Incidentally, while the left- and right-hand ends of a construct have to be opposite in meaning, they don't have to express a positive versus negative evaluation. The construct 'technically skilled–socially skilled' is quite neutral and descriptive, unless of course the topic is one which demands technical skills and not social skills, or vice versa.) Do feelings predominate? Do the constructs concern activities and action?

Working through the grid, you may also wonder about some of the finer points of the procedure, which are summarized in Table 13.2.

Finally, you might become curious about the possible applications of repertory grid technique. Grids have been used predominantly in the personnel and training field (job analysis, performance appraisal, training needs analysis, training course development, employee mentoring and counselling, team building), but there are also some applications in the study of financial decision-making; in assisting in the development of business policies and strategies by management teams; in the field of market research (during the 'qualitative stage'); and in quality control (to identify the factors involved in subjective judgements about product quality). A review of most of these applications is provided in Jankowicz (1989). If you decide to use the repertory grid for part or all of your empirical work, and want more details about the procedures involved, the best handbook by far is Stewart and Stewart (1982), although Gammack and Stephens (1994) pack a lot of information, including some good comments on the limitations of grid technique, into 19 readable pages.

Analysis of a single repertory grid

Having completed a grid yourself, you'll appreciate how straightforwardly you can read the data back from someone else's grid.

- List the elements.
- List the constructs.
- Look at the extreme ratings: where are the '1's and where are the '5's; what does this tell you about the position of elements on constructs, and the meanings being expressed?

Whether this is informative depends on what you'd have expected about the individual before you looked at his or her grid! However, more detailed analyses are possible, all of which involve answering questions about the relationships expressed in the grid.

- What are the relationships between the elements? To find out which elements are construed similarly, and which ones differently, take the elements in pairs, find the absolute difference between the ratings on each construct, and sum these differences down the grid across all the constructs. When you've done this for all the element pairs, the lowest sum will indicate the most similarly construed elements, and the highest, the most differently construed. Whether this is informative depends on the topic of the grid and the particular elements involved; for example, in your own grid, if the most different elements were 'Myself as I am' and 'Myself as I'd like to be', that would surely be thought-provoking!

■ What are the relationships between the constructs? To find out which constructs are rated most similarly, use the same procedure of summing differences between pairs of ratings, but this time, work across the grid taking two constructs at a time. Also, you'll need to do this twice over. Each construct has two ends, and a relationship may be low if you take a pair of constructs one way round, but high if you reverse the direction of one of the constructs in the pair. Suppose you have five elements rated:

Morose	1 4 5 1 3	Lively
Dependable	5 2 1 5 3	Untrustworthy
(differences	4 2 4 4 0)	

This gives a difference sum of 14, which is large: there seems to be little relationship between Moroseness and Dependability. On the other hand, and remembering that the left-hand end of the construct defines the '1' of the scale, and the right-hand end of the construct defines the '5' end of the scale, the same meaning would have been expressed by:

| Morose | 1 4 5 1 3 Lively |
| Untrustworthy | 1 4 5 1 3 Dependable |

Here there is a difference sum of 0. The relationship is in fact very high: you're saying that the more a person is Morose, the more he or she is Untrustworthy! So, when you're analysing construct differences, calculate the differences between two constructs directly; and then reverse one of the constructs by subtracting the ratings from 6 (for a five-point scale) or 8 (for a seven-point scale), and recalculate, switching the construct round as I've done above. **Remember, the meaning you're expressing remains the same**, since you keep to the convention that the left-hand end of the construct always defines the '1' end of the scale. An element rated '5' on a scale running from Dependable = 1 to Untrustworthy = 5, is rated '1' on a scale running from Untrustworthy = 1 to Dependable = 5.

This sort of difference analysis is most informative when you've got prior grounds for supposing that some differences will be high and some low, or when you're investigating a particular hunch about the way in which your respondent thinks. Take another look at Figure 13.1. The respondent was **supplied** with one of the constructs by the researcher, by being given the construct 'Overall, an easy trading link to establish and develop – Overall, a more difficult trading link'. He was then asked to rate all the trading partners on it. The obvious differences to calculate were those between his own construct and that one, to discover which of his own were most similar: in other words, to see on how he defines successful trade. (In fact, the construct matching most closely with 'Easy–Difficult' is 'Have the technical experience to appreciate the product – Lacking technical sophistication in this market'. This senior manager tends to define the development of his east European trading partnerships in terms of the partners' understanding of the technical ways in which things are done in the industry, back home in the west.)

You might care to go back to your own grid and look at the difference between each of your elements and the 'Self as I am' element. Which of your friends and colleagues do you construe as being most similar to yourself? Who is matched most closely to 'Myself as I'd like to be', that is, who comes closest to your ideal?

It's possible to carry out more powerful and complete analyses of single grids using cluster analysis and principal component analysis, both of which focus on differences between ratings as we've done above, but these techniques are beyond the scope of this book. If you want to find out how to do a cluster analysis of a grid, try Jankowicz (1982); if you want to analyse grids by microcomputer, STATVIEW is a commonly available general-purpose package which includes principal components analysis, while REPGRID is a very user-friendly special-purpose package running on Apple Macintosh machines, which provides both forms of analysis and also elicits grids interactively in the first place: see Gaines and Shaw (1990); Shaw and Gaines (1989). Finally, for a thorough review of grid packages for various computers and operating systems, see Sewell *et al.* (1992).

Aggregating the results of several grid interviews

Calculating difference scores for selected comparisons on more than a few grids can be very time-consuming. Very often, what you're looking for in a group of grids is an organized listing of all the different constructs which the sample of respondents holds about some common topic. Assuming that you used the same set of elements with all your respondents, it's a straightforward task to carry out a content analysis of all the constructs. Have a look at section 11.2 and Table 11.3 for the general procedures involved; your unit of analysis would be each individual construct, and you'd pool all the constructs of the whole group of respondents before proceeding with the content analysis.

A more grid-specific form of content analysis has been described by Honey (1977). It fits the situation in which you're interested in the different ways in which a group of people construe an issue of importance to them, having started your grid interview by **supplying** a construct which expresses that issue. This is just what happened in the grid shown as Figure 13.1, where the issue concerned the nature of the relationships between trading partners, and the 'Overall, easier link–Overall, more difficult link' construct was supplied by the researcher. Honey's content analysis sets out to classify all the constructs in a set of grids, and to present as examples of each category, just those constructs which are highly matched (have low difference scores) with the supplied construct. The basis of the procedure is quite simple.

- For each grid separately, calculate the difference score between each construct and the supplied construct, remembering to reverse one of each pair in the way I described above, and using the lower of the two difference scores involved in each comparison. Write the score beside the construct involved.
- Go through the whole set of grids, develop a set of content-analysis categories in the usual way, and code each construct into its category. (You'll find it useful to transcribe each construct, annotated with its difference score, on to a separate file-card: coding is then a simple matter of putting the cards into separate piles, each pile being one category.)
- Ask a friend to repeat this step using your original categories. Are the first and second sets of codings the same – in other words, is your content analysis reliable? Argue with yourself or your friend until you agree on a final set, and repeat the coding one more time, both of you. Calculate one of the reliability indices described in Figure 11.1 for the first and the second codings, hoping for an improvement the second time round!
- From each pile, select the constructs with the three lowest difference scores, to represent the category.
- The result will be an account of the different ways (categories) of thinking about an issue (the supplied construct) which a group of respondents reveal.
- When reporting your findings, report the original and improved content analysis reliability figures.

Depending on the issue, this may be very informative in itself. Moreover, it can supply you with the questions to ask of, or alternatives to offer to, a larger group of respondents by means of a subsequent structured questionnaire or interview guide.

Bearing in mind the discussion in Chapter 6, in which the importance of issues rather than variables in project work was emphasized, you'll find that the grid interview is a very powerful way of exploring the ways in which managers and professionals think about the issues themselves. Bearing in mind my warnings about the need to avoid contaminating your findings with your own prejudgements, it's apparent that the grid interview is powerful precisely because it speaks in the language (the constructs) of the respondents themselves. And finally, given the importance of negotiating a place for your own research interests and questions in investigating your respondents' concerns, the use which grid technique makes of negotiation as a form of interaction (in agreeing elements, and in its use of occasional supplied constructs added to the pool of the respondent's own, elicited constructs), seems particularly well suited to business and management project work.

13.2 ATTITUDE SCALING

Empirical work for business and management projects often involves the measurement of your respondents' attitudes. You may want to find out what they feel about a particular issue or problem, being interested in the strength and direction of their feelings about it: whether they're strongly in favour of, weakly against, and so on. You have three ways of doing so: by structuring your items into rough-and-ready five- or seven-point rating scales; by developing your own precise scale; or by using a scale which has been pre-researched and published elsewhere.

Rating scale items in structured questionnaires and interviews

I'm sure you're very familiar with items of this kind. In the case of a five-point scale, the respondent is requested to express the strength of his or her agreement or disagreement with an item, by placing a mark on some point on a scale which runs from 'Strongly agree' to 'Strongly disagree'; this scale is represented by a line with four divisions, or by a set of five boxes. Analysis would be by tallying the responses to each item across the whole group or subgroup of respondents, to see how many people answered 'Strongly agree', how many answered 'Agree', and so on. The average score for each item could be calculated for the group as a whole, and for subgroups. This approach is useful and straightforward if you want a rough-and-ready indication of the strength of feelings among the group.

Very often, it's particularly helpful to ascertain people's reasons for providing the ratings they did, particularly if they chose the negative end of the scale, and you can combine the item with an immediate follow-up item to the effect 'If your response was "Disagree" or "Strongly disagree", please indicate your main reason in the space below', carrying out a content analysis of the reasons given when you present the results. Figure 13.3 provides an example of an item of this kind, taken from a larger set in the study of Irish police sergeants referenced in Table 9.3.

If you're looking for greater precision, however, you may feel a little uncomfortable about this form of scaling. Your respondents' internal scales of judgements may vary substantially, so that someone who's fairly cautious would answer 'Agree' to an item to which a less cautious person would answer 'Strongly agree', when both hold the same strength of attitude. This sort of thing can be troublesome (especially in situations which evoke caution, e.g. those in which managers appraise their subordinates); what was a five-point scale turns into a three- or even two-point scale, because most of your respondents avoid extreme ratings even when one might suspect they're merited.

One very good way round the problem is to express the wording of the item in such a way that you're enabled to label each of the scale positions with an **operational description**: a description of an observable event, or a statement of what would have to happen for the respondent to be able to tick one point on the scale rather than another in making a response. The bottom part of Figure 13.3 shows an example.

An alternative solution is to abandon the rough-and-ready five-point scale, and do some prior research in order to discover the way in which feelings are distributed among the population whose attitudes you want to measure. In other words, to design your own precise attitude scale.

The development of a precise attitude scale

There is a second reason for designing a pre-researched scale. Attitudes are complex, and people who hold an overall attitude on an issue may respond one way to one aspect, but very differently to some other aspect of the issue. If you assess them on just one scaled item, your result won't be very reliable. It's far better to use several different items which cover various aspects of the issue in question, and derive some kind of combined score.

Admittedly, for most business and management projects, this level of precision would be too time-consuming, and would be too narrow in scope, to be worth troubling over; however, there are some topics, especially at undergraduate and professional level, in which you could do very useful work by making the development of such a precise scale the main thrust of your project. Attitudes to a new policy, working practice, or outside organization spring to mind, especially if the issue is likely to be a

under-graduate

profes-sional

Q.16. How satisfied or dissatisfied are you with the sense of teamwork which exists between yourself and other sergeants?

Very satisfied	Satisfied	Neither one nor other	Dissatisfied	Very dissatisfied

Please indicate your answer by ticking one of these boxes. If your answer is 'Dissatisfied' or 'Very dissatisfied', please use the space below to tell us why, in a few words

(a)

How satisfied or dissatisfied are you with the sense of teamwork which exists between yourself and other sergeants?

	Very satisfied	Satisfied	Neither one nor other	Dissatis.	Very dissatis.	Total	
	70	140	8	22	2	242	No.
	28.9	57.9	3.3	9.1	0.4	99.6	%

Mean = 4.04

Content analysis of causes of dissatisfaction

No. of replies

1. There is no opportunity for teamwork – colleagues meet only rarely at work due to shift arrangements etc.   11
2. There is no teamwork, but an attitude of 'I'm alright'. There is no concern for other areas and no cooperation or interest.   8
3. Colleagues are interested in teamwork when it will benefit themselves   4
4. No answer given   1

Total   24

(b)

How satisfied are you with the services of our technical information department?

Please rate the quality of our service by putting a tick in the box which best expresses your view.

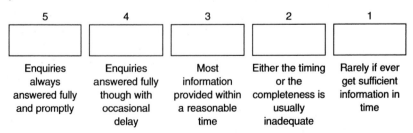

5	4	3	2	1
Enquiries always answered fully and promptly	Enquiries answered fully though with occasional delay	Most information provided within a reasonable time	Either the timing or the completeness is usually inadequate	Rarely if ever get sufficient information in time

(c)

Figure 13.3 Samples of rating scale items. (a) The item as in the questionnaire; (b) the item as analysed; (c) an example of an item with operational scale-point descriptions.

recurring one and your organization would like to have a scale for use on repeated occasions.

There are several alternative techniques at your disposal, of which the most feasible are Likert's method of summated ratings, and Thurstone's method of equal-appearing intervals. Figure 13.4 shows the steps involved in each. Both of them involve two stages: a design stage, in which you use a group of people in order to develop the scale, and a usage stage, in which you measure the attitude of a different group of people, your actual research sample.

all

Likert's approach is based on the rationale that, if you intend to assess the strength and direction of an attitude by summing the ratings of a number of items, you must first ensure that the items which you're adding together do indeed measure the same attitude. The problem is that you have no independent measure of the attitude concerned which would allow you to check this, and so you adopt a 'bootstrapping' approach. That is, you take the total score over all the items as an indicator of 'whatever the scale as a whole measures', and each item is evaluated against this. (Obviously, after you've eliminated the unsuitable items, the total score will be different, and so will 'whatever the scale as a whole measures'; it's likely to be more precise, since the items that you're left with will relate more closely to it.) Basically, the procedure outlined in Figure 13.4(a) develops the coherence of the whole scale, and leaves it up to you, in devising the items in the first place, to ensure that the appropriate attitude is being tapped.

An alternative approach, if you don't know how to calculate a correlation coefficient, is to proceed according to Figure 13.4(a) up to step 4, and then to focus your attention on two extreme groups of respondents: those whose total scores are highest (say, the top 25%), and those whose total scores are lowest (the bottom 25%). For each item, calculate the difference between the average score on that item of the top group, and the average score on that item of the bottom group. **If this difference is low**, reject the item. Clearly, if it doesn't distinguish between those with high total scores and those with low total scores, it doesn't coherently measure 'whatever the scale as a whole measures'. How low a difference do you use? Well, you're seeking to reject between two-thirds and a half of all the items, to end up with a final set of 20, so a pragmatic rule of thumb would be to set a benchmark value for the difference which would allow you to retain 20 items.

Whichever method you use, you should ensure that the wording of the final set of items is arranged so that agreement with the attitude means scoring '5' for half the items (Group A), and '1' for the other half (Group B). You do this to control any tendency for respondents to answer unthinkingly. When you use the scale with your final sample of

(a) The Likert Scale
1. Write 50–60 items you believe to measure the attitude in question.
2. Ask a test panel of 100 respondents to respond to all the items.
3. Cast responses into a table showing each person's response to each item.
4. Sum across the table to derive a total score for each person.
5. For each item, correlate the scores it received (its column) with the total score column.
6. Items with low correlations don't measure 'what the scale as a total' measures: so they're not tapping the attitude: reject them.
7. The remaining items (aim for 20 or so) form the final scale . . .
8. . . . on which a person's attitude would be measured by summing the ratings of the items ticked.
9. **Note:** ideally, when calculating the correlation, the value in the total column should be the total minus the item being considered.

e.g. 'The policy of this government seems to be to give in to as many pressure groups as it can'.

Strongly agree	Agree	Neither	Disagree	Strongly disagree
1	2	3	4	5

Respondent No.	Item No. 1	2	3	4 ... 50	Total Score
1	3	5	4	1 4	150
2	1	2	2	2 3	50
3	4	3	4	3 3	200
4	5	3	3	4 4	250
:	:	:	:	: :	:
100	2	3	3	1 5	100

Column 1 correlates highly (r = 1.0) with total score column, so retain the item for the final scale.
Column 2 correlates poorly (r = 0.3) with total score column, so reject the item from consideration.
And so on, for all items.

(b) The Thurston Scale
1. Write 100 or so items that you believe measure the attitude in question.
2. Ask 50 people **not** to agree/disagree, but to judge how favourable–unfavourable each item is, by putting it into one of 11 groups from 1 = Favourable to 11 = Unfavourable.
3. An item distributed by the judges as in the first example is unsuitable (people can't agree on it!) and would be rejected.
4. An item distributed as in the second is, by the same token, usable.
5. You'd look for a final set of 20 items on which judges agree; all spread across the width of the '11-point scale'.
6. Place these in random order and give to the respondents whose attitude you wish to measure. Ask them simply to **choose the ones with which they agree.**
7. The mean of their scale positions indicates the attitude, its direction and strength.

Example 1: Item 1 is distributed as below:

Very favourable   Very unfavourable

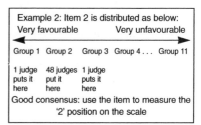

Group 1   Group 2   Group 3   Group 4 . . .   Group 11

5 judges put it here   15 judges put it here   5 judges put it here   25 judges put it here

No consensus: reject the item

Example 2: Item 2 is distributed as below:

Very favourable   Very unfavourable

Group 1   Group 2   Group 3   Group 4 . . .   Group 11

1 judge puts it here   48 judges put it here   1 judge puts it here

Good consensus: use the item to measure the '2' position on the scale

Figure 13.4 Procedural guide. (a) the Likert summated rating scale; (b) the Thurston equal-appearing interval scale.

respondents, you ask each respondent to choose one of the five alternatives for each item; you then reverse the ratings for the items in Group B (by subtracting from 6 in the case of a five-point scale) to restore the direction in which they're scaled, and sum the ratings of both groups of items to get a total score for the respondent concerned. The lowest possible score is (1 × the number of items) and highest possible score is (5 × the number of items) for a five-point scale, and so you can place your respondent somewhere between these two extremes.

Likert's method provides powerful and precise attitude measures and, because the end result is a set of five-point items that look familiar to respondents, people feel comfortable in using them. There is one problem, however, arising from the fact that individual item scores have to be added to get the attitude score. You could get the same score either by ticking the '1' box for half the time and the '5' box for the other half, or by ticking the '3' box every time. Yet surely these are rather different attitudes? The first represents some kind of ambivalence, while the other would appear to indicate neutrality. But the problem is, we don't know what 'neutrality' on such a scale is, and it's a rather large assumption to say it's the middle score on the scale.

Thurstone's method is designed with this problem of the mid-point in mind. The design stage requires people to judge the scale position of each item directly, using a procedure which arrives at a set of final items which are spread evenly across the whole scale, including the mid-point. (At steps 3 and 4 in Figure 13.4(b), the position of a given item on the scale is derived by calculating the median value of all the groups it's put into by the judges; its spread across the groups is derived by calculating the interquartile range of the groups it's put into by the judges. Only items with low interquartile ranges are selected.)

As you might have anticipated, the validity of the scale you obtain by Thurstone's technique depends on the attitudes of the people you first use as judges, and depends on the assumption that people can adopt a neutral stance when asked to act as judges. This issue has been extensively researched, and a straightforward guideline has emerged: when choosing your group of judges for the design stage, avoid people who, in your opinion, are likely to have extreme views on the attitude in question.

If you plan to develop one of these forms of attitude scale, you might want to refer to a more detailed account than the above. Edwards (1957) presents a variety of techniques very clearly, and provides worked examples. You would also need to have a nodding acquaintance with simple statistical calculations, such as those for computing the mean, median, and interquartile range, with the correlation coefficient as an option in the case of the Likert scale. You might care to check your calculations with your tutor before using the scales with your sample of respondents.

The use of pre-researched attitude scales

Finally, you could save yourself a lot of development work by finding a published, pre-researched scale, which measures the attitude in which you're interested. The most convenient source of such scales is a two-volume collection put together by a team of researchers and practitioners associated with British Telecom; you'll find it referenced either under MCB (1984) or Stewart *et al.* (1984a; 1984b); it's under the latter entry that it appears in my bibliography. The blue volume 1 provides a variety of personal satisfaction measures, and is more likely to contain scales assessing personal attitudes; but you should check the yellow volume 2, to see if there's anything suitable in its collection of organizational measures.

It's well worth including one or more of these scales in a longer questionnaire or interview schedule, at any level of project, (from undergraduate to Masters); you could also use a suitable scale from this collection as an adjunct to any semi-structured technique that you're using. Before doing so, it would be useful to obtain the original account in which the development of the scale is described; these are listed in each volume. Finally, take note of any particular copyright restrictions that may be mentioned.

13.3 OBSERVATION TECHNIQUES

When all's said and done, and all the semi-structured and fully structured techniques have been taken into account, your eyes are still a very good research instrument. You don't have to depend on extensive dialogue with other people to begin to understand what's going on! However, standing and staring in a disorganized manner won't get you very far, and both of the techniques which I shall outline depend on a more structured approach.

Structured observation

Some of the most interesting and important findings about the nature of managerial work and its problems have been obtained by observational means. Stewart's research on how managers spend their time (Stewart, 1967) asked managers to act as their own observers and record their activities in diary form; it is still quoted as a source of ideas, hypotheses, and guidance in understanding the problems involved in different kinds of management role.

Mintzberg's work on the same issue (Mintzberg, 1973) helped to change our views about management as a planned, purposeful activity; its observation categories are still used in studies which seek to relate what managers do, to their effectiveness (e.g. Martinko and Gardner (1990), an article which reproduces Mintzberg's category headings themselves, with some additions). Isenberg's study of middle and top management (Isenberg, 1984) has refocused our attention on the importance of the personal interpretations that influence management decision-making and action, helping to legitimize the individual as the unit of analysis in management research; it's a good account of a semi-structured approach. Finally, if you plan to carry out observations of problem-solving groups, you should take note of Bales' Interaction Process Analysis category system (Bales and Slater, 1950) which led to some very influential findings on group dynamics and influenced early work on leadership style.

If you want to include an observational phase in your project work, two basic procedures are open to you. You can use a pre-existing analytic scheme, such as Mintzberg's, or you can develop and apply your own. Mintzberg's can be used as a complete unit, or you might take just the one of his three main category schemes that is most relevant to your needs. He offers schemes for classifying managerial events, purposes of contact (together with a separate scheme for classifying the inititator of contact), and managerial roles. How to develop your own scheme is outlined below. However, some form of scheme is strictly essential, if you're to avoid being overwhelmed by the flood of observations that is potentially available to you in even the simplest business or management situation.

Developing and using your own scheme involves you in a process of analytic induction, a brief account of which is provided in section 6.4 under the rubric of Grounded Theory. Becker and Geer (1982) describe the following three stages involved in the case of observation technique.

1. **Selection and definition of problems, concepts and indices**, in which you try and place initially observed single events into a conceptual perspective and begin the search for further indicators of the ideas, concepts or themes that you think are involved. So, for example, if a manager mentions the pace and burdens of his or her particular job, your thoughts might turn to the concept of stress, and you begin to identify ways of categorizing stressors in the management environment; or the notion of time management may occur to you, and a variety of efficiency measures become possible. In this stage, the credibility and status of your informants, the extent to which the comments were elicited by you or volunteered by the informant, and the extent to which social influences prevail, are particularly important.
2. **Checking frequency and distribution of phenomena**, in which you decide whether the events are widespread enough and typical enough to repay systematic recording, and in which you do the main data-

collection itself. How frequent is the comment or behaviour concerned, what forms does it take (the beginnings of a categorization scheme), and do other events confirm the significance and importance of the behaviour involved? This is the place for the collection of observations using whatever category scheme (or schemes: it's likely that the events you're studying will require several) you construct. Other techniques, such as the repertory grid or a semi-structured technique like the key informant interview, may provide you with the material for a content analysis which results in a category scheme.

3. **Construction of models** which provide a general framework within which the observations can be described, and into which general concepts may be introduced to allow an explanation of the events in question. (On the distinction between a description and an explanation, refer again to Table 8.7.) This model will relate the events to particular factors and influences in the organization being studied, and allow statements about the necessary and sufficient conditions required for the events to occur, statements about what is important and what isn't, and statements which relate the present situation being studied to some wider class of situations as described by the concepts you drew on initially. Here, you're commenting on the significance and generalizability of your conclusions to other organizations.

This type of observation forms a very useful technique if you're using case study method. During all of this time, you'll need to carry pencil and paper (tape recorders are, as I've mentioned before, a mixed blessing); you'll need to tolerate a measure of uncertainty and ambiguity; and you'll want to discuss your emerging ideas with other people. For all of these reasons, your role as observer must be publicly known, and you should have taken an early decision on whether you're there as a participant observer or as a non-participant.

The latter is too big a question to be resolved here, since it depends on the specifics of the situation you're in. But in any event, you will always influence the events you observe to some degree, regardless of whether you participate or not; you'll always have problems of over-identification with what's going on which need to be guarded against; and you'll always encounter situations and events in which things happen so quickly, or which have such personal implications, that the role of the dispassionate observer is difficult to maintain. Jorgensen (1989) is a useful guidebook on these and related issues, and Waddington (1994) reinforces these points in an account which summarizes his classic case study of the Ansell's Brewery strike.

Depending on whether you're involved in the more systematic stage of data-collection, this may or may not be a problem. A student of mine was doing an observation study of activities in a hospital ward, one of his objectives being to draw conclusions about staffing levels. Being a kind-hearted soul, he'd occasionally help the harassed nurse to turn some of the heavier post-operative patients in their beds during the night-shift when assistance couldn't be obtained, which does seem to negate the purpose of the observation activity! This is a form of over-identification which must be avoided.

Being a lively and curious person, he'd dress up in surgical robes and attend operations immediately after his nightly observation period was completed, taking advantage of the surgeons' mistaken belief that the only 'student' on the wards could be a medical student; in this case, the observations weren't compromised, and he enjoyed himself immensely. This seems quite an appropriate level of identification with the issues being studied. There is a very interesting discussion of the personal implications of participant observation in Gans (1982).

The field experiment as observation

As you may recall from section 10.2, experiments are feasible in those situations in which you can structure events so tightly that control becomes possible. Here, you're concerned with the control of extraneous variables that compete with the independent variable in influencing changes in the dependent variable, and also with the kind of control that permits you to manipulate the independent variable itself. The experiment than becomes a form of highly structured observation, in which you formally ignore everything but these variables, while informally keeping an eye on anything else that might have a bearing on the validity of your findings and their interpretation.

Occasionally you may be lucky and discover that events have arranged themselves in such a way that at least two levels of some independent variable fall naturally to hand (one group of managers go on a course and another group don't; one division adopts a new policy and another doesn't). You're faced with a **found or natural experiment**, in other words, and you're faced with three problems:

- to define a suitable dependent variable sufficiently operationally so that informative conclusions about the impact of the independent variable become possible;
- to ensure that your measurement of the dependent variable doesn't intrude excessively on the behaviour of the people you're observing;
- to find a rationale for deciding which of the variables that you couldn't control matter, and which don't.

I leave it to you to recognize a suitable occasion if it should ever occur.

You might find Webb *et al.* (1966) a useful source of ideas, particularly in handling the second kind of problem.

In the normal course of events, however, experiments must be made to happen, and one way to accomplish this is by structuring a form of questionnaire in such a way that the various subgroups of respondents fall into different levels of the independent variable in which you're interested. I've already suggested this as a rationale for the analysis of conventional structured questionnaires (see Section 12.1), and, provided it's possible for you to arrange subgroups according to a precise experimental design, you can obtain an impressively high level of experimental control. A study by Van Clouse (1990) provides a good example.

Van Clouse presented a group of students with a questionnaire at the beginning and end of a course in entrepreneurship, in order to measure changes in their perceptions of the factors to be taken into account in making business start-up decisions. In this case, presence on the course is the independent variable, and the extent and nature of the changes form the dependent variables. Following a carefully pre-validated procedure, in which the validity of the questionnaire was established and the reliability of the participants' responses demonstrated, he was able to show that there were statistically significant changes in students' perceptions on many of the factors which the entrepreneurship course was designed to influence.

Strictly speaking, as he didn't measure changes amongst a group of students who did **not** attend the course, there was only one level of the independent variable, and it is technically incorrect to conclude that it was the course which brought about the changes. Indeed, he could, one imagines, have administered his questionnaire twice over to a group of students who did not attend the course for comparative purposes, but he chose not to. However, to provide a control group of this kind would be difficult in many of the situations in which you might plausibly conduct a field experiment of this type, and he used the evidence of questionnaire reliability, and the informal reasoning that the changes were as one would expect, given the contents of the course, to attribute the changes to the course itself.

If you find yourself with an issue or topic which lends itself to this approach, the following guidelines should be followed.

■ Identify some grouping of respondents which represents at least two levels of an independent variable in which you're interested: for example, position in the organization, or known views on some important issue.

■ Construct a questionnaire-based measure of this variable. This may be a simple, single question which asks them to state their position in the organization or their views on the issue, as in the above example. Alternatively, it may be a more sophisticated index which is the result of combining responses to several questions. For example, if you wanted to find out whether 'high-flyers' in your organization made systematically better decisions than run-of-the-mill employees, you might have to ask several questions covering such issues as number of years employed, and number and level of positions held in the organization, in order to construct a measure of career progression.

- Decide on the dependent variable or variables: some indicator of the issues in which you're interested, that you think may be influenced by the independent variable.
- Construct one or more questions which assess this variable. In the case of the 'high-flyers', for instance, your questions about the quality of their decisions might be incorporated in the same questionnaire, in the form of technical problems to which there were recognizable right or wrong answers. (This is essentially what van Clouse did: he asked his students to say what emphasis they placed on a number of factors which are necessary for successful business start-ups, and he checked with existing entrepreneurs and with colleagues that these factors were realistic, and that the judgements being elicited were appropriate.) Alternatively, you might get this information from other sources: in the case of our running example, from their supervisors' views of the adequacy of the decisions they make, or even from some quasi-objective indicator. Salesmen can be judged on the sales they make, bank lending officers by the number of loan defaults occurring among businesses to which they lend, and so on.
- Analyse the data to see if there is any systematic relationship between the independent variable and the dependent. In practice, this would involve casting the answers to the questions measuring the dependent variable into a table with at least two columns: one for the first level of the independent variable and one for the second – high-flyers' responses in one column, and those of run-of-the-mill employees in the other, in terms of the above example.
- The analysis would involve you in making the assumption of no difference in the responses, and examining them to see if the observed differences were sufficiently large for you to reject this assumption. A variety of statistical tests are available to aid this decision, and you might find the discussion under the Analysis heading of section 12.1 useful here.
- If the difference were indeed statistically significant, you would be able to attribute it to the independent variable only if your design permits you to. As usual, this would have to have been considered at the outset, when you constructed the questionnaire itself. It would include such

issues as the robustness, reliability, and validity of the measures you chose; a decision to take repeated measures with the same group of people, as opposed to making separate measures on independent groups of people and the extent to which this might influence the inferences you can draw; and the presence of uncontrolled variables which might plausibly account for the result which you obtained.

Using this version of experimental technique depends on a familiarity with the principles of experimental design in general, and on the use of appropriate analytic statistics, the two being interrelated. Much of this involves standard procedures outlined in a variety of textbooks. If you find that the introductory account in Anderson (1966) is insufficient, you could try the following: Campbell and Stanley (1966) on general experimental design in field settings, or Green and Tull (1978) on experimental design in marketing applications in particular. Cook and Campbell (1979) are particularly good on issues of design for field observation.

Writing it up | 14

If you haven't done any previous project work before, you won't have realized to what extent the act of writing, the very activity of composition, influences the development of your ideas, your arguments and your hunches. The sooner you start writing the better. If you think about it, you'll recognize that you need to go through three stages in order to construct a completed project document. The first stage involves adding data taken from primary and secondary sources specifically related to your topic, to data taken from your own stock of general knowledge; while the second stage requires you to turn those data into information by building an argument which achieves your project objectives. All of your efforts will be pointless, however, if you give insufficient attention to the third stage, in which you have to communicate that information to your reader in a way that he or she finds convincing. The first two have been dealt with in earlier sections; my purpose in this chapter is to provide you with guidelines on the third stage.

14.1 BASIC REQUIREMENTS: FORMAT AND DEADLINES

Section 4.4 provided you with some introductory material on the length, layout, timing and structure of your document in order to make you aware of what you were facing. This material is worth a brief second glance now that you're well advanced with your work.

Length

Writing to length is important. You might argue that quality, rather than length, is a primary consideration, and you'd be right in general terms. However, some institutions (especially the professional bodies) see the project as an exercise in the communication skills essential to a manager, and feel quite strongly that you should be able to get your message across within a set limit.

The best way to do this is to divide your maximum length, as specified in the programme regulations, into sections or chapters, allocating an appropriate number of words or pages to each. Writing is not an exact process, and you'll find it useful to pretend that you're aiming to produce one more section than you actually need, allocating pages to it when you make this initial estimate, and keeping these in reserve to account for the sections which, once you've written them, turn out to be longer than you estimated. This may seem pedantic, but the discipline is useful. An over-extended project may raise a suspicion that you've 'padded out' your project with unnecessary information, may indicate a lack of originality in what is an undigested compilation of material, and suggests that you haven't given sufficient thought to the message you're trying to convey.

Layout and make-up

Once you have finished placing words on the page following the suggestions made in section 4.4, you'll need to bind the pages together.

MBA

diploma

Institutions have their own regulations but, as a general rule, Masters and many Diploma project documents need to be bound by a professional bookbinder. The actual colour of the covers is often specified for you. Your institution should be able to give you a list of local bookbinders while, if you happen to live near to Stockton on Tees, Dorking, Newcastle under Lyme or Halifax you will find a branch of Remploy which offers a specialist dissertation bookbinding service. Their prices are very competitive at around £25 per copy, with extra charges if you wish to incorporate photographs or video/audio cassettes in a multi-media format; allow for a turnaround period of ten days, or seven days in an emergency.

under-graduate

profes-sional

Undergraduate project reports should at the very least be spiral-bound with a punching-and-binding machine; peg-and-strip arrangements in which the plastic strip is melted to the pegs in a process of heat-treatment, with plasticized card for front and back covers, make for a satisfactory binding.

all

The wording on the title page, and sometimes on the front cover, is normally as follows: title; author surname and initials; the words 'A thesis' (or 'dissertation') 'submitted to [name of your institution] in partial fulfilment of the requirements for the degree of [name of your qualification]'; the month and year of submission. Professional bodies may have their own variants.

Timing

I've said it before and I'll say it again: deadlines are essential. If you have the feeling that you might miss them, talk to your tutor. You see, there are only two options available to the tutor:

- to allow you a few extra days taken out of the period allotted to him or her to read the document before submitting the grade to the appropriate examination board, bearing in mind any external examining arrangements involved;
- to submit no grade to the examination board, making an arrangement with you for submission to the next board. This may be a term, a semester, or a year later, may well hold up your graduation, and might use up one of the two chances which most regulations permit for submissions (including the chance to resubmit work that was initially failed). There may also be a penalty in the form of deducted marks in one form or other.

Structure

Take a glance at Figures 4.1 and 4.2, and now that you're *in medias res*, refresh yourself on the associated discussion. Now that you have a good feeling for the scope of your project, it helps if you think of yourself as being involved in one of three situations:

- the short document;
- the longer document without implementation;
- the longer document with implementation.

The short document. Your work is best structured as a management report, in which the title gives an exact description of what you are doing rather than an allusive or literary gloss on the subject-matter. ('An evaluation of three strategies for overseas trade' is an exact description; 'Coping with cultural differences: implementing trading strategy' contains an allusion to the main conceptual material contained in the document.) It should open with an executive summary, in which objectives are followed by recommendations; supporting information comes next; a description of methods and techniques is given where recommendations depend on them, usually next but sometimes in an appendix. The arguments for various actions given relevant background information comes at the end. The remaining material should be organized in order to amplify and support this summary, and you might consider labelling the major sections with a hierarchic numeric system (1.0 containing 1.1, 1.2 etc.; 1.1 containing 1.1.1, 1.1.2, etc.), or numbering each paragraph sequentially.

The longer document without implementation. This is probably the most common alternative, and the structure will take one of the two forms as summarized in Figures 4.1 and 4.2. It will depend on whether you wish to organize material around several distinct issues, with a separate review and discussion of secondary data being followed by methodology and primary research findings for each issue; or whether you feel you are dealing with one main issue which runs throughout the material. The former is common at MBA level and is an argument for distinct sections or chapters, one for each issue, all (not each!) being preceded by overall objectives and company background material, and succeeded by material which summarizes, integrates, discusses and concludes. The latter is more usual at undergraduate level, and the general material in section 4.4 applies.

The longer document with implementation. If you have the opportunity to implement recommendations arising from the earlier parts of your project, in which you constructed an argument for some course of action and mustered primary and secondary data in support of a choice from a set of alternatives, your reader will be particularly interested in the outcomes of that action. So your document should be structured accordingly; make sure that you give sufficient emphasis to the outcomes, presenting fresh data as evidence, discussing the outcomes, evaluating the wisdom of the particular action you recommended, and drawing conclusions for the future. This is really an argument for allowing plenty of pages (perhaps half of your complete document) to everything that followed the action which you initially recommended.

14.2 THE USE OF LANGUAGE

There are many useful accounts which will help you with the humble business of writing. George Orwell's classic essay is one to read now if you haven't encountered it before (Orwell, 1957), and Strunk and White (1972) provide a goldmine of useful detail in only 78 pages; Burgess (1975) will tell you as much as you'll ever need to know about the theory of language, while Turk and Kirkman (1989) is probably the most relevant to your immediate needs.

The last of these asserts that the notion of 'proper', grammatical English is somewhat outmoded, and argues that you should discover and implement the rules of acceptable usage, and current convention, instead (Turk and Kirkman, 1989: 15). Though I might disagree on matters of detail ('datum' or 'data', for instance; 'medium' or 'media'), there's no doubt that you need to be familiar with the style and conventions which apply when you write for an academic audience in the business and management field.

What's 'style'? It's said of **people** that they either have it or they don't; but **literary** style, in case you wondered, consists of the method or methods by which you obtain the effect you wish to achieve in your reader. Like fashion style, it is something which you deliberately adopt in order to obtain the effect you intend. Table 14.1 lists some recommendations given in Turk and Kirkman (1989), to which I've added some relevant stylistic suggestions which are worth addressing individually.

Your own aims

Don't confuse your aim of building a convincing argument with the aim, and associated objectives, of the project itself. Indeed, weaker students have been known to cite their substantive objectives; the aim of being convincing; and one or more of the objectives given in section 2.2 and Table 2.1, in sentences such as 'The objective of this dissertation is to examine and evaluate the outcomes of divisionalization on the marketing strategy of the company, to convince you, the examiner, that all the relevant arguments have been marshalled, and to be of assistance to the company.' The objective **of the student's project work** concerns divisionalization and its impact on strategy, and the examiner will refer to this substantive objective periodically to see how well the argument is achieving it. An objective **of the project process** relates to the wish to be convincing; while Tables 4.1 to 4.4 suggest that presentation is important in assessment, it's just a part of what is assessed. Finally, the objective **of the project as an educational method** is in a different category altogether. While the examiner may discern ways in which the work might help the company and form an opinion on the extent to which project method has succeeded educationally for the student, he or she is not the best judge of company benefit and will restrain enthusiasm or despair arising from these grounds in giving a mark. Don't confuse categories when stating your objectives!

Try not to be breathless. You can be convincing by sharing your convictions, and expressions of personal opinion are permissible – but only if they're warranted by evidence. Statements of company views or policies can be quoted as observations you have made, but you need to be careful about their status as evidence: 'We are a People Company' is a valid report of something you have seen in the company brochure and may state something about the company's espoused image for publicity purposes. Lifted straight from the brochure and used as evidence, however, it doesn't engender confidence that the company does indeed care for the people it supplies or employs.

Table 14.1 Devising a style suited to an examiner in business and management

The question to pose	A suitable answer	Stylistic implication
What is your aim?	To build a convincing argument leading to a conclusion which is sensible given the issues investigated and the data obtained.	Ensure your assertions are logical, supported or supportable by evidence, and take exceptions into account. Avoid personal or company opinions and feelings to which the above doesn't apply.
Who are your audience and what is their aim?	To pass you or fail you, depending on whether they are convinced by the argument, with the minimum expenditure of time and effort on their part.	Write in an authoritative but not opinionated manner (quote sources!) using simple and readable sentence constructions. Provide summaries where needed.
What attitude do they hold?	Supportive, taking account of any special difficulties you encountered. They're cheering you on, hoping they can pass you so that they don't have to read the document afresh when you resubmit it after an initial failure.	Include conceptual, situational and organizational constraints within your argument and indicate if and how you dealt with them. Personal difficulties are best left to a separate statement.
What is their background?	Already knowledgeable in the field and willing to learn more, of above-average intelligence, and used to absorbing large amounts of written information in a hurry.	Reference your assertions, elaborate concepts and ideas only when necessary, include relevant asides selectively to maintain interest. Polysyllabic words and sentences are welcomed; though only if briefer formats do not suffice.
What do they really need to know?	Enough to convince them that you have learnt the relevant parts that they know, together with sufficient new reasoning and data to be convinced by your argument.	Ensure the basics of the subject are covered, summarize periodically, and include self-referential statements indicating that you are tracking the argument you are building.

After Turk and Kirkman (1989)

Your reader's aims

Your examiner will do his or her best to do your work justice when the mark is allotted, but you must make this as easy as possible.

Long sentences are dangerous, since the reader's concentration may be distracted by qualifying clauses. Faced with two other project documents, each of between 10 000 and 50 000 words, and the scripts of two or three taught courses to mark (some of which may involve answers to up to four questions from each of a class of 100 people), all within a period which varies between one week and six weeks, he or she will appreciate everything you do to make the experience of reading your document an interesting and pleasant one, since you are competing for his or her attention with many other people. Um. Far better to have said 'The lecturer may be faced with six other project documents to read, each of them 50 000 words long, and yours will be particularly appreciated if it's readable and interesting. There could also be three or four examinations to be marked, each one consisting of answers to four questions from each of 100 students. You're competing for attention at a very busy time.'

And so, several longish sentences seem a better alternative, especially as they lend themselves to a rhythm which pulls the reader's attention along.

Short sentences command attention.

Your reader's attitude

While being supportive, the tutor would prefer you to keep your personal cries for help separate from an account of conceptual difficulties encountered and methodological problems addressed. A conversation backed by documentation, or a letter submitted with your document, are a better way of drawing the examiner's attention to problems caused by illness, files lost through criminal breaking and entry, and all of the other accidents which have been known to happen to project documents. Justified or not, including them in the document suggests special pleading and is best avoided.

Your reader's background

It is safe to assume that your examiner knows the subject-matter well, and doesn't require you to explain simple terms or to plod through basic definitions and concepts. Your problem lies in judging what he or he is likely to view as 'simple' and 'basic', but by the time you are writing the main part of the document you should have formed an impression from the secondary sources you've read. Stop the flow to define and explain:

- when you feel it is critical to your argument;
- when you are taking an unusual stance;
- when you're trying to do something new with the material to hand.

Although your reader will be used to coping with large volumes of information, you can help by providing bulleted summaries periodically (especially when presenting empirical findings). He or she will find it difficult to handle situations in which poorly digested data lie congealed within an unclear presentation, especially when both are compounded by errors of thinking and logic. A list of the most criminal errors of reasoning is given as Table 14.2: commit them at your peril.

What your reader really needs to know

In amplifying Table 14.1 and the original suggestions given in Turk and Kirkman (1989), I find I'm addressing the irreducible core of your project document: the essence which remains when the outer layers have been pared away. What is it all ultimately about? Here's a checklist which would seem to apply to all project documents.

- That you have identified your objectives, stated them clearly, and referred back to them in writing your conclusions.
- That you are familiar with basic secondary sources, drawing on them to formulate your efforts within an appropriate academic context.
- That you understand the organizational background sufficiently well to demonstrate that your objectives are appropriate, your topic relevant, and the issues you select for investigation realistic.
- That you can demonstrate that your methods and techniques of primary data-gathering are capable of answering the research questions you ask, being aware of their limitations.
- That you can build a critical argument which pulls all of the above together.
- That you can turn primary data into information which is relevant to your argument, congruent with the secondary data, relevant to the issues you are exploring, and essential to the conclusions you draw and the recommendations you make.

You will provide him or her with all of this only if you provide clear guidelines and signposts through your material, directing and controlling his or her attention. By doing this, you tell the reader that you are capable of thinking through your material to the point at which you have become a very competent **teacher** of what you know about the topic of your research. To be a teacher is to possess knowledge, and to know how it is

Table 14.2 Seven errors of reasoning calling to Heaven for vengeance

The kamikaze argument
Your assertions may state a case, or contradict and hence argue with someone
else's statements. What they shouldn't do is argue with themselves. Two
statements which contradict one another are easily spotted if they're in the same
paragraph, and may be recognized even when separated by lots of intervening
text – especially if they're strong statements, or central to your thesis. Of course
you can change your mind in your project document: but this is best done
intentionally, and usually, when the primary data warrant it.

The plain stereotype
Certain phrases are like 'motherhood' and 'apple pie' on the one hand, or
'anarchy' and 'democratic rights' on the other: they may express banalities,
seduce the listener into a brainless response, and prevent originality of thought.
Take care when you use words like 'leadership', 'participation', 'vital' and
'objective'. Of course there are occasions on which they're exactly appropriate,
but these aren't as frequent as you might think. Conversely, there is

The misinterpreted stereotype
An idea may express a conventional wisdom, and may be couched in stereotyped
terms. But you need independent evidence to decide if it's weighty or trivial: to
recognize that a stereotype exists is not sufficient to decide if the ideas it involves
are in error or, indeed, plausible.

The cardboard cutout
Your project can only sample a person's actions and ideas: the complete
individual is more complex than your methods allow. People can appear
inconsistent (particularly in behaving in ways that appear to contradict their
utterances). That doesn't necessarily prove thoughtlessness or insincerity on their
part, and you always need independent evidence to establish the position which
people hold.

The sloppy consistency
You can usually turn up evidence which leaves your beliefs intact without testing
them out. 'The company survived; the profits were high; therefore the profits led
to the survival.' If you believe that, then you're ignoring a multitude of
alternative explanations: for example, cashflow. Just because your evidence
appears consistent with your beliefs, doesn't make them true.

The articulate nonsense
A manager may be effective but unable to define it or explain it in words.
Conversely, the ability to make propositional statements about one's beliefs and
actions is consistent with wisdom but isn't a necessary or sufficient condition. An
explicit argument isn't necessarily true.

The galloping hypothesis
A plausible possibility can be expressed in one paragraph, taken for granted in
the next, and assumed to be true in the remainder of your text. Reiteration will
irritate rather than convince: unless you provide some evidence to support your
assertion.

After Watson (1987)

best shared with the reader; it is a reflexive, self-aware process, and so another suggestion is that you demonstrate your competence by the occasional self-reference. Comment on your intentions, draw attention to weaknesses in your argument (while demonstrating that you can imagine how they can be improved); let your reader know when you are arguing from a position of strength.

This needs to be done subtly.

- 'The main weakness in this argument is x, y and z' comments on what you are doing and shows you **know** what you're doing without the explicit intrusion of 'I'. 'The main weakness of my argument' might be appropriate on rare occasions but is likely to lead to excessive self-consciousness as you grope for a consistent style.
- 'Another advantage to this position is that . . .' is entirely appropriate, while 'Yet another advantage . . .' is light and readable, but carries the danger of turning into facetiousness if a long list is to be presented. 'And there are yet more advantages to come [you lucky reader you] . . .' is a trap to avoid.
- 'It remains to present the views of the senior managers' sample, in order to . . .' shows that you're building an explicit argument; 'I now intend to present the senior managers' views and will next . . .' is a little too plodding, especially if you use it often in building a series of bridges across different sections of your account.

If you take the conclusion that my own style in writing this book is best avoided, that would be entirely correct, since my intentions about my reader were necessarily different from yours. Some project topics lend themselves to a section or chapter written in a very personal, experiential style, where the qualitative and the personal are an integral and intended part of your research design. However, this takes skill to carry off successfully, and you'd probably want to take your tutor's opinions on an early draft. In general, then, I'd suggest that you follow the excellent advice given in chapter 5 of Strunk and White (1972): 'Place yourself in the background' (with a suitable emphasis on the second word as well as the last). The rest of that chapter is worth reading in detail, (though to my mind a lot of it is about personal **voice**, as much as it is about style).

14.3 NON-SEXIST LANGUAGE AND POLITICAL CORRECTNESS

There is a stylistic rule which suggests that you use active constructions rather than passive (**I am writing this clause** in the active voice, while **this clause has been written** in the passive). Unlike the rules which suggest that you should be grammatical and take care over the accuracy of your spelling (both of which can be handled automatically if you use a word processor, the former less successfully than the latter), there will be many occasions on which you'll need to break it.

For example, one is occasionally driven to use the passive voice rather than the active when framing phrases that avoid sexist language constructions; indeed, one of the arguments against the use of non-sexist language is that it leads to awkward sentence constructions. On the other hand, there are many good reasons for avoiding sexist terms and constructions in your writing, and in drawing your attention to Table 14.3, I can only suggest that you take it seriously, and that a clear style is compatible with non-sexist constructions given a little practice and forethought.

Another argument against non-sexist language is that it reflects political correctness, and that there can't be any place for PC in a document which is meant to be the outcome of untrammelled intellectual thought. You have to be careful to avoid sexist – and racist – constructions, while eschewing PC. There is perhaps just the one example of PC in the list. The purpose of this particular compilation of non-sexist terms is to help minimize discrimination against **women**, male examples are therefore omitted, and the assumption is made that one must never run the risk of insulting a woman through the thoughtless usage of language. Few would argue against any of that. However, if one **intended** an insult then 'bitter old spinster' would be much more effective than 'bitter old unmarried undivorced woman'. (And likewise, 'seedy old bachelor' makes for a more pungent insult, if an insult is intended, than 'seedy old unmarried, undivorced man'.) To include it as an example in a document where male examples are, appropriately enough, excluded results in political correctness.

Political correctness is an evil since it constrains freedom of action: (Phillips, 1994a), a brief article which she has expanded into a book, Phillips (1994b). However, it isn't necessarily political correctness to constrain language (for what are grammar, orthography, and style but forms of constraint?) if the consequent impact on thinking makes for the lessening of prejudice, and it is important for you to avoid sexist and racist constructions as best you can. Choosing alternatives is often a matter of taste. For example, I prefer 'he or she' to 'they' since this construction replaces 'he' which is singular, while 'they' is a plural; yet, in a brief article accompanying Phillips', Wordsworth (1994) points out that there are other instances of plural words with singular meanings, e.g. 'ones' (as in 'Which sweets do you prefer?' 'The red ones.').

Table 14.3 Avoiding sexist language. The material is taken directly from a publication by the National Union of Journalists' Equality Council, to whom acknowledgement is made for kind permission to reproduce it. Clearly, it is directed at journalists, as some of the comments and contexts make clear, but the guidelines are valuable for anyone involved in project work in a field (management!) where males outnumber females by at least 4:1, for many reasons, some dubious. One may thoughtlessly give an impression of offensiveness, or, perhaps worse in a piece of applied research, offend an examiner by giving an impression of thoughtlessness. See the discussion of political correctness in the text

---

The NUJ Equality Style Guide

Most newspapers, magazines and books discriminate against women so automatically it is almost unconscious.
Here are suggestions for avoiding bias:

Instead of	Try
businessman	business manager, executive, boss, business chief, head of firm, etc., businesswoman/people
cameraman	photographer, camera operator
newsman	journalist or reporter
fireman/men	firefighter, fire service staff, fire crews
ice cream man	ice cream seller
policeman/men	police officer, or (plural) just police
salesman/girl	assistant, shop worker, shop staff, representative, sales staff
steward/ess, airhostess	airline staff, flight attendant
chairman	chairperson/woman, in the chair was . . . , who chairs the committee
best man for the job	best person/woman
man or mankind	humanity, human race, humans, people
manhood	adulthood
man-in-the-street	average citizen, average worker
manpower	workers, workforce, staffing
manning	staffing, jobs, job levels
manmade	synthetic, artificial, manufactured
Ford men voted . . .	Ford workers voted . . .
male nurse	nurse
woman doctor	doctor
housewife	often means shopper, consumer, the cook
mothers	often means parents
girls (of over 18)	women (especially in sport)
spinster/divorcee	these words should not be used as an insult
he, his	often means he or she, or his or hers – or sentence constructions can be changed to use they or theirs
Mrs, Miss	if your publication insists on courtesy titles, at least offer women the choice of being called Ms
Mr John Smith and his wife Elsie	Elsie and John Smith
authoress	author – avoid /ess where possible
dolls, birds, ladies, Mrs Mopp	these, and the puns arising from them are not funny
pin-ups	are they really news?
spokesman	official, representative

Try the double standard test – would you use this description of a man?

14.4 CONCLUSION

As with the previous section, all of this chapter is about conviction in one form or another. Indeed, this whole book explores ways of convincing someone else that you have something valuable to say, and that you have evidence to support it. Your goal, ultimately, is to present accurate and convincing information to your tutor and the examiners; although the relevance and realism of your work is most important, it's the academics, rather than the colleagues in your organization, that your argument has to convince. Prove what you claim.

After losing Calais to the French, Mary Tudor is said to have declared 'When I die, you will find the word "Calais" engraved on my heart.' Just in case you're ever autopsied, ensure that the words 'I proved it' are written on yours.

I wish you every success in this endeavour.

Bibliography

Items in bold are particularly recommended as casual bedside reading, to give you a flavour of the organizational and management environment in which your project work will be done, together with some contrasts: see the discussion in Section 2.2.

Allport G.W. (1981) 'The general and the unique in psychological science' in Reason P. and Rowan J. (eds), *Human Inquiry: a Sourcebook of New Paradigm Research* Chichester: Wiley.

Anderson B.F. (1966) *The Psychology Experiment: An Introduction to the Scientific Method* Belmont, CA: Brooks-Cole.

Annett J. and Duncan K.D. (1967) 'Task analysis and training design' *Occupational Psychology* 41, 211–21.

Ashton D. (1989) 'The case for taylor-made MBAs' *Personnel Management* July, 32–5.

Aspinwall K. (1992) 'Biographical research: searching for meaning' *Management Education and Development* **23** (3) 248–57.

Baetz, M.C. and Beamish, P.W. (1989) 'North American experience with business policy field projects' *Management Education and Development* **20** (1), 112–23.

Baker M.J. (1976) 'The written analysis of cases' *Quarterly Review of Marketing* (1).

Bales K.F. and Slater. (1950) *Interaction process analysis: a method for the study of small groups* Cambridge, MA: Addison Wesley.

Bannister D. and Fransella F. (1985) *Inquiring Man: Theory of Personal Constructs* London: Croom Helm.

Barzun J. and Graff H.E. (1985) *The Modern Researcher* London: Harcourt, Brace, Jovanovich.

Becker H.S. and Geer B. (1982) 'Participant observation: the analysis of qualitative field data' in Burgess R.G. (ed.) *Field Research: a Sourcebook and Field Manual* London: George Allen & Unwin.

Bennett R. (1986) 'Meaning and method in management research' *Graduate Management Research* **3** (3), whole part.

Berger R.M. and Patchner M.A. (1988) *Implementing the Research Plan* London: Sage.

Beynon H. (1988) 'Regulating research' in Bryman A. (ed.) *Doing Research in Organizations* London: Routledge.

Blau P.M. (1964) *Exchange and Power in Social Life* New York: John Wiley & Sons.

Boisot M. (1994) *East–West Business Collaboration: the Challenge of Governance in Post-Socialist Enterprises* London: Routledge.

Boje D.M. (1994) 'Organisational storytelling: the struggles of pre-modern, modern and postmodern organisational learning discourses' *Management Learning* **25** (3), 433–61.

Brindberg D. and McGrath J.E. (1985) *Validity and the Research Process* London: Sage.

Brown L.D. and Kaplan R.E. (1981) 'Participative research in a factory' in Reason P. and Rowan J. (eds), *Human Inquiry: A Sourcebook of New Paradigm Research* Chichester: John Wiley & Sons.

Buchanan D., Boddy D. and McCalman J. (1988) 'Getting in, getting on, getting out, and getting back' in Bryman A. (ed.) *Doing Research in Organisations* London: Routledge.

Burgess A. (1975) *Language Made Plain* London: Fontana-Collins.

Burgess R.G. (1982a) 'The role of theory in field research' in Burgess R.G. (ed.) *Field Research: a Sourcebook and Field Manual* London: George Allen & Unwin.

Burgess R.G. (1982b) 'Some role problems in field research' in Burgess R.G. (ed.) *Field Research: a Sourcebook and Field Manual* London: George Allen & Unwin.

Burgess R.G. (1982c) 'The unstructured interview as a conversation' in Burgess R.G. (ed.) *Field Research: a Sourcebook and Field Manual* London: George Allen & Unwin.

Burgoyne J.G. (1994) 'Stakeholder analysis' in Cassell C. and Symon G. (eds), *Qualitative Methods in Organizational Research* London: Sage.

Buzan A. (1989) *Use your Head* London: BBC Publications.

Campbell D.T. and Stanley J.C. (1966) *Experimental and Quasi Experimental Designs for Research* Chicago, IL: Rand McNally.

Cassell C.C. and Symon G. (1994) 'Qualitative research in work contexts' in Cassell C.C. and Simon G. (eds), *Qualitative Methods in Organisational Research* London: Sage.

Chambers C. (1985) 'The missing ingredient' *Management Education and Development: Special Issue, Men and Women in Organisations* **16** (2), 180–3.

CIM (undated) *Senior Management Entry Schemes: Entry by Management Experience: Amendments: Specification for Entry by Marketing Management Experience* Maidenhead: Chartered Institute of Marketing.

CIPFA (1993) *CIPFA Syllabus and Regulations* London: Chartered Institute of Public Finance and Accountancy.

Clegg S.R. (1992) 'Postmodern management?' *Journal of Organisational Change Management* **5** (2) 31–49.

Cohen J. (1960) 'A coefficient of agreement for nominal scales' *Educational and Psychological Measurement* **20**, 37–46.

Cook T.D. and Campbell D.T. (1979) *Quasi Experimentation: Design and Analysis Issues for Field Settings* Chicago, IL: Rand McNally.

Copetas A.C. (1993) *Bear-Hunting with the Politbureau* **New York: Touchstone, Simon and Schuster.**

Cottle T.J. (1977) *Private Lives and Public Accounts* New York: New Viewpoints.

Davies J. (1992) 'Careers of trainers: biography in action, the narrative dimension' *Management Education and Development* **23** (3) 207–14.

Dillman D.A. (1978) *Mail and Telephone Surveys: The Total Design Method* Chichester: Wiley.

Doswell R. and Nailon P. (1976) *Case Studies in Hotel Management* London: Barrie & Jenkins.

Dunphy D. and Stace D. (1988) 'Transformational and coercive strategies for planned organizational change: beyond the O.D. model' *Organization Studies* **9** (3) 317–34.

Easterday L., Papademas D., Schorr L. and Valentine C. (1982) 'The making of a female researcher: role problems in fieldwork' in Burgess R.G. (ed.) *Field Research: a Sourcebook and Field Manual* London: George Allen & Unwin.

Eden C. and Sims D. (1979) 'On the nature of problems in consulting practice' *International Journal of Management Science* **7** (2) 119–27.

Eden C., Jones S. and Sims D. (1979) *Thinking in Organisations* London: Macmillan.

Eden C., Jones S. and Sims D. (1983) *Messing about in Problems* **Oxford: Pergamon Press.**

Edwards A.L. (1957) *Techniques of Attitude Scale Construction* New York: Appleton-Century-Crofts.

Farrell P. (1992) 'Biography work and women's development: the promotion of equality issues' *Management Education and Development* **23** (3) 215–24.

Fiedler, F.E. (1967) *A Contingency Theory of Leadership Effectiveness* New York: McGraw-Hill.

Filley A.C. (1989) 'Collective judgement: a judgemental process for planning and analysis' *Journal of Organisational Change Management* **2** (1) 58–60.

Forster N. (1994) 'The analysis of company documentation' in Cassell C. and Symon G. (eds), *Qualitative Methods in Organizational Research* London: Sage.

Fox A. (1966) *The Timespan of Discretion Theory: an Appraisal* London: Institute of Personnel Management.

Frazer V.C.M. and Dale B.G. (1986) 'UK quality circle failures: the latest picture' *International Journal of Management Science* **14** (1) 23–33.

Frey J.H. (1983) *Survey Research by Telephone* London: Sage Publications.

Gaines B.R. and Shaw M.L.G. (1990) *REPGRID2 Manual* Calgary, Alberta: Centre for Person-Computer Studies, 3019 Underhill Drive NW, Calgary, Alberta, Canada T2N 4E4.

Gammack J.G. and Stephens R.A. (1994) 'Repertory grid technique in constructive interaction' in Cassell C. and Symon G. (eds), *Qualitative Methods in Organizational Research* London: Sage.

Gans H.J. (1982) 'The participant observer as a human being: observations on the personal aspects of fieldwork' in Burgess R.G. (ed.) *Field Research: a Sourcebook and Field Manual* London: George Allen & Unwin.

Giere R.N. (1979) *Understanding Scientific Reasoning* London: Holt, Rinehart & Winston.

Gill J. and Johnson P. (1991) *Research Methods for Managers* London: Paul Chapman.

Gilovich T. (1991) *How we Know what Isn't so: the Fallibility of Human Reason in Everyday Life* New York: Free Press.

Glaser B.G. (1978) *Theoretical Sensitivity: Advances in the Methodology of Grounded Theory* Mill Valley, CA: Sociology Press.

Glaser B.G. and Strauss A.L. (1967) *The Discovery of Grounded Theory: Strategies for Qualitative Research* Chicago, IL: Aldine.

Golde P. (1970) *Women in the Field: Anthropological Experiences* Chicago, IL: Aldine.

Goldstein M. and Goldstein F. (1978) *How We Know* London: Plenum Press.

Gorman M. and Sahlman W.A. (1986) 'What do venture capitalists do?' Proceedings, Babson Congress, University of Calgary, Alberta.

Gowler D., Legge K. and Clegg C.W. (1993) *Case Studies in Organizational Behaviour* London: Paul Chapman.

Green P.E. and Tull D.S. (1978) *Research for Marketing Decisions* Englewood Cliffs, NJ: Prentice-Hall.

Groebner D.F. and Shannon P.W. (1981) *Business Statistics: a Decision-Making Approach* New York: Merrill.

Haley U.C.V. and Stumpf S.A. (1989) 'Cognitive trails in strategic decision-making: linking theories of personalities and decisions' *Journal of Management Studies*, **26** (5) 477–97.

Harré R. (1981) 'The positivist-empiricist approach and its alternative' in Reason P. and Rowan J. (eds), *Human Inquiry: a Sourcebook of New Paradigm Research* Chichester: John Wiley & Sons.

Hartley J.F. (1994) 'Case studies in organizational research' in Cassell C. and Symon G. (eds), *Qualitative Methods in Organizational Research* London: Sage.

Hemingray T. (1988) 'BA(BS) Year 3: Placement and Project Handbook'. Internal mimeo, Middlesbrough: Teesside Business School, University of Teesside.

Hemingray T. (1994) 'Modular Business Scheme: Placement and Project Manual'. (Internal Mimeo) Middlesbrough: Teesside Business School, University of Teesside.

Hemry G.T. (1990) *Practical Sampling* London: Sage.

Henwood K.L. and Pidgeon N.F. (1992) 'Qualitative research and psychological theorising' *British Journal of Psychology* **83** (1) 97–111.

Heron J. (1981) 'Philosophical basis for a new paradigm' in Reason P. and Rowan J. (eds), *Human Inquiry: a Sourcebook of New Paradigm Research* Chichester: John Wiley & Sons.

Hofstede G. (1991) *Cultures and Organisations: Software of the Mind* Maidenhead: McGraw-Hill.

Holden N. and Cooper C. (1994) 'Russian managers as learners and receivers of western know-how' *Management Learning* **25** (4) 503–522.

Holsti O.R. (1968) 'Content analysis' in Lindzey G. and Aronson E. (eds), *The Handbook of Social Psychology* Wokingham: Addison-Wesley.

Honey P. (1977) 'The repertory grid in action' *Industrial and Commercial Training* 11, 452–9.

Hosking, D.M., Morley, I. (1988) 'The skills of leadership' in Hunt, J.G., Baliga, B.R., Dachler, H.P. and Schriesheim, C.A. (eds) *Emerging Leadership Vistas* Boston, MA: Lexington.

Howard K. and Sharp J.A. (1983) *The Management of a Student Research Topic* Aldershot: Gower.

Hunt A. (1975) *Management Attitudes and Practices towards Women at Work* London: HMSO.

Hunt D.E. (1987) *Beginning with Ourselves: in Practice, Theory, and Human Affairs* Cambridge, MA: Brookline Books.

Hunter-Brown C. (1984) 'Information search guide' in Martin J. and Spear, R. (eds) *Project Manual, Block VI of Technology, a Third Level Course* Milton Keynes: The Open University Press.

IPD (1993) *Professional Education Scheme: Syllabus* Institute of Personnel and Development (Institute of Personnel Management), London: IPD, July.

Isenberg D.J. (1984) 'How senior managers think' *Harvard Business Review* **62** (6) 81–90.

Jankowicz A.D. (1982) 'The FOCUS cluster-analysis algorithm in human resource development' *Personnel Review* **11** 15–22, and erratum **12** (1) 22.

Jankowicz A.D. (1987) 'Intuition in small business lending decisions' *Journal of Small Business Management* **25** (3) 45–52.

Jankowicz A.D. (1989) 'Applications of personal construct psychology in business practice' in Neimeyer G. and Neimeyer R. (eds), *Advances in Personal Construct Psychology* Greenwich, CT: JAI Press.

Jankowicz A.D. (1994) 'The new journey to Jerusalem : mission and meaning in the managerial crusade to eastern Europe' *Organization Studies* **15** (4) 479–507.

Jankowicz A.D and Pettitt S. (1993) 'Worlds in collusion: an analysis of an eastern European management development initiative' *Management Education and Development* **24** (1) 93–104.

Jankowicz A.D., and Walsh P. (1984) 'Researching the Sergeant's role' *Garda News* **3** (8) 6–13.

Jones H. (1992) 'Biography in management and organisational development' *Management Education and Development* **23** (3) 199–206.

Jones M.O. (1988) 'In search of meaning: using qualitative methods in research and application' in Jones M.O., Moore M.D. and Snyder R.C. (eds) *Inside Organisations: Understanding the Human Dimension* London: Sage.

Jorgensen D.L. (1989) *Participant Observation: a Methodology for Human Studies* London: Sage.

Kane E. (1985) *Doing Your Own Research: Basic Descriptive Research in the Social Sciences and Humanities* London: Marion Boyars.

Kelly G.A. (1955) *The Psychology of Personal Constructs* New York: Norton.

King N. (1994) 'The qualitative research interview' in Cassell C. and Symon G. (eds), *Qualitative Methods in Organizational Research* London: Sage.

Klecka W.R., Nie H.H. and Hull C.H. (1975) *SPSS Primer: Statistical Package for the Social Sciences* New York: McGraw-Hill.

Kornhauser A. and Sheatsley P.B. (1976) 'Questionnaire construction and interview procedure' in Selltiz C., Wrightsman L.S. and Cook S.W. (eds), *Research Methods in Social Relations* New York: Holt, Rinehart and Winston.

Krueger R.A. (1988) *Focus Groups: a Practical Guide for Applied Research* London: Sage Publications.

Lancaster G. and Massingham L. (1988) *Essentials of Marketing: Text and Cases* Maidenhead: McGraw-Hill.

Likert, R. (1961) *New Patterns of Management* New York: McGraw-Hill.

Lodge D. (1988) *Nice Work* Harmondsworth: Penguin.

London, M. (1988) *Change Agents* London: Jossey-Bass.

McCormack M.H. (1984) *What They Don't Teach You at Harvard Business School* London: Collins.

Mączynski, J. (1991) *A Cross-cultural Comparison of Decision Participation Based on the Vroom-Yetton Model of Leadership* Report no. PRE 23 Institute of Management, Technical University of Wroclaw, Poland.

Mair M. (1989) 'Kelly, Bannister, and a story-telling psychology' *International Journal of Personal Construct Psychology* **2** (1) 1–14.

Mair M. (1990) 'Telling psychological tales' *International Journal of Personal Construct Psychology* **3** (1) 121–35.

Mangham I.L. (1986) 'In search of competence' *Journal of General Management* **12** (2) 5–12.

Mann R.D. (1959) 'A review of the relationships between personality and performance in small groups' *Psychological Bulletin* **56**, 241–70.

Marshall J. (1985) 'Paths of personal and professional development for women managers' in Boydell T. and Hammond V. (eds), *Men and Women in Organisations: Special Issue, Management Education and Development*

Martin J. and Spear R. (1985) *Project Manual, Block VI of Technology, a Third Level Course* Milton Keynes: Open University Press.

Martinko M.J. and Gardner W.L. (1990) 'Structured observation of managerial work: a replication and synthesis' *Journal of Management Studies* **27** (3) 329–57.

Mason D. (1988) 'Gissa project!' *Times Higher Education Supplement* 18 March.

Miles M.B. and Huberman A.M. (1994) *Qualitative Data Analysis: an Expanded Sourcebook* London: Sage.

Miller D.C. (1977) *Handbook of Research Design and Social Measurement* New York: David McKay.

Millman, T. and Randlesome C. (1993) 'Developing top Russian managers' *Management Education and Development* **24** (1) 83–92.

Mintzberg H. (1973) *The Nature of Managerial Work* New York: Harper & Row.

Mishler E.G. (1986) *Research Interviewing* London: Harvard University Press.

Misumi J. (1985) *The Behavioural Science of Leadership* Ann Arbor, MI: University of Michigan Press.

Moran R.T. and Johnson M. (1992) *Cultural Guide to doing Business in Europe* London: Butterworth-Heinemann.

Morgan D.L. (1988) *Focus Groups as Qualitative Research* London: Sage Publications.

Morita A. (1988) *Made in Japan* London: Fontana.

Morris L.L., Fitz-Gibbon C.T. and Freeman M.E. (1987) *How to Communicate Evaluation Findings* London: Sage.

Murdoch J. and Barnes A.J. (1986) *Statistical Tables for Science, Engineering, Management and Business Studies* London: Macmillan.

Nelson R.D. (1980) *The Penguin Book of Mathematical and Statistical Tables* Harmondsworth: Penguin.

O'Cinneide B. (1986) *The Case for Irish Enterprise* Dublin: Enterprise Publications.

Orbell J. (1987) *A Guide to Tracing the History of a Business* Aldershot: Gower Press.

Orwell G. (1957) 'Politics and the English language' in *Inside the Whale and other essays* Harmondsworth: Penguin.

Ouchi W.I. (1981) *Theory Z: How American Business can Meet the Japanese Challenge* Reading, MA: Addison-Wesley.

Parlett M. (1981) 'Illuminative evaluation' in Reason P. and Rowan J. (eds), *Human Inquiry: a Sourcebook of New Paradigm Research* Chichester: John Wiley & Sons.

Parsons C.J. (1973) *Theses and Project Work* London: George Allen & Unwin.

Parsons, T., Bales, R.F. and Shils, E.A. (1953) *Working Papers in the Theory of Action* Glencoe, IL.: Free Press.

Perreault W.D. Jnr. and Leigh L.E. (1989) 'Reliability of nominal data based on qualitative judgements' *Journal of Marketing Research* **XXVI**, May, 135–48.

Pfeffer J. (1981) 'Management as symbolic action: the creation and maintenance of organisational paradigms' in Cummings, L.L. and Staw, B.M. (eds) *Research in Organisational Behaviour* Vol. 3, Greenwich, CT: JAI Press.

Pheysey D.C. (1993) *Organisational Cultures: Types and Transformations* London: Routledge.

Phillips E.M. and Pugh D.S. (1987) *How to Get a Ph.D.* Milton Keynes: The Open University Press.

Phillips M. (1994a) 'The strange death of liberal England' *Spectator*, 17 September.

Phillips M. (1994b) *The War of the Words* London: Virago Press.

Porter L.W. (1963) 'Job attitudes in management: IV perceived deficiencies in need fulfilment as a function of size of company' *Journal of Applied Psychology* **47** (6) 386–97.

Raimond P. (1993) *Management Projects* London: Chapman & Hall.

Randlesome C., Brierley B., Bruton K., Gordon C. and King P. (1993) *Business Cultures in Europe* London: Butterworth-Heinemann.

Read S.J., Druian P.R. and Miller R.C. (1989) 'The role of causal sequence in the meaning of actions' *British Journal of Social Psychology* **28** , 341–51.

Reason P. and Rowan J. (1981a) *Human Inquiry: a Sourcebook of New Paradigm Research* Chichester: Wiley.

Reason P. and Rowan J. (1981b) 'Issues of validity in new paradigm research' in Reason P. and Rowan J. (eds), *Human Inquiry: a Sourcebook of New Paradigm Research* Chichester: Wiley.

Reeves T.K. and Harper D. (1981a) *Surveys at Work: a Practitioner's Guide* Maidenhead: McGraw-Hill.

Reeves T.K. and Harper D. (1981b) *Surveys at Work: Student Project Manual* Maidenhead: McGraw-Hill.

Riebel F.-H. and Amini S. (1985) 'Research and teaching' *Der Tropelandwirt: Zeitschrift für die Landwirtschaft in den Tropen und Subtropen* Special Issue **24**, 9–23.

Roberts C. (1985) *The Interview Game and how it's Played* London: British Broadcasting Corporation.

Rothwell S. (1985) 'Is management a masculine role?' in Boydell T. and Hammon V. (eds), *Men and Women in Organisations: Special Issue, Management Education and Development*

Salmon P. (1992) *Achieving a Ph.D.: 10 Students' Experiences* London: Trentham Books.

Saxton J. and Ashworth P. (1990) 'The workplace supervision of sandwich degree placement students' *Management Education and Development* **21** (2) 133–49.

Schlackman B. (1989) 'Projective tests and enabling techniques for use in market research' in Robson S. and Foster A. (eds), *Qualitative Research in Action* London: Edward Arnold.

Schön D.A. (1983) *The Reflective Practitioner* London: Temple Smith.

Selltiz C.S., Wrightsman L.S. and Cook S.W. (1981) *Research Methods in Social Relations* London: Holt, Rinehart & Winston.

Sewell K.W., Adams-Webber J., Mitterer J. and Cromwell R.L. (1992) 'Computerised repertory grids: review of the literature' *International Journal of Personal Construct Psychology* **5** (1) 1-23.

Shaw M. and Gaines B. (1989) *REPGRID and User's Manual* Calgary: Centre for Person-Computer Studies, University of Calgary.

Siegel S. and Castellan N.J. (1988) *Nonparametric Statistics for the Behavioural Sciences* Maidenhead: McGraw-Hill.

Siehl C. and Martin J. (1988) 'Measuring organisational culture: mixing qualitative and quantitative methods' in Jones M.O., Moore M.D. and Snyder R.C. (eds), *Inside Organisations: Understanding the Human Dimension* London: Sage Publications.

Smith B. (1990) 'Mutual mentoring on projects: a proposal to combine the advantages of several established management development methods' *Journal of Management Development* **9** (1) 51–7.

Smith J.M. (1972) *Interviewing in Market and Social Research* London: Routledge and Kegan Paul.

Smith, P.B. and Peterson, M.F. (1988) *Leadership, Organizations and Culture* London: Sage.

Smith P.B., Misumi J., Tayeb M., Peterson M. and Bond M. (1989) 'On the generality of leadership style measures across cultures' *Journal of Occupational Psychology* **62** (2) 97–109.

Snyder R.C. (1988) 'New frames for old: changing the managerial culture of an aircraft factory' in Jones, M.O., Moore, M.D. and Snyder, R.C. (eds) *Inside Organisations: Understanding the Human Dimension* London: Sage Publications.

Sternberg R.J. (1988) *The Psychologist's Companion: A Guide to Scientific Writing for Students and Researchers* Cambridge: Cambridge University Press.

Stewart B., Hetherington G. and Smith M. (1984a) *Survey Item Bank vol 1 Measures of Satisfaction* Bradford: MCB University Press.

Stewart B., Hetherington G. and Smith M. (1984b) *Survey Item Bank vol 2 Measures of Organizational Characteristics* Bradford: MCB University Press.

Stewart R. (1967) *Managers and their Jobs: a Study of the Similarities and Differences in the Ways Managers Spend their Time* **London: Macmillan.**

Stewart V. and Stewart A. (1982) *Business Applications of Repertory Grid* Maidenhead: McGraw Hill.

Stoeckeler H.S. and Hasegawa M. (1974) 'A technique for identifying values as behavioural potentials in making consumer housing decisions' *Home Economics Research Journal*, **2** (4) 268–80.

Stogdill R.M. (1948) 'Personal factors associated with leadership: a survey of the literature' *Journal of Psychology* **25**, 35–72.

Stogdill R.M. and Coons R.M. (1957) (eds) *Leader Behavior: its Description and Management* Columbus, OH: Bureau of Business Research, Ohio State University.

Strunk J.W. and White E.B. (1972) *The Elements of Style* London: Collier Macmillan.

Sudman B. (1976) *Applied Sampling* London: Academic Press.

Tayeb M. (1988) *Organizations and National Culture: a Comparative Analysis* London: Sage.

Teesside Business School (1987) 'Submission to CNAA: Masters in Business Administration' Middlesbrough: Teesside Polytechnic.

Teesside Business School (1988) 'Student's Project Brief, Diploma in Personnel Management' (Internal Mimeo) Middesbrough: Teesside Business School, University of Teesside.

Teesside Business School (undated) *Assessment Criteria for the Diploma in Management Studies* (Internal Mimeo) Middesbrough: Teesside Business School, University of Teesside.

Thibaut J.W. and Kelley H.H. (1959) *The Social Psychology of Groups* New York: John Wiley & Sons.

Tommerup P. (1988) 'From trickster to father figure; learning from the mythologisation of top management' in Jones M.O., Moore M.D. and Syuder R.C. (eds), *Inside Organisations: Understanding the Human Dimension* London: Sage Publications.

Torrington D. (1972) *Face to Face: Techniques for Handling the Personal Encounter at Work* London: Gower Press.

Tremblay M.A. (1982) 'The key informant technique: a non-ethnographic application' in Burgess R. (ed.) *Field Research: a Sourcebook and Field Manual* London: Allen & Unwin.

Turk C. and Kirkman J. (1989) *Effective Writing* London: E & FN Spon.

Tversky A. and Kahnemann D. (1982) 'Judgement under uncertainty: heuristics and biases' in Kahnemann, D., Slovic, P. and Tversky, A. (eds), *Judgement under Uncertainty: Heuristics and Biases* New York: Cambridge University Press.

Tyson S. and Kakabadse A.P. (1987) *Cases in Human Resource Management* London: Heinemann.

van Clouse G.H. (1990) 'A controlled experiment relating entrepreneurial education to students' start-up decisions' *Journal of Small Business Management* **28** (2) 45–53.

Waddington D. (1994) 'Participant observation' in Cassell C. and Symon G. (eds), *Qualitative Methods in Organizational Research* London: Sage.

Watson G. (1987) *Writing a Thesis: a Guide to Long Essays and Dissertations* London: Longman.

Webb E.J., Campbell D.T., Schwartz R.D. and Sechrest L. (1966) *Unobtrusive Measures: Nonreactive Research in the Social Sciences* Chicago, IL: Rand McNally.

White J., Yates A. and Skipworth G. (1979) *Tables for Statisticians* Cheltenham: Stanley Thornes.

Whitehead J. (1994) 'How do I improve the quality of my management? A participatory action research approach' *Management Learning* **25** (1) 137–53.

Whyte W.F. (1982) 'Interviewing in field research' in Burgess R.G. (ed.) *Field Research: a Sourcebook and Field Manual* London: George Allen & Unwin.

Williams C.B. and Stevenson A.H. (1963) *A Research Manual for College Studies and Papers* London: Harper & Row.

Woodall J. (1992) *Models and methods of management development in Poland and Hungary* in Kirkbride, D.S., Rowland, K. and Shaw, B. (eds) Proceeding of the Third Conference on International Personnel and Human Resources Management Ashridge, July.

Wordsworth D. (1994) 'Mind your language' *Spectator*, 17 September.

Yin R.K. (1994) *Case Study Research: Design and Methods* London: Sage.

Zeithaml V.A. (1990) *Delivering Quality Service: Balancing Customer Perceptions and Expectations* Glencoe, IL: Free Press.

Glossary

This list of definitions of key ideas, terms and techniques, referenced to the page on which the definition first appears, deals largely with issues of methodology, and is useful at all stages of your project. It is particularly helpful if you care about the precision of the language you will use in your project report.

Alternative: For the purposes of this book, a string of words which expresses a potential answer to a question [224]; see also *Item* and *Response*.

Area: A broad field of scholarly endeavour: an academic discipline, business function, or course title [34].

Aspect: A more detailed facet of a *Field* (*q.v.*), which provides you with the topic of your project [34].

Census: The measurement of a complete population, rather than a sample; worth considering in in-company work [164].

Construct: A particular way in which an individual expresses the meaning s/he intends [256].

Content analysis: A technique used to categorize the answers to open-ended questions, so that the meanings expressed in the data can be classified, coded, and tabulated [206].

Controlled variables: The variables which would get in the way of a causal explanation of the relationship between independent and dependent variable, and whose effects you try to eliminate. The impossibility of doing so without distorting what you're doing is frequently the reason for avoiding experimental methods in project work [187].

Data: Specific findings and results, which may or may not be meaningful [143]; see also *Information*.

Dependent variable: The variable which forms the focus of your observations, and which you hope will express the effects of your activity in manipulating the independent variable [187].

Design: A particular approach to the collection of data, which combines validity of findings with economy of effort [153]. For example, Examining Contrasting Modes of Operation [154]; Time-Sampling [154]; Before–After [154]; Repeated Measures [278]; Independent Groups [278].

Effectiveness: Has to do with constraints on the applicability of technically acceptable recommendations [48].

Efficiency: Has to do with technical possibility and feasibility [48].

Empathizer: A role in project work in which you offer your services as a sympathetic problem-solver [117].

Empirical data: The result of new observations, made in order to check out your assertions [88].

Epistemology: An enquiry into how it is possible for people to know things [87].

Expert: A role in project work in which you utilize coercive power arising from your specialist knowledge or techniques [117].

Facilitation: Posing a series of questions which stimulate, maintain, and direct the flow of discussion in a focus group [217].

Field: A component of an *Area* (*q.v.*) being a sub-discipline, a theme within a business function, or some issue dealt with by a course [24].

Flashcard: A card on which the alternative answers to a question in a fully structured questionnaire are printed, to assist the respondent in remembering the options available to him or her [251].

Found experiment: Also known as a 'natural experiment', being a situation in which events occur in such a way that at least two levels of an independent variable happen to be available, and an appropriate dependent variable suggests itself [275].

Fully structured technique: A technique in which the content and sequence of questions, and the form of answers, have been determined in advance [175].

Hermeneutic technique: One way of determining the meaning and significance of an utterance, written statement, or event by interpreting the symbols in which these are expressed. Depends crucially on the understanding of the context, and plausible to the extent that consistency with an appropriate conceptual background, and triangulation with other techniques, are explicitly demonstrated [176].

Hypothesis: The formal statement of a deduction that if a theory is true, then a relationship can be found between at least two variables [89].

Hypothetico-deductive method: A set of procedures in which a hypothesis is deduced from a theory and expressed in terms of a relationship between one or more variables, each operationally defined. Measurements are made in order to test the hypothesis and verify the theory [89].

Illustrative quotation: An attractive and interesting way of stating and substantiating your main findings, requiring careful presentation [180]; compare with 'Narrative Account' and 'Tabular Presentation'.

Independent variable: The variable you regard as possibly the cause of the effect being observed, and which you set out to control directly; in project work, this is rarely possible without distorting data or information [187].

Information: Data expressed in such a way that they remove uncertainty and create meaning [44, 143].

Item: For the purposes of this book, a string of words by which you elicit data from a respondent [224]; see also *Alternative* and *Response*.

Literary style: The method or methods by which you obtain the effect you wish to achieve in your reader [283]; see also *Voice*.

Measurement: The making of observations [89].

Mentor: Someone who's already completed the level of course which you're studying, and done a project as part of it [32].

Method: A systematic and orderly approach towards the collection of data so that information can be obtained from those data [172]. Not to be confused with

Methodology: The analysis of, and rationale for, the particular method used in a project [174].

Narrative account: A very common way of presenting the findings of business/management projects, by blending empirical information with reasoned argument in connected prose; the key to success is the quality of the reasoning [162]; compare with *tabular presentation* and *illustrative quotation*.

Negotiator: A role in project work in which you handle the task of problem definition and resolution in cooperation with the people you're studying. More likely to be successful than either the *Expert* or the *Empathizer* roles (*qq.v.*) [117].

New Paradigm: A non-positivist approach to the study of people, at work and elsewhere: an appropriate alternative to positivist approaches for most in-company projects [91].

Nonprobability sampling: A variety of techniques for drawing a sample in such a way that findings will require inference, judgement and interpretation before being applied to the population; often the only, or most sensible, thing to do in the circumstances [155].

Open-ended technique: A technique in which respondents are asked to answer your questions in their own words [195].

Operational definition: A careful statement of what you need to measure in order to observe two variables varying [89].

Operational description: A description of an observable event, particularly useful in labelling the different positions on a rating scale [267].

Pilot work: An essential stage of work, during which you identify and resolve doubts about the content, structure, and design of the questions you intend to ask your respondents, by conducting a trial on a small subgroup [193].

Plagiarism: 'Copying' from someone else's work; a crime which, if intentional and proven, is terminal [46].

Population: A complete set of people, occurrences or objects from which a sample will be drawn [155].

Positivism: The philosophical assumptions which underlie hypothetico-deductive method, which assert that this method is the only rational way of knowing things; that the purpose of theory is application; that truth can always be distinguished from untruth; and that truth can be discerned either by deduction or by empirical support and by no other means. Highly misleading when taken as a model for all in-company project work, though it may apply to some [90].

Probability sampling: A variety of techniques which attempt to ensure that a sample is representative of the population in such a way that findings can be directly generalized to the population [156].

Psychological significance: In contrast to statistical significance, a statement of the confidence with which you are prepared to accept that a set of results are meaningful and relevant; a property of the *design* (*q.v.*) of your investigation [240].

Purpose of a project: To create an opportunity for the application of concepts and techniques acquired during the taught programme, in a management practitioner environment, in order to complete the formal learning experience, and to be of use to the sponsor [8].

Qualitative analysis: A set of techniques which takes people's experiences and their verbal expression seriously, while checking their value, meaningfulness and applicability when generalizing conclusions [173].

Quantitative analysis: A set of techniques in which the frequency of occurrence of reponses is counted. Very powerful when applicable, the results need cross-checking and are often the result of the ease, rather than relevance, with which the chosen technique has been applied [174].

Reliability of measurement: The precision of measurement, such that the same result would be obtained on re-measurement, assuming the situation had not changed [89].

Replication: In comparative case study work, a method of selecting companies to study which ensures they represent different positions on one or more issues or variables, an infinitely preferable alternative to random sampling [180].

Response: For the purposes of this book, the utterance or action a respondent makes to indicate his/her views in reply to a question [224]; see also *Item* and *Alternative*.

Sample: A set of people, occurrences or objects chosen from a larger population in order to represent that population to a greater or lesser extent [155].

Sampling frame: A list, often divided into subgroups, of a population, used in order to draw a sample and to keep track of its representativeness [155].

Scholarship: The careful and accurate use of evidence; care in the discovery and attribution of sources; thoroughness in the coverage of subject-matter; respect for truth and the validity of data and assertions; in short, a major defence against the charlatan and the demagogue [52].

Semi-structured technique: A technique in which the content and sequence of questions is not fully specified in advance [195].

Stakeholder analysis: A description of the people to whom particular issues matter, together with the reasons, both personal and systemic, why they matter. Very useful as a technique in case study method [181].

Statistical significance: A statement of the confidence with which you are prepared to accept that the results in a sample reflect the realities in a population. Offering exact precision of your chances of making a mistake, but not necessarily the same as *psychological significance, q.v.* [240].

Tabular presentation: A common way of presenting survey results, in which tables of frequencies and proportions of answers to your questions are accompanied by verbal statements of the information contained in each table [180]; compare with *Narrative account* and *Illustrative quotation*.

Technique: A step-by-step procedure for gathering and analysing data [172].

Testing: Drawing conclusions about a hypothesis [89].

Theory: Generally, a belief expressed in words or through action [79]. In hypothetico-deductive method, a formally expressed general statement which has the potential to explain things [89].

Thesis: A statement of your belief and intention in doing your project; a statement of the kind of conclusion which you believe your data may support [83].

Triangulation: The use of one method to cross-check the results of another. Very useful in all cases, and essential in qualitative work [175].

Validity of measurement: The accuracy of measurement, such that the process or event you intended to measure, is indeed properly measured [89].

Verification: The drawing of implications from empirical conclusions to theory [89].

Voice: An attribute of your written material that conveys your own, *personal* style and perspective [288].

Subject index

References to important tables and figures are shown in italic. Entries in **bold** are references to examples and anecdotes in the text which may be particularly useful in suggesting an idea for a topic if you're having difficulties in identifying one.